PENGUIN BOOKS

## THE RUFFIAN ON THE STAIR

Rosemary Dinnage was brought up in Oxford and Canada. She has worked in publishing, as a translator, in journalism and as a research psychologist. For eight years she was Research Officer at the National Children's Bureau, where she wrote a series of books on child care. She is now a freelance writer and a frequent contributor to literary journals in Britain and the USA.

She has published a biography of Annie Besant in the Penguin series 'Lives of Modern Women' (1986) and *One to One* (Penguin 1989), a collection of interviews with people who have undergone psychotherapy.

Rosemary Dinnage lives in London and has two grown-up sons.

ROSEMARY DINNAGE

# THE RUFFIAN ON THE STAIR

## REFLECTIONS ON DEATH

PENGUIN BOOKS

PENGUIN BOOKS

Published by the Penguin Group
Penguin Books Ltd, 27 Wrights Lane, London W8 5TZ, England
Penguin Books USA Inc., 375 Hudson Street, New York, New York 10014, USA
Penguin Books Australia Ltd, Ringwood, Victoria, Australia
Penguin Books Canada Ltd, 10 Alcorn Avenue, Toronto, Ontario, Canada M4V 3B2
Penguin Books (NZ) Ltd, 182–190 Wairau Road, Auckland 10, New Zealand

Penguin Books Ltd, Registered Offices: Harmondsworth, Middlesex, England

First published by Viking 1990
Published in Penguin Books 1992
10 9 8 7 6 5 4 3 2 1

Copyright © Rosemary Dinnage, 1990
All rights reserved

The acknowledgements on page xi constitute an extension of this copyright page

The moral right of the author has been asserted

Printed in England by Clays Ltd, St Ives plc

Except in the United States of America, this book is sold subject
to the condition that it shall not, by way of trade or otherwise, be lent,
re-sold, hired out, or otherwise circulated without the publisher's
prior consent in any form of binding or cover other than that in
which it is published and without a similar condition including this
condition being imposed on the subsequent purchaser

# Contents

To James Horrigan
1934–1989

Madame Life's a piece in bloom
    Death goes dogging everywhere:
She's the tenant of the room,
    He's the ruffian on the stair.


W. E. Henley

# ACKNOWLEDGEMENTS

Grateful acknowledgement is made for permission to reproduce the following copyright material:

*Beowulf*: excerpt from the translation by Michael Alexander (Penguin Classics, 1973), copyright © Michael Alexander, 1973. To Penguin Books Ltd.

John Bowlby: chapter from *Attachment and Loss* (vol. III). To the Tavistock Institute of Human Relations and the Hogarth Press.

S. C. Humphreys and Helen King: excerpt from *Mortality and Immortality: The Anthropology and Archaeology of Death* (1981). To Academic Press.

Claude Lévi-Strauss: excerpt from *Tristes Tropiques*, translated by John and Doreen Weightman. Copyright © Librairie Plon, 1955. Translation copyright © Jonathan Cape Ltd, 1973. To Jonathan Cape Ltd.

James Joyce: excerpt from 'The Dead' (published in *Dubliners*). To the Executors of the Estate of James Joyce, Jonathan Cape Ltd, and the Society of Authors.

Thomas Mann: excerpt from *The Magic Mountain*. To Martin Secker & Warburg and Alfred A. Knopf, Inc.

Czeslaw Milosz: lines from 'On the Other Side', copyright © 1988 by Czeslaw Milosz Royalties, Inc. From *The Collected Poems, 1931–1987*, published by The Ecco Press (1988) and Penguin Books Ltd (1988). To The Ecco Press and Penguin Books Ltd.

Jean-Paul Sartre: excerpt from *Words*, translated by Irene Clephane. To Hamish Hamilton.

Hanna Segal: excerpt from 'A Psychoanalytic Approach to Aesthetics' (published in *New Directions in Psychoanalysis*, ed. M. Klein). To Tavistock Publications.

Richard Wilbur: lines from 'The Pardon'. To Faber and Faber Ltd (*Poems 1943–56*) and Harcourt Brace Jovanovich, Inc. (*Ceremony and Other Poems*, copyright 1950 and renewed 1978 by Richard Wilbur).

Virginia Woolf: excerpts from *The Diary of Virginia Woolf* Volume Two: 1920–1924, copyright © 1978 by Quentin Bell and Angelica Garnett. To the Executors of the Estate of Virginia Woolf, the Hogarth Press and Harcourt Brace Jovanovich, Inc.

# INTRODUCTION

'How can you expect people to talk about death?' asked a friend about this book. If fear of death (whatever exactly that is) lies behind all lesser fears, then one might suppose that no one can really talk honestly about it; but having, for a previous book,* listened to people talking most searchingly about themselves, I have confidence in how much they find they can say.

As in that book, I cannot claim that the talks recorded here are in any way representative – it is not feasible, for instance, to interview a child, so a description of a child's bereavement is included here instead. But my hope has been that, by tapping a person's thoughts on one subject, I also tap into a life and a way of seeing and dealing with the world. Of course the right questions to ask are only realized when the enterprise is over; I see now that I might have formulated some specific question on how it is that, in face of its ending, we do have confidence in life. Fortunately a kind of answer to this does often emerge from the talks.

Writers who have speculated about death (and they all have, even when the message is in invisible ink) have said that it is everything and it is nothing. On the one hand life is seen as dwarfed by death, overwhelmingly influenced by it in every aspect. Johnson felt the whole of life to be nothing but keeping away thoughts of death, and Henry James, embarrassed, declared life 'a predicament before death'; Plato claimed that the thinker's whole task is to train for death; Arthur Koestler has said that without the word 'death' in our vocabulary, there would be no civilization – 'the cathedrals collapse, the pyramids vanish into the sand, the great organs become silent'. On the other hand Wittgenstein, like Freud, pointed out that logically death is not

* *One to One*, Viking, 1988; Penguin Books, 1989.

something we can talk about – 'Death is not an event in life. It is not lived through' – or, as the Hofrat in *The Magic Mountain* says, 'We come out of the dark and go into the dark again, and in between lie the experiences of our life. But the beginning and the end, birth and death, we do not experience; they have no subjective character, they fall entirely into the category of objective events, and that's that.'

But, except in the most pedantic sense, is this true? When people talk about death, as they do here, they are not talking about the instant of death, of which, except by seeing others die, they cannot have any experience; they are talking about whatever in their experiences and fantasies has *meant* death. In everything but literal fact, everyone has died deaths – perhaps even, or particularly, children. So death – or Death – is there in every imagination and given every possible shape. To Browning he is the Arch Fear, cold and mist and fog in the throat; to the Prince of Salina in *The Leopard*, a girl in a brown travelling dress and a straw hat with a speckled veil; to Wilfred Owen in the trenches of the Great War, a sleazy companion:

> Out there, we've walked quite friendly up to Death;
>   Sat down and eaten with him, cool and bland, –
>   Pardoned his spilling mess-tins in our hand.
> We've sniffed the green thick odour of his breath, –
>   Our eyes wept, but our courage didn't writhe.

To innumerable writers death has meant, on the contrary, an immaculate quiet, a delicious drowsing without bad dreams, relief from the struggle of living; as Empson says, 'We are happy to equate it to any conceived calm.' To the Sora people described in this book by Piers Vitebsky it is a state where you long for a gossip and a drink; to Jonathan Miller it is a bear's skull, a glimpse of an organdie dress; to Christine, a street full of strangers. Death is a safe port, an icy hand, a jewel, a carriage for two, a ship, a little pin, a pale flag, an old peasant with a sack, a bird's flight, a prince, a doorway, a pale horse, a bridegroom, the cure of all diseases. Only Thomas, here, has described the first unelaborated fear simply of not being.

But Thanatos, where it means everything that is opposed to

life and vitality, must in fact start from that very sense of loss and fear and blankness in childhood; to Thomas it somehow attached itself to a threepenny bit on the desk, to Sartre as a five-year-old it meant a glimpse into a cellar:

I saw death ... It took the form of a hole: this was at Arcachon; [we] were visiting Madame Dupont and her son Gabriel, the composer. I was playing in the garden of the villa, scared because I had been told that Gabriel was ill and was going to die. I was playing at horses, half-heartedly, and galloping round the house. Suddenly, I noticed a gloomy hole: the cellar, which had been opened; an indescribable impression of loneliness and horror blinded me: I turned round and, singing at the top of my voice, I fled.

The sinister vacuum associates itself with the powerful fear of loss of identity, which is natural in a child's shakily acquired ego, but continues, to a greater or lesser degree, to haunt us through life – many of the people I talked to said it was not death they feared but senility, loss of their recognizable selves. So Czeslaw Milosz describes hell as somewhere where nothing is quite recognizably what it seems – there is 'as-if vodka' and 'as-if time', gramophones play tunes that never existed:

> hungry dogs lengthening and shortening their muzzles,
> And changing from mongrel to greyhound, then
> dachshunds,
> As if to signify they were perhaps not quite dogs.

To the adult, death logically has two distinct aspects – thoughts of one's own death and bereavement when others die – but to children there may be no clear distinction. When a child loses someone, even just by absence, it is a death; death not only of the lost person, but a threat of death to the child's own self which depended on the person. So whoever in adult life struggles with the sorrow of bereavement also still has to struggle with a blow to their own vitality, with the problem of their own survival, how it can be sustained and whether it is legitimate. Rosemary Gordon in her interview here describes ways in which such loss can frighten and deaden people.

In *The Ancient Mariner* Coleridge, who was so often subject to a deathly dejection, sets out this struggle between deadness and aliveness. The wind that keeps the mariner's ship moving is the breath of life; it is threatened and destroyed by dreadful recurrences of stagnation. The idea of death is never far from the idea of killing, and the mariner kills life in the form of the albatross. In revenge, the world dries up; image follows image of punishing drought and dumbness. What seems like the return of life proves to be the Nightmare Life-in-Death, that particularly terrifying combination that recurs everywhere in folklore and ghost stories and horror films. When she wins the dice game, the mariner is left at the extremest point of his paralysis and isolation, living on among the accusing corpses and unable to die or to pray; until the mood changes with the long and beautiful image of the moon, and its accompanying stars that seem still and yet are alive and moving: 'and everywhere the blue sky belongs to them, and is their appointed rest and their native country and their own natural homes, which they enter unannounced, as lords that are certainly expected, and yet there is a silent joy at their arrival'. Order and joy are restored; the mariner is freed to bless the beauty of the water-snakes – before, they were 'a thousand thousand slimy things' – and water and wind and movement bring back life.

So Browning goes on to the triumph over the Arch Fear – 'the black minute's at end'; and so Owen turns Death into a friend – 'We laughed at him, we leagued with him, old chum.' So in his diaries Kafka, after sitting up all night to write his first great story 'The Judgment', sees the act of writing it as a kind of death survived: 'How everything can be said, how for everything, for the strangest ideas, a great fire is prepared in which they perish and rise up again.' These opposite poles of feeling – of deadness and vitality – are what we juggle with when we try to think of death. And when an actual death occurs, it involves a number of tasks: to express grief, to realize what is involved in surviving, to construct a transition from life to death, and eventually to carry the transition through to the restoration of life. In most cultures society has formulas for these tasks, into which the individual can fit his or her own emotions. It is a truism, but has to be repeated, that in developed Western societies these forms have become sketchy or lacking; Philippe Ariès declares that it was when death really began to be feared that it ceased to be talked about. Roy Porter in his discussion here has described how we have lost the earlier expectation that we should be masters of our own deaths. People today do nevertheless work out private formulas and demarcations for themselves. All the feelings and fears we see expressed in less self-conscious cultures, however bizarre the expression seems to us, are, I believe, still very much part of the furniture of our own minds.

Society's recorded death rituals among them express every aspect of these four tasks, every permutation of these feelings, all 'possible oppositions between time and timelessness, memory and oblivion, movement and stillness, activity and its suspension, incompleteness and completion', as the anthropologist S. C. Humphreys says (1981). The smaller the society, the more the elimination of one of its members is felt as an attack upon its corporate strength. Few of the societies that anthropologists have studied are without rituals for expressing both this public and the private grief. Grieving – usually the task of women – may involve not only cries and dirges but smashing, tearing, and self-mutilation, of which the Jewish ritual cutting of a garment described by Albert Friedlander is a remnant. After a person is gone a vacuum is left; and everywhere the natural impulse is to fill up the gap – whether in the shape of a requiem mass or a dance or a carved stone – with a celebration of the solemnity of the transition from one state to the other.

> High over head they hoisted and fixed
> a gold *signum*; they gave him to the flood,
> and let the seas take him, with sour hearts
> and mourning moods. Men have not the knowledge
> to say with any truth – however tall beneath the heavens,
> however much listened to – who unloaded that boat.

So in *Beowulf* the dead chieftain Scyld is launched on his journey away from life, in a boat loaded with gold and weapons and treasures to honour him. In myth and poetry the image of a journey is the central one to express the great transition. It embodies the fact that though dying in actuality is a matter of incomprehensible swiftness – at one minute a whole, living person, at the next a vacancy – for the survivors there is a long process during which that person goes through many transformations, absences, and returns, moods of malignity and benevolence, before the new status is established. The dead one has to paddle a canoe westwards, go through a dense wood, be irrevocably ferried across a river; the unbelievable parting, the journey, and the re-establishment into a new status cannot be effected without time and work. As the anthropologist Robert Hertz wrote at the turn of the century, 'The brute fact of physical death is not enough to consummate death in people's minds; the image of the recently deceased is still part of the system of things of this world, and looses itself from them only gradually by a series of internal partings.' Death, he says, is 'always received with the same indignant amazement and despair'; for society, it strikes at the faith it has in itself. But at the end of the rites of transition, 'the last word must remain with life' (1960).

The vacated body meanwhile is always the focus of mixed feelings of fear and love; it is so like, and *not* like, the person we talked to half an hour ago. The sense that for a time it still contains the spirit is there when Edward Blishen talks of his father's death, and in the rituals of Catholicism and Judaism described in two of the interviews; the body of the newly dead is to be kept company, not left alone and solitary. In the many cultures where there are two separate funeral rituals, the second one celebrates the departed one's orderly arrival in the finally dead state – honoured, remembered, and pacified according to the prescribed rites.

In her diary Virginia Woolf describes transitions of feeling about the death of Katherine Mansfield, who was both an intimate and a rival:

At that one feels – what? A shock of relief? – a rival the less? Then confusion at feeling so little – then, gradually, blankness & disappointment; then a depression which I could not rouse myself from all that day . . . Visual impressions kept coming & coming before me – always of Katherine putting on a white wreath, & leaving us, called away; made dignified, chosen. And then one pitied her. And one felt her reluctant to wear that wreath, which was an ice cold one. And she was only 33 . . . For two days I felt that I had grown middle aged, & lost some spur to write. That feeling is going. I no longer keep seeing her with her wreath. I dont pity her so much. Yet I have the feeling that I shall think of her at intervals all through life.

This suggests one aspect, for us, of the dead – their pitifulness. 'Who will feed her?' the child Wendy asks about her mother who has died. They still ask to be fed, whether with wreaths or food or ritual observances; the Berawan tribe in Borneo solicitously offer their dead a puff of their cigarettes. The great Achilles, when Odysseus meets his shade in the underworld, says that he would rather live as a poor peasant's servant than reign as master over the dead. In 'All Souls' Day' D. H. Lawrence laments the 'poor dead' enduring their perilous transition – 'a long, long journey after death/to the sweet home of pure oblivion' – and repeats Beowulf's image of the death-ship:

> Oh, from out of your heart
> provide for your dead once more, equip them
> like departing mariners, lovingly.

And in Joyce's story 'The Dead' a man in full life thinks of his wife's long-dead lover – a shadow out in the cold, but pacified at last in the peacefulness of falling snow:

It was falling, too, upon every part of the lonely churchyard on the hill where Michael Furey lay buried. It lay thickly drifted on the crooked crosses and headstones, on the spears of the little gate, on the barren thorns. His soul swooned slowly as he heard the snow falling faintly through the universe and faintly falling, like the descent of their last end, upon all the living and the dead.

The forlorn dead and the triumphant living join here in reconciliation.

But the other side of pity for the dead is fear – an uncertain fear of their anger over their deprived state, over our still being in possession of what has been wrenched away from them. It is as if we kept them alive by our thought, and when we let them die we have failed them. Funeral rituals show both grief at their frailness and anxiety lest they exact revenge for it. In the Sora community that Piers Vitebsky describes, this danger is quite open, and mediums argue it through in dialogues with the disgruntled departed, who after a time let themselves be persuaded to relent and send blessings. Similarly Joseph Malual is torn by the idea that perhaps his dead mother in her loneliness took away his daughter for company. As Lévi-Strauss says (1955), successful mourning work 'is as if a contract had been concluded between the dead and the living; in return for being treated with a reasonable degree of respect, the dead remain in their own abode, and the temporary meetings between the two groups are always governed by concern for the interests of the living'.

Christianity – though malign spirits were until recently part of its eschatology – introduces a much more benign notion of the state of the dangerous dead; and yet associations of guilt and anxiety are not entirely banished. Jonathan Miller describes a sense of them as hungry children with their noses pressed to the restaurant window; a notion reminiscent of the much more terrible image in *Wuthering Heights* – that story of a passionate haunting – of the ghost of Cathy Linton tapping at the window and crying, 'Let me in.' There is somewhere, too, a fear of death by association – possessions, relatives tabooed – which is perhaps really a fear that our own Thanatos-grief will be so strong that it will override Eros and lead us to follow our dead.

Freud has argued that frightening fantasies of the dead as being hostile are a projection of our own hostility to them – hostility that we felt while they were alive, or anger at them for leaving us. This may be one element in a complex knot of feelings, but only one. (Who could be hostile towards a beloved dog, for instance? – yet Pat Hart describes her twinge of anxiety lest her dog should be jealous of its replacement.) Simply surviving – which inevitably involves replacements and consolations – poses the problem of enjoying one's own persisting vitality after the other has finished his or her share of it. The idea of life as a limited substance to be apportioned, bartered with, given, stolen, comes naturally to us – is there ever enough for all? Who is to enjoy it, and who lose it? The concept of sacrifice, central in Christianity as in so many other religions, follows on from this idea of life as a precious, limited essence which it is possible to offer back.

So for survivors there is always the task of establishing peace and continuity with the dead – forgiving them their terrible absence, being forgiven by them for continuing life. Their strangeness has to be faced; Richard Wilbur in 'The Pardon' begs his dog's forgiveness for recoiling from the corpse, and dreams his tremendous reappearance:

> Last night I saw the grass
> Slowly divide (it was the same scene
> But now it glowed a fierce and mortal green)
> And saw the dog emerging. I confess
>
> I felt afraid again, but still he came
> In the carnal sun, clothed in a hymn of flies
> And death was breeding in his lively eyes
> I started in to cry and call his name . . .
> I beg death's pardon now. And mourn the dead.

And Pat Hart imagines that at midnight her two dogs, the dead and the living, get up and play together.

Several other people who talk here express their sense of the lost person's benign continuation. Cathy Taggart struggles with a fear of her father's uncanniness, to find eventually that he is helping her to go on living; just as Joseph Malual expresses his deep belief that his father has guided him ever since his early death. A survivor may feel that he or she is now the container for the person's spirit, as when five-year-old Wendy acts out her mother's way of talking, or when St Augustine feels his dead friend to be precariously preserved in him: 'I felt that my soul and his soul were "one soul in two bodies": and therefore was my life a horror to me, because I would not live halved. And therefore perchance I feared to die, lest he whom I had much loved, should die wholly.' The persisting ghost may be elusive and tantalizing as, again, in *Wuthering Heights* – 'I could *almost* see her, and yet I *could not*! . . . She showed herself, as she often was in life, a devil to me!' – or patient, speechless, devoted, as is the shade attending Thomas Hardy:

> What a good haunter I am, O tell him!
> Quickly make him know

> If he but sigh since my loss befell him
>     Straight to his side I go.
> Tell him a faithful one is doing
>     All that love can do
> Still that his path may be worth pursuing,
>     And to bring peace thereto.

The ghosts come in dreams too, in various guises that reflect their fluctuating status. Jules de Goncourt records a dream in which he and his inseparable brother (then dead) walk down the street, both in deep mourning, receiving condolences, while simultaneously he is aware in the dream of the death announcements, spread out on the billiard table. In a dream told to me, a widow spent a happy day with her husband playing in a children's playground until, at the end, he sat her down and said, 'I must tell you now. I'm dead.' Virginia Woolf, so much of whose work is concerned with death and with re-creating people she had lost, goes on noting changes in her feelings for Katherine Mansfield. First the ice-cold wreath (as at the end of *To the Lighthouse* Mrs Ramsay, as Woolf's mother, seems to come back, 'raising to her forehead a wreath of white flowers'); five years later she dreams of her lying surrounded by sad-faced women; later still, Katherine Mansfield is shaking hands and talking with Woolf, though both know she is dead, and the dream seems 'a curious summing up' of all that has passed since she died. Piers Vitebsky meets a Sora guide carrying a lamp, though they fail to reach the Sora underworld. Jonathan Miller sees his father wistful, swept away by a crowd, somehow one of the thousands that died at Pompeii.

Dreaming is a way of remembering, and remembering is always seen as vitalizing, as a task that the living owe the dead. In the Sora underworld, when you are no longer remembered, your spirit turns into a butterfly. Searching for Tiresias in the underworld of the primitive Greeks, Odysseus calls out the shades and has them name themselves, and by doing so briefly restores the memory of who they are. In his interview here Ben Helfgott, having lost all his family, can say that as long as they are in his memory they are still living. Relics, memorials, keepsakes, contain in tangible form the memory of the dead person's essence; when two of the contributors talk about visiting old gravestones, it is with a sense that they are giving the dead a persisting thread of life. And the blessing is given back. The Anuak people of the Sudan carry about with them fragments that represent a legacy from their dead: a bit of a particular kind of wood with which an old man built good fences, a piece of bark from a tree where someone enjoyed sitting.

So there is a continuous balancing of life against death, continuous work to restore vitality wherever there has been an ending. When what has been lost is honoured, recollected, and established, as it were, into a new order of posthumous existence, the sense of continuity can begin to be established again for the people who suffered the loss. Re-creations of every kind – art or ritual, solemn or private – spring up in the gap that is left. Edward Blishen describes here his sense that a person should not be totally wasted by death, but conserved by the writer; the analyst Hanna Segal (1955) sees Proust's whole fictional world under this aspect:

He came back after a long absence to seek his old friends at a party, and all of them appeared to him as ruins of the real people he knew – useless, ridiculous, ill, on the threshold of death. Others had died long ago. And on realizing the destruction of a whole world that had been his he decides to write, to sacrifice himself to the re-creation of the dying and the dead.

Proust himself, in the same metaphor in which Lydia describes the survival of cuttings from her garden, evokes this belief in our power of regrowth:

I may say that throughout the whole of that year my life remained fully occupied with a love affair, a veritable liaison. And she who was its object was dead. It is often said that something may survive of a person after his death, if that person was an artist and put a little of himself into his work. It is perhaps in the same way that a sort of cutting taken from one person and grafted on to the heart of another continues to carry on its existence even when the person from whom it had been detached has perished.

And, relating the death of Bergotte at an art exhibition, he has him die with his mind fixed on a tiny patch of yellow wall from the background of a Vermeer painting – 'That's how I ought to have written'; and, pursuing the puzzle of how an artist works over and over a minute patch of paint without reward, Proust sees an intimation that 'the idea that Bergotte was not permanently dead is by no means improbable'.

In *The Prelude*, which is all a celebration of survival, Wordsworth re-creates two succeeding scenes in which desolation was transformed for him: the deserted moor where as a young child he stumbled on a gibbet; and a lonely crag where he waited impatiently to go home from school. Soon after he reached home his father died. But the wind and mist and rain, the bleak stone wall and single bare tree become something which nourishes him and to which he can go back in imagination and 'drink as at a fountain'.

A kind of surrendering is implied in these transformations, a loosening of the terrible grasp on each moment of time that John Snelling talks about here. Katherine Mansfield's own journal of her last few years traces an increasing calm as she relinquishes a demand on life – 'How hard it is to let go – to step into the blue. And yet one's creative life depends on it and one *desires* to do nothing else.' Three years before her death at thirty-three she had this dream:

I went to sleep. And suddenly I felt my whole body *breaking up*. It broke with a violent shock – an earthquake – and it broke like glass. A long terrible shiver, you understand – and the spinal cord and the bones and every bit and particle quaking. It sounded in my ears – a low, confused din, and there was a sense of flashing greenish brilliance, like broken glass. When I woke up I thought there had been a violent earthquake. But all was still. It slowly dawned upon me – the conviction that in that dream I died. I shall go on living now – it may be for months, or for weeks or days or hours. Time is not. In that dream I died. The *spirit* that is the enemy of death and quakes so and is so tenacious was shaken out of me ... And, oh, how strong was its hold upon me! How I *adored* life and *dreaded* death!

This freeing goes with a sense of blessing: blessing the watersnakes; or the moment when Tolstoy's Ivan Ilyich, angry and dying, makes peace with his family. It implies a degree of reconciliation – the moorland graves under a benign sky at the end of *Wuthering Heights*. 'I've fought you all my life,' says fireman Dick Clisby here, 'now you can have me!'

## References

Hertz, R. (1960). *Death and the Right Hand*. Translated by R. and C. Needham with an introduction by E. E. Evans-Pritchard. New York: Free Press.

Humphreys, S. C., and King, Helen (1981). *Mortality and Immortality: The Anthropology and Archaeology of Death*. London: Academic Press.

Lévi-Strauss, C. (1955). *Tristes Tropiques*. Translated by John and Doreen Weightman. London: Jonathan Cape. (First published in French, 1955.)

Segal, Hanna (1955). 'A Psychoanalytic Approach to Aesthetics'. In *New Directions in Psychoanalysis*, edited by M. Klein. London: Tavistock.

# THOMAS

        I don't know when it started – I couldn't put a date on it. But it was the only thing I ever thought about, night after night. Certainly it was by the time I was four. There is an odd thing about it – I had a threepenny bit on my desk and for some reason that symbolized the whole terror. That's just a circumstantial thing that I remember. No significant person died – I didn't have anything like that to show me what was involved. I just realized, because I had an atheistic upbringing – I realized what death meant. I knew that my parents could not solve this problem. So in the end I'd be crying and when they came up I'd always invent a nightmare, because I couldn't hear it from them that there was nothing to be done. I never dared to ask them, because I was too afraid the answer would be that that's the way it is. I knew that was the answer.

It was the thought of eternal non-existence. I think a lot of children mostly fear the break-up of the family and the loss of their parents – they start asking how old you are. That is part of the fear. But it's also your own death, your own eternal ending. It was only a physical fear in the sense that there were lots of going-to-sleep things that used to happen. I used to have a recurrent – not a dream, a half-sleepy state where there would be a slope, getting steeper and steeper and steeper. And this was terrifying. It was down, down, down. For me that was a sort of image of the eternity of my non-existence. It was fantastically vivid and utterly terrifying.

I thought I must have been adopted, like so many children. I was up at the top of the house, the only child at the top of the house. Very scared. One other thing I remember – well, we lived in Woodstock Road, so the St Giles's graveyard was a few hundred yards away. I remember quite a complicated thought I used to have: I was very anxious because as far as I could see there was no space left in the graveyard, and I wanted very much for us all to be buried together, although I also knew it was no good – it wouldn't *really* mean us being together.

I don't think I ever had any sort of vague hopes – well, I suppose I wanted there to be something after death . . . I doubt if all that was connected with my teaching moral philosophy now. I think the immediate result of it was becoming a kind of mystic consumer as an adolescent. First it was Hinduism – my best friend's uncle was connected with someone like the Maharishi; and then, well, Sufism, Christianity, Buddhism . . .

No, I didn't tell anyone as a child, it was too . . . It was: time would go on for ever and ever and you wouldn't be there. For ever; I mean really for ever. Actually I'm slightly nervous of talking about it because it's ceased to be a problem in some way, and the idea that I might . . . If I get too confident about it, it might come back. I don't want to restart the mechanism.

I couldn't sleep as a child; and if you don't sleep you think more. And you know how you always imagine, if there was a fairy, what one wish would you have, and that you mustn't wish for *all* your wishes to be granted because that would be cheating; my one wish was always to be able to go to sleep. Oh, to wish to live for ever – I knew that was unrealistic. It didn't change as I got older, at least not for a long time. No, I didn't ask my parents about death. It was secret, I didn't want to talk about it, because I didn't want to hear what I knew confirmed. Or rather, I couldn't look someone in the face and see them too acknowledging this fact of death.

The first I heard about God was when I was at school, when I was about five. It probably didn't make much impression on me – it did on my sister, she started saying prayers and so on. I don't think there was any interesting development in my views about it when I was a child, I just remember it as this terrible thing. And it was truly awful. Every night I knew what was going to happen once the light was out. So I read a lot, kept a light underneath the bedclothes. I think every child realizes the same thing, but usually there's a successful process of repression. Who knows what's relevant or not? – but apparently I was virtually deaf in infancy, I didn't speak till I was over two, and I didn't walk till very late. They thought I might be mentally subnormal till I had my tonsils out. Perhaps this early silence did something to me.

I would say I was very unhappy as a child – mainly because of that, because of the thoughts of death. Also going to school – even when I was seven I knew what I had to do was get a scholarship, and I was worrying already. My father was a non-existence in my childhood – he was always working. My mother – she would tend to lose her temper; I was very bad, I was a wild, tantrum child, I would kick down doors.

Teenage – well, perhaps my interest in various religions was connected . . . Hinduism – that was just because my best friend was involved. He got killed later, when I was about twenty-six; that's the most significant death I've known. That was really terrible, and I realized that . . . Perhaps I shouldn't talk about it and bring it back. I think actually that was the first thing that stopped me being freaked out about death – one thought, well, if he's gone that way one could go that way too. He was killed while he was doing anthropology fieldwork in South America – a very gifted and odd person. It was just the thought that if he's dead, it doesn't matter so much; it's not that I think something happens afterwards.

It's true that you just can't believe it, even so . . . Ever since he died I've had dreams in which he would be alive; and in the dream I'd say, 'Yes, but this is only a dream.' And even more complicated dreams where after I'd said that this is only a dream, it would then be, 'No, this is really true!' Within the dream, as it were. It was just a refusal to accept it, I suppose. I think at the beginning after he died I did daydream too about meeting up with him after life was all over, wishing that that could be true. Desperately. It also meant that . . . I'm still afraid of getting letters, ever since I had that letter about his death in my hand. I put them away and don't look at them. It's funny.

The childhood fear, it was being worried about . . . Yes, it was fear of eternal non-existence connected up with the idea of infinite space and infinite time. I suppose that's part of the insignificant-speck syndrome. I think Joseph, my son, has those thoughts; he's six. I don't know. In my twenties it was still there; I remember at the beginning of marriage, the actual fact of marriage somehow made death more real, as a natural termination of this state. Instead of being aware of the living person, I would be aware of the bones.

It must have been known in the family when I was a child that I was very afraid of death, because I was taken to see *Oliver* as a treat, and there's a point at which he worked, I think, as an undertaker's assistant, and everyone was frightened that I wouldn't be able to bear this scene. I remember reading the school magazine, and every year there'd be a report about someone who'd tragically died young; and I thought, oh well, statistically it's got to be one of us, and I decided it was going to be me. That I'd die before the age of nineteen. So I haven't done too badly. But I was always planning to commit suicide as a child, just to show them. Because I was always getting into terrible trouble. But now . . . Having your own children makes a lot of difference – you couldn't do it. Though I have even now sometimes had the feeling that if it's too difficult I don't want to go on.

I sleep a bit better now, but it's still bad. But no, this is the extraordinary thing – which is why I'm tempting fate in talking to you – it *has* changed. Julian Barnes in his first book had a character who used to be obsessed with death – till thirty, and then it just stopped. One hypothesis was that it was having a son that did it. One always looks for the least flattering explanation of why things happen to one . . . Perhaps there is something in the view that people feel that they're perpetuating themselves when they have children. It seems to me to be completely irrational. But it does coincide – Joseph was born when I was thirty, and that was about the time it got better. I do still think about it sometimes, the terror, but you have to be terribly careful. The idea that I could start it up again would be so awful . . .

My friend dying – I'd say that was the most crucial thing in my life. We got involved in Islam together. That was quite serious, because it was a genuine mystical organization, based in Algeria with a place in Paris. But what it actually did was to turn me into a true agnostic, after having flirted with Christianity and all the rest – these absurd notions of a Christian God, this was all wiped clean. Oh, it's all terribly beautiful, yes. I think there's a class of people, like Iris Murdoch for instance, who don't really believe but they do wish it was true, and they can't stop being interested. What I find repugnant about Christian prayers is the actual sort of beseeching God for something, because it's such utter nonsense. Yes, the sense of helplessness in adversity I think must be the main motive for religious belief. When I was a Muslim I'd be saying the prayers five times a day – well, I faced in the right direction and said something. But one thing about Islam was that there was no pleading prayer, the prayer was just something you had to do, praising not supplicating.

But I think the Muslim thing turned me back into a proper agnostic, atheist if you like; it cleaned out all the Christian accretions. What it was about, all the way through, was some project of self-improvement, being a good person in the world; it wasn't future-directed in any way. Because the promise of mystical enlightenment is that you lose all time, therefore you no longer fear death. It doesn't necessarily mean that you think there's life after death. But I copped out of all that, because I met my wife, and she was very much into a materialistic way of life; I gave up vegetarianism, I quite enjoyed the repudiation of all my hippy values. I don't think I'd had mystical experiences anyway, it was more the sense of community, being involved with others, feeling you were in it together. Maybe that did improve things, I can't quite remember now.

Sometimes, yes, I have thought very occasionally that all of it, all the bad stuff, has been worth it for *this* bit, for what's happening right now. A sunny day early in the autumn . . . But I can imagine recovering the sense of terror. I think what it is now is that I'm too occupied with my present concerns to have the terror – I feel this is the key, having a job that you're really interested in. And all I think about is, am I going to finish this bit of philosophy? I feel that I'd need ten years to write all the stuff I want to write, that's more what worries me now. The acquisition of worthwhile short-term worries is the best defence!

I don't think there's mind apart from brain, no, I'm a convinced materialist. But I do think there's a mystery about how physical processes can give rise to, let alone *be*, mental processes – it's not only not self-evident, it's deeply counter-intuitive. I think one of the difficulties about this is that when people think of the problem they always think about themselves, and people, but when you think about dogs, the problem doesn't worry you; you're sure that they see and they smell and they can feel pain, and you're sure that that's all physically based and nothing more. Still, I do think that there's a mystery, and I don't think that anyone has any idea about how to begin to solve it. For me that doesn't have any nice consequences about survival or an immaterial soul. No, I don't have any difficulty in knowing that anything so complex as a human being just disappears, because I think of the profligacy of nature, the micro-engineering of a mosquito – such extraordinary complexity thrown away ... I think of it as nature sort of wildly overshooting, splurging her gifts around; with human beings it's just more of the same kind of profligacy. These extraordinary brains and sensibilities, produced in millions, and then just thrown away, disappearing in eternity. I don't think man's a special case, I think the theory of evolution explains it all. It's a very beautiful theory, come to think of it, a marvellous and inspiring theory, though it has grim consequences for us.

I don't actually have the terror now. But I suspect it might get worse again when I get older – apparently there's some study that shows that fear of death rises steadily until the age of about sixty and then drops sharply after that. I think I became much more hypochondriac after losing the big fear of death, and I wonder if the one has just somehow converted into the other. There are two fears, I can see that – one of dying and one of death. The *locus classicus* for that is the two characters in Arthur Koestler's novel *Dialogue with Death* – they discover that one is only afraid of dying, and the other is only afraid of death. I can't imagine saying that I'm only afraid of dying and not of death itself.

*The Makropoulos Case*, do you know about that? It's an opera by Janáček. There's an article about that by Bernard Williams; he argues there that it's actually terrible, because the woman lives on and on and stays the same age and she gets desperately sad and bored ... That's one thesis, that death is a good thing because we couldn't take much more life than we get. But I don't find that convincing – as long as you don't age, there are always new books to read, there's music to listen to, there's the countryside to enjoy. But, yes, the ending does structure our thought about things, very deeply. From an early age; because we all cotton on.

It doesn't seem to me that Christianity is any help, because the key thing there is the resurrection of the body, and the traditional image of what happened was: first nothing, and then the next thing you know is that you're getting out of your grave and rising up to heaven ... It's not obvious that to believe in immortality you have to believe that the soul exists independently of the body; one strong tradition denies that, and insists on the resurrection of a body, to have memories and experiences and so on. The Hegelian thing, that we're all just aspects of the one absolute spirit – I think that wouldn't comfort many people, because what they care about is their individuality.

No, I don't see how there could be something that could survive the death of the brain. Even if telepathy were true, that would just mean there were processes in the natural world that we didn't yet understand. There is one wonderful theory: because it's so hard to explain how mind can arise from matter, the only decent thesis is to suppose that matter is already mental in some way. That matter is real, but that there's some fragmentary consciousness in every particle. Quantum physics – no, I don't think that that changes anything – there's a terrible amount of rubbish talked about it. It's true that there is one lesson of modern science, which is that everything is really far, far stranger than we thought – so strange that no hypothesis can really be ruled out. And neurophysiologists – everyone says that they all go into a mystical phase when they retire. It's interesting, because they've spent their whole lives dealing with the brain, and end up feeling dissatisfied.

But as for mystical feelings about survival, that's just the tremendous force of native egoism – people can't believe in their own extinction. It doesn't seem the right kind of reason for believing in survival, it doesn't make you feel they might be right. Just a kind of transcendental egoism. And the near-death experience, that's just a brain-state, something like the *déjà vu*. And there is that thing, that when you're in great danger you can suddenly feel great – I had that when I went over the handlebars of my motor bike. Just feeling absolutely wonderful. Everything slows down, complete calm. I'm sure that's real, but it doesn't *mean* anything either in terms of survival. I guess it's easier, then, if you have a sudden death, not a long-drawn-out one – the point about sudden death is that you *are* aware, you come together, time slows down enormously. A second or two of awareness is enough.

Joseph said the other day – I was saying something about pain, being badly burnt was the worst thing that could happen to you – and he very peremptorily said, 'No it isn't, the worst thing that can happen to you is death.' How he learned about death, I don't really know – it's in conversation all the time, you swat insects . . . I never killed insects, and that neurosis remains, in that I hate to kill one now. It was the sense that one was oneself as swat-able as a fly, or as transient as a fly. I remember thinking that to be grown-up, that was going to be salvation – you could keep the light on at night. And it seemed clear to me that grown-ups weren't thinking about death all the time, and I assumed that that would happen to me. Well, it may be true. But poor old Rach- maninov, for instance – he couldn't think about anything else.

People who aren't afraid, I think most of them just don't know what death *means*. But suppose you knew you would just be painlessly killed and not know anything about it, would you think that was a bad thing to happen? I'm not sure it would be. The idea is that it's terrible, because then you've lost a chunk of years – no, that's a sort of tradesman's attitude to one's life, I can't conceive of thinking of it like that. The standard theory of moral philosophy is that it's a great evil for a person to be suddenly cut off; but it seems to me that the evil is knowing that it's going to happen. If it happened without your knowing, it wouldn't matter. There's that marvellous poem of Larkin's about a hospital . . .

Wittgenstein said it was a mistake to be afraid of death itself; he said that 'death is not an event in life, it is not lived through'. But actually I feel it's a sort of moral failure, not to be afflicted as I used to be. Because if you *are* no longer afflicted, it's only because you've succeeded in drugging yourself with distractions. But, of course, saying that, I'm tempting fate . . .

I don't know how I'll feel when my parents die. I've always

assumed that when people get to a sufficient age you just don't feel bad about it. Consciously or not, you have been absorbing the message that there is this span for them. And also you're trying to balance the suffering of their decay against their death. But I do think perhaps – again, not consciously – you might feel that they're sort of longstops, they stand between one and death. And when they go the vista opens out ... I'm sure one would feel that. And the question of leaving things unsolved with one's parents ... Like Hardy's poems, the 1912 to 1913 poems to his wife – she had died suddenly, and there was so much he wanted to have said to her. But you can't do it – you can be aware of all that, and yet you can't have that significant talk with your parents. But don't you feel that at some level there's a mutual understanding on both sides? I don't talk much to my mother, and yet I do hope that there's some awareness of that sort on her side.

I do see that eternal existence is a frightening idea too. Tolkien talked about death as man's gift – that may come from Norse mythology. Our whole thinking about life is implicitly that it's going towards some ending. If one did have eternal life it would have to be a *kind* of life that one wouldn't want to end; one would just move within a smallish shell of concerns which reached a few years into the future. As it is, I think you do learn, with a bit of luck, to appreciate things that are transient.

I think I'm probably not a good person to interview because I've dropped the terror now – I hope so anyway. I'm still not sure whether I've been able to get it across to you, the total terror and how long it lasted. For instance, my eldest child was a mistake really, because at the time I thought, I'll never have a child because I wouldn't want it to go through what I went through. I thought it was obviously immoral to have children, because of the terrible suffering that fear of death would cause in childhood.

I feel I should have more rich experiential detail to tell you, but I've lost touch with it. I'm sure there was a lot more to it. There were times when it seeped into everything, there was no point in anything. The extraordinary physical sensation when the thought of eternal non-existence struck! Every time. Something in the throat, I don't know: there are lots of physical accompaniments. It's like a sort of white electricity.

You know what Dostoevsky said – that shivering on a ledge in hell for all eternity was better than non-being. Not true, of course, but still . . .

## Trudy Brown

I'm in launderettes – very mundane, isn't it? I'm a
very practical person. Only psychic on the side, really. You'll find
I'm a very doubting spiritualist; I mean, although I'm a medium I
find it very hard to quite totally accept it all. Yes, it makes for a
lot of difficulties within my psychic development, because I'm
only a ninety per cent believer.

It's an interesting thing, how I became a medium. First of all,
my mother was always interested in psychic matters, and her
family . . . Well, they never knew much about it, but they used to
push the glass around on a table and that sort of thing. My father
disapproved, he thought it was a load of rubbish. But my mother
believed, and I grew up sort of believing and always very interested. And I always found at school if we played about with the
glass on the ouija board that if I put my finger on it, it always
went – everybody swore I was pushing it, but I wasn't. In fact I
could sit and look at it and know what it was going to say,
without even touching it, so to this extent I was always somewhat
psychic. I do think it's there in everybody, in that probably
everybody could play the piano but some play it better than
others. But there has to be . . . Well, either it's a special tuning, or
a special need, or you're chosen and maybe it's your path in life to
be a medium. Certainly it's not an easy one. And so that's how it
started.

I remember when I was about fourteen I came up from
school – the war was on, and I was away at school – and I went
to the Pembridge Place Spiritual Association with my mother;
and the medium was demonstrating and she pointed to me and
said to me, 'You're going to be a medium one day and stand on
this platform.' And I thought, oh, what a load of nonsense!
Because I've never *seen* things; I can't look in the corner and see
a ruddy great Red Indian standing there; I know things, but at

that time it seemed terribly impossible. In the event, when I graduated as a medium I stood in that church on the platform and demonstrated clairvoyance. Isn't it interesting?

No, as a child I never saw anything or talked to anything . . . My one experience, and it really isn't much: I was about nine, I had pneumonia and pleurisy together and I was very ill. I remember lying in bed, I've never forgotten it, and then all of a sudden I was up on the ceiling looking down. I can still remember looking down, seeing myself in bed, and some new shoes that my mother had bought that I'd decided I'd never wear, under the chair. I can't remember if I was scared. I can only remember the amazement of being up in the corner of the room and looking down, and I've never forgotten that. I don't know how long it lasted. That was my only experience.

My husband wasn't exactly a believer, but he was a very open man, so when anybody died we used to go to a medium, or once in a while anyway. But I'm very down to earth, you know, very inclined to doubt. I'm not dedicated – I do lots of things, bridge, travel, and so on. People have said it makes me a better medium. There are gullible people who do a lot of harm to the movement, people who think that spirit moves everything – you know, I've heard people say, 'Well, I need a gardener and spirit will send me a gardener so that I can get on with my work'! I think, what nonsense! I don't believe that your guides tell you what to do; I mean, people come to me and say, 'Do my guides tell you what I should do about moving home?' I say, 'No, I think if you're going to move home that's your decision, that's what you're here learning about – the guides are not telling you when to sell your stocks and shares.'

Anyway, my husband and I used to go to the odd sitting with a medium. My husband's mother died, and my parents died very soon after each other, and I'd always been interested anyhow, so occasionally we went. I did find that when we talked to people, I used to have these little cold winds blowing up and down my hands – it was most odd, as though somebody was puffing cold wind – so I sort of got to believe that spirit was there. Anyhow, my husband began to believe, not because of any one thing but because over a period of time we got so much circumstantial evidence. My father's mother, who was a difficult old lady – she came through. And she never believed; and the medium said, 'Your mother's standing here', and he said, 'It's most amazing, because she's passed over, but she's saying to me, "It's a load of poppycock"!' Which is actually what she used to say! So that was the sort of thing, over a period of time all these things happened.

I used to go to my parents' grave and cry; and one day a medium said – it sounds as though I was always going to mediums, but I wasn't – one day a medium said to me, you know, 'Why do you go to their grave and cry? – that's not where they are.' So this was the sort of comforting thing which one got. And then once I was sitting in front of the television with my husband and I felt . . . It was very odd, it was just an ordinary evening – my brother-in-law was very ill, but it wasn't particularly bearing upon me; and I felt myself drifting away. I didn't realize this at the time, but I actually went into trance. My husband told me afterwards that somebody came through, and sort of spoke to him – he was rather surprised, but he was always very good at coping with anything that happened – and this voice, this person said, 'I can't talk to you very much'; he said, 'Your wife is too strong, she's sitting on my mind.' I've never forgotten that! When I came round, I thought I'd been asleep. But my voice had been saying these things. My husband had asked about my brother-in-law, would he be all right; and apparently the guide said yes, as far as they knew he'd be all right, but he said something about life is like a candle, you know, someone blows and the candle goes out.

And then I went with my niece to see a medium and the medium said, 'You know, you really ought to develop.' I was in my forties. 'You really ought to develop, because, you know, you should be a medium.' I really hadn't wanted to get involved, I'd left it, I hadn't done anything about it; I'd sort of half believed it and half not. You know, you think to yourself, well, maybe I made the whole thing up. Anyhow, to finish off – we actually stopped at the College of Psychic Studies, and my niece went in and made an appointment for me to start development classes.

And I came home, and my husband had just retired – he retired early – and life was going very well, it had always gone pretty well. And I thought, I'm not going to develop now, I'm not going to start doing things which might stop me going away on holidays with my husband, or doing this or that; so I phoned and cancelled it. And then about a week later my husband died, very suddenly.

He had an aneurysm – he hadn't been ill, he was fifty-seven. He just broke up. It happened one Saturday morning – he didn't feel well, his blood pressure was low, and they took him into hospital and he died that night. It was dreadful. I don't know how those people who don't believe in survival can stand it. Because, I mean, one minute the person is there – and the next minute *gone*. *Just* out of reach. As though you could almost pull them back, and yet you can't.

The following evening I was sitting in there, in the chair, absolutely knocked, as you can imagine, with the shock. My brother was sitting there, and my niece. And I felt as though I was getting smaller and smaller, as though I was shrinking inside my own body, smaller and smaller and smaller. And that's all I remember; but I went into trance, and my brother and my niece were absolutely amazed. My niece actually wrote it all down in the beginning of a library book she was reading, and we were never able to take the book back to the library! My guide came through and said, well, now I was going to do a lot of work, and they'd had to wait for my husband to pass before I could really start to do the work. They didn't say they *made* him pass – they said they had to wait until he passed because I wouldn't be ready till then. And that we were to try not to mourn too much, because there was a lot of work for me to do.

Guides – they've had many lives, lived on earth many times, and as I understand it they've progressed beyond ever coming back to earth, but they're doing you a service – they work with you and for you. They would be people who would have passed on a long time ago, who probably met you in different lifetimes. They'll try to influence and advise you to the best if they can; for instance, I have a guide who I've been told mainly does the communicating, but there's a group of them, a fellowship, but they'll talk through one who for whatever reason is more able to communicate with me.

So I started after the guides told me, after my husband died. I wasn't sure what to do; I went to see Benjamin, Benjamin . . . I can't think of his second name. He was a most fantastic old-fashioned medium who's since died. I went about a week after my husband's death. I was all in black, so I obviously looked like a widow, or I could have lost a child . . . But I went to see him and he was absolutely fantastic, he said, 'Ah, I'm glad you're here, your husband's been here waiting for you', and that was marvellous. And he said to me – I was wearing long black gloves – he said to me, 'Show me your husband's watch you're wearing.' So I showed him the watch. 'Yes,' he said, 'but that wasn't the watch he was wearing in hospital, was it? That watch is still in the hospital.' And it was. So he was really good.

He said lots of things about my husband; but then the most interesting thing was, he went into trance, and a guide came through and said to me, 'You're going to do a lot of work, we've already told you, you're going to do a lot of spiritualistic work.' And I said, 'Well, what should I do about it?' And he said, 'Nothing – it will happen.' When he came out of trance, the medium was amazed that he'd been in trance; he was a very old man, and he said, 'I haven't been in trance for fifty years.' And in fact he took me downstairs to his wife and said, 'Tell my wife I've been in trance' – it was so funny.

No, I don't go into trance normally. When somebody comes in and sits with me, I bring up the power, I say a teeny little prayer to myself, you know – sort of 'Don't let me down, kid!' No, in a nicer way! And the person comes in, and things go through my mind, almost like a tune. I say, 'Well, I'm seeing a lady, I think it must be your grandmother – she had so-and-so and she did so-and-so.' And they might say, 'No, that's not my grandmother, that's my husband's mother' – I'm never quite sure. 'Yes, well, she says so-and-so about you.' And they say, 'Yes, that's right.'

You have to clear your mind of other things, but I can talk to them and be listening at the same time, so they don't have to sit in silence. Some untrained mediums are open too much, and that's terrible; but we were taught to close down . . . I mean, I'm talking to you now, but I'm getting nothing at all about your life because I'm closed down, I'm not open, the telephone exchange is not working. I know that people always look at me and think to themselves, I wonder if she's seeing into my mind, I wonder if she's going to tell me something. But I'm not, because I'm not open to it all the time.

The training was very hard; you start off sitting in a class, which I always call the babies' class, where she teaches you to open up, which is making yourself aware of psychic power within you. It's banding your body with light, so that you're closer to spirit – it's a question of concentration. Yes, it's difficult when you don't see anything at the end of it, but you begin to feel when it's right ... The hardest thing in the beginning is giving clairvoyance, because, for me, I don't actually hear a voice talking, it just goes through my mind. So in the beginning it's very hard to say, 'Well, I'm seeing a man with a top hat on', or whatever it is. You see, there's a big class and you go to who you like – you're drawn to a person – and you say, 'All right, Joan, I'm coming to you, I'm seeing a man with a top hat.' And they'll say, 'No, I don't understand that' or 'Yes, I do', and you draw up the power again and you try again. Eventually you get a feeling; I should imagine like a pianist playing a wrong note, as you give it you know it's wrong, there isn't that real note of truth in it.

When I stand up in a hall or demonstrate in a church, it's usually right. Sometimes it's not. There can be all sorts of reasons for that. Maybe I'm putting it wrongly to a person. If I say to somebody, 'I've got your mother, and she was quite short and plump', maybe she was only plump in her old age and the person is remembering her as a young woman. Or I'm saying, 'She had a great sense of humour', maybe she didn't, maybe she only ever laughed if somebody fell over – I'm picking up the sense of humour and giving it wrongly. So a lot of it, when people don't understand, is because I'm translating what I'm getting in my mind badly. Not very often, though. Sometimes you get some-body who comes up to you afterwards, or writes to you after a sitting, and says, 'You know, I didn't know who you were talking about – when I got home, of course, my daughter reminded me that it was my old Aunt Fanny.' That happens quite a lot – people don't remember, don't think. Very often somebody comes to a sitting, and they're absolutely set on getting their husband, or their daughter, and they get somebody else; and they don't even think. 'No, no, no, I don't know who that is at all.' And a medium tends then to stop; I reckon you have three goes, and if the person says no, you give it up.

It's not something that we can control, who comes through; maybe Great Aunt Fanny has something to say which is important, and the husband is standing back. But when they cut you off it's very hard, it's like being punched in the stomach, you know. They say, 'No, no, I don't want that'; but *they*'re not making the call, they're only receiving the call. Sometimes somebody comes because there's something specific they want to say to you. For instance, supposing you were planning – I mean, I'm only making this up – but supposing you were planning to remarry, your husband might not want to come and say to you, 'That's the wrong man', but your Great Aunt Fanny might come in and say, 'You want to be careful who you're thinking about marrying.' I once had a lady, and I said to her, 'Your husband's here' – and she said, 'I don't want to speak to *him*!' She really did! In this world there must be people that you don't particularly want to hear from – I mean, somebody phones you up and you think, oh God, I don't want to talk to her. But then they may have something that they really need to say to you.

I'd been told by my guide to do nothing, it would happen; and it really is interesting, everything's just happened to me, I never pushed. My brother, who didn't believe at all, had a very bad back and he'd started going to a healer just before my husband died. He didn't believe in it, but oddly enough the treatment had helped him, he was sleeping better. So just after my husband died he said to me, 'Look, I've got an appointment with the healer today and why don't you come with me', and I said, 'I don't want to.' He said, 'I won't go otherwise, I won't leave you alone.' So I said, 'All right, I'll go.'

So I went. It was nice and warm, and there was music. I was very sad, someone was trying to heal me, and I actually went into trance again – I know it sounds as though I'm always going into trance, but it's only three times in a whole lifetime that I've been in deep trance – and in the trance my guide said, 'We're going to come and help you with the healing, we're going to bring you strength.' And apparently they, as a group, the healers, had been told a week before by a medium that there would be another healer. So when I came round she said, 'Please join us.' This was before I started my training in the development class. I said, 'I don't know anything about healing.' She said, 'Never mind, come.'

So I started to come, and it really saved my life. I went twice a week, laying my hands on people; I didn't know what I was doing or why, but it was just the fact of going, and the group who did the healing were so kind, and it gave me something to do. And then in the healing group somebody said to me, 'You really ought to go and train as a medium, you know, because you're very clever' – because I used to pick up odd bits and say to people so-and-so, and they'd say, 'Yes, how did you know?' I didn't know how I knew. So that's how I went to be trained in the end.

Yes, I felt my husband very strongly by my side – but whether he was really by my side or whether I wanted to feel that he was, I can't tell you. But, as I say, this is my scepticism coming out. I did feel that my husband was very close, and it gave me enormous help. If somebody you loved was gone and you felt they'd gone for good, it must be awful, I don't know how you cope with that. I've got a very dear friend that that happened to recently. My belief in spiritualism did help me enormously – first of all the companionship helped me, and also my firm belief that there was a hereafter, and that they were still around me.

When I was told, 'All right, I can train you to be a medium – are you prepared to work on the platform?' I must confess that I said yes, not because I wanted to work on the platform, but I thought, ah, I'll be able to talk to my husband, and my mother and father, you know, absolutely great! Of course in actual fact I never have been able to talk to my husband or my parents. Because how can I know it's not my own mind? You see, it comes through my mind like a tune; now if I tell you things, I don't know you from Adam and it's got to be right, but if I think to myself my husband is saying so-and-so, is he saying it or am I imagining it? Occasionally I feel my husband says to me, 'Don't be a bloody fool' – but then I think, ah well, that's probably me putting into my husband's mouth what he would have said and what I know myself to be true.

But I'm now so convinced he's around, and of course I've got messages . . . I've helped train students, and when the students are having great trouble in communicating, one of them will say to me, 'Your husband's here', and I know that to be true; and then they'll get something quite good, because my husband is helping them, you know. And that gives them confidence, because there's nothing worse if you're learning to be a medium than if you can't get anything right, you just think, oh, I'm never going to get it. So I know my husband's around.

I know people say that the messages could be a kind of telepathy rather than evidence of survival, but it always seems to me that if you were that skilled in telepathy you could get a jolly good job in a music-hall, you wouldn't need to be a medium at three pounds a throw or something. I think actually at some point . . . I've heard Christians say that you have to affirm your faith, and I think you need to make that leap of faith, I think that's necessary. If it all came so easily, you would think it nothing, but you need that little bit of effort to say, 'OK, of all the possibilities, I believe that my husband's still there.'

There are people who don't believe at all, and really that's up to them. I don't think it's necessary for everybody to believe; but I find that people who come to see me have already got a faith, they don't need to be convinced in that way. Times have changed – of course the Victorian mediums were very different. That's been explained, by a guide; the Victorians needed to *see* miracles to believe – they were very down-to-earth people. Today we accept so much; we accept television and the radio, we know that somebody's been on the moon, we don't so much need to see things to believe. I was trained to give proof – that is, to be able to tell you about your mother or your grandmother, and specific things about them, and I was very pleased to be able to do this. But I find that people come because they're worried about themselves, they want to know where they're going. I think more people are conscious that their way of life is not just something that's haphazard, that it has a plan or purpose or things happen for a particular reason. And they often come to mediums to know about that.

What I think happens is that while on earth you learn about things that you can't learn about in any other sort of place, because earth is physical, and so you learn about coping with money and about love and anything else you want to know, hatred, and training yourself – it's a school of learning. And I think you come back to earth many times to learn different things, and that you opt to know what you're learning. So that you might lead a life on this earth which appears to be very pointless, but maybe you're learning to be of service. I often think to myself, perhaps somebody like Marilyn Monroe was supposed to be learning about coping with beauty and money, and never did succeed. Or maybe she did, but she had to learn that very hard way. So I think that we are all doing paths which might seem to be very unimportant, but they're not – they're all part of training your soul. It's always difficult to know why there are outright villains, though. It could be that they're turning in a way from what they should be, or it could be perhaps that people are bouncing off them – maybe somebody is acting the part of the villain in order that other people should learn.

I don't believe there could be anything evil in the guides who come through, I don't believe there could be. Bad souls are not connected with people like you and me. They're floating about by themselves. I think it's silly for people to do the ouija table and this sort of thing, I think you can get riff-raff, by and large. I mean, I've played with it as a child, but I've got a strong mind, and you tend to discard it. But some people will get themselves hooked; now, whether in their minds they think there's somebody evil there or whether there *is* somebody, I can't tell, because I don't know. But I think that there are spirits floating around who are looking constantly towards earth and who are wanting to get back.

My guides once said that people's illnesses are for different reasons, and sometimes the reason for their illness is to help other people. I mean, that's a hard thing to say, but if you get away from thinking that everything that happens on earth is very important, things can take on a different . . . I can say this, but I don't totally practise it by any means, I easily succumb to irritation. But I see that if you start to look at it from a different point of view ... For instance, it's said by a lot of people, I believe, that children who die very young of cancer and things like this, very often they're old spirits who've opted to come back as a service, because the living and the dying as a child can often do great things for a family – sometimes it brings them together, it gives them an awareness. You see? And as long as you're judging it all from this earth it seems to be cruel and hard, but if you judge it as being part of a pattern, then you look at it differently. If it doesn't matter, if life doesn't matter as such, if you can get away from thinking that living is the most important thing ... I mean, if somebody could only talk us round to thinking that dying was the great graduation ...

No, I don't fear death at all, I don't think I do. If somebody pointed a gun at me this minute my heart would start thudding, that's a natural reaction, and I'd probably say, 'Please don't shoot me', because that's me, I'm human. I think if I were very ill – I mean, I'm sure I would be frightened – but I think I would have times when I would say to myself, 'Well, really, I don't mind – I'm sorry for the people I'm leaving behind, but I'm glad to go.'

Well, as for what happens after death ... There are all sorts of stories. First of all, I've heard from a lot of people who've both died and not died – you know, there are all these books about the near-death experience – that dying is very peaceful, in that you rise above your body like I did when I was a child, you watch people trying to resuscitate you, you don't realize for a time what's happening because, I suppose, you think you're in a coma or whatever it is. And then usually somebody that you've loved comes to meet you and take you over ... Isn't that nice? My mother was a spiritualist, she was very ill at the time, though I don't think she was thinking about it, and she said to me about a day before she died – nobody really knew she was about to die – she said, 'You know, Grandpa was here, sitting in the chair.' Her father. And I said, 'Oh, Mummy!' I wasn't much of a believer. And she said, 'Yes, he was. And I said to him, "I can't go yet, Daddy, I can't go, because my brother isn't married."' I think he probably was there – I think he came, and when she died he took her across.

You go back into spirit, you see, and I think that for a time you're looking towards earth, if you've got children and some people that you're interested in. That's why you communicate, that's right, because maybe there are things you want to say, or they need you. I think as time goes by – and there's no such thing as time, so that makes it very difficult – their interest lessens. For instance, I don't think my great-grandparents care a fig about me. So then you're going back into your own group, and you're looking – 'What am I going to do next? What do I still need to learn about? Perhaps I still need to learn about suffering, I don't know.' The people you're involved with over there are people that you've been involved with in other lives. You see back over your life, you realize the things that you haven't done, and the mistakes you made which you can learn by. And then at some stage you come back again in a different guise. So each soul is evolving all the time; and there comes a time when some of the great gurus on earth have evolved and they don't come back any more – I think Jesus was a great spirit. Then people like Henry the Eighth, who are always coming back, are very basic spirits and have an awful lot to learn.

No, I don't see how there could be a *personal* God. I think myself that we need a personal God because we're people, so therefore we bring God down to being a nice benevolent old man. I think it's more a question of a plan in the universe. But then a plan does take in the idea that somebody has thought it out. I saw a very interesting film in America recently; they had great scientists and mathematicians – I heard one of them say that the more you study the galaxies and the universe, the more religious you get.

So I don't know . . . I do pray – I have little words with my guides, sort of sweet threats, like 'You help me, kid, and I'll help you.' Yes, if somebody was desperately ill, I'm sure I'd pray – I suppose it would be to God, because I'm human and I'd say, 'Don't let it happen.' Of course I still cry about my husband; and I've been absolutely inconsolable about my dog – he had to be put to sleep yesterday. Animals do survive. I can only tell you what I've heard, which is that they have sort of group souls, it's like a pool. I think it's very nice that domestic animals – not as individuals, but the group soul – have opted to be of service to mankind. And sheep and cows and all the things that we kill so indiscriminately – they're here to do a service. And somebody once told me that if you love an animal very much, it sets it on its road to becoming a human soul. I quite often, when I'm giving clairvoyance, see cats or dogs with people.

I was up at Stevenage Church, giving a clairvoyance, and there was a lady sitting there – I knew she'd lost a baby. I didn't want to say it to her directly, because that's a very bald thing to say, 'You've lost a baby.' I said, 'You know someone who's lost a baby.' And she said, 'Yes, I do.' I said, 'Well, tell your friend it was the right thing to do – it couldn't be helped, it had to happen that way'; so she said, 'Thank you.' I said, 'By the way, tell your friend she will have another baby.' Afterwards the chairlady said to me, 'I'm so glad you went to that woman – you know it was *her* baby.' I said, 'Yes, I knew that.' And the chairwoman said that the child was spina bifida, and the mother was given the chance to have it aborted or not, and she had it aborted. Apparently one of her kind friends had said to her, 'You'll never have another baby, because God is punishing you', and she'd been trying about a year and hadn't become pregnant. Now I reckon she will have another baby – whether I was right or whether I was wrong – because I think that probably somebody saying to her, 'You know, it's all right, it had to be' would remove the guilt.

I tell people I'm not a fortune-teller. You have to get somebody in the spirit who the sitter will recognize; the power comes into you, and it's at various levels, and in order for it to be clairvoyant the power has to be right up here. I was in America a few months ago, and I talked to a group about how you develop, and at the end I said, very rashly, 'Well, I suppose you really want to see some clairvoyance now.' And they all said, 'Oh yes!' So I said to a lady, 'Right, your mother's here'; I said, 'Your mother's laughing, she's saying she was a good cook, but you never liked her cooking.' And this lady said to me, 'My mother was a terrible cook, everything was so greasy!' So anything else I told her after that, I knew I was on the right level.

They come across as we knew them; or perhaps as they like to think of themselves, at the time when they had a lovely figure or blond hair, for instance. I knew someone who went to a sitting, and her friend came through saying she had lovely dark hair she could sit on; well, she hadn't had that for twenty years before she passed over. And her own mother – she'd got very fat, because she'd had a baby at forty-three and had breast-fed it and thought you had to eat for two. Well, when she came across she said, 'Tell her I'm as light as a feather, I could dance!'

What interests me about myself is that I've never done anything, everything has just happened to me naturally. My teacher's guide came through himself – that's very rare – and he said I had a lot of mediumistic work to do on my own. That's why I've been left on my own. I had no children, though I wanted them; my husband died, my sister died. I was told that this path was right for me, because of the work I had to do.

## PIERS VITEBSKY

The Sora are a 'tribe' in central India, in the hills of Orissa. It's a fairly out-of-the-way area, which is why you still have tribes like this, supposed to be the original inhabitants before Aryans or Dravidians arrived; but since they're a non-literate culture there are no real records. In one way you could say they're not Hindu, or they're pre-Hindu, in another way you might say that Hinduism itself is built up from a foundation of these kinds of religions. As an anthropologist I was interested because I knew they went into trance and had dialogues with the dead – there were earlier references which made it clear that they did this.

It took a long time to work it all out, and I'm still not sure of everything. Yes, I learned the language while I was there; you can't manage to discuss these things otherwise, you can't talk about this sort of thing through interpreters. And if you're alone there, that's the only human company and they won't leave you to be lonely, so you have to learn it. The children were especially patient in the early stages.

What really strikes you when you go there is that in every village, almost every day, people hold these dialogues with the dead. And you'll see a shaman – a female shaman usually – sitting on the ground with her legs stretched out in front of her, eyes closed, and talking. And there's a small group of people packed around her, arguing back with the spirits, weeping sometimes, cracking obscene jokes at other times, peals of laughter – every new spirit that comes demands a drink.

'Natural' death – no, that's a concept I'd be surprised if many cultures apart from our own have arrived at. If you have an

Piers Vitebsky's *Dialogues with the Dead: The Discussion of Mortality among the Sora of Central India* will be published by Cambridge University Press in 1990.

animistic world view, that means that you impute a human kind of consciousness to virtually everything – the landscape, the environment, and also to experience, including the kinds of experience that cause illness and death. In other words it's a theory of causality which is free of the very enigmatic notion of randomness – the theory of probability and so on, which even for us only makes sense on a large, statistical level. If you try to apply it to individual cases it's meaningless. So for the Sora, death is always caused by a previously dead person. (The previously dead person may have made a deal with a living sorcerer on the side, but that's incidental.) The main point is that it's only previously dead people who have the power to cause more death.

So if you're seriously ill and some spirit turns up and owns the responsibility through the shaman's voice – 'Yes, *I*'m doing this' – then you, and your family round you, say, 'What's the big idea, why are you doing this?' And the spirit may say, 'I'm angry with you because you didn't do me a sacrifice', or whatever; or it may say, 'I love you so much I can't bear to be without you down below in the underworld, so I'm making you come and join me.' Either way, out of anger or out of love, the dead will still cause this suffering and this death in you. It's a very piquant ambivalence. Whoever you are, you were close to many people who've died, particularly your parents and your closest relatives; but even your friends, regular drinking-partners, lovers, people you used to work with regularly in the fields, any of these kinds of associations can be the excuse for a spirit to attack you. What I felt in the end was that when a spirit attacks you it is in some sense reminding you of its presence – 'Here I am, don't forget me – because I'm part of what's gone into making you.'

The dead person has lost his body – it's cremated immediately after death and they're not particularly interested in the corpse, though the ashes are carefully buried. But it's the soul, the consciousness, which counts – it becomes something called *sonum*, which is their word for the consciousness of the dead. You can talk about a *sonum* of so-and-so; you can also talk about *sonum* as a kind of state of being – he has become *sonum*, he's no longer living. And the morning after the cremation you hold an inquest, and the shaman sits down and she summons various *sonums*, all the close relations who are already dead, some of whom say, 'It's nothing to do with me, I didn't do it!' and others ... Well, finally one will come and say, 'I did it', you see; and then there'll be some reason. But it's all very tentative at this stage.

And then the dead person himself will come, and you interrogate him – 'Which *sonum* took you? What did it feel like, just as you were going down the path? What did it feel like when you collapsed?' At the inquest you start putting together a picture of all the circumstances surrounding a person's death – who were his enemies, who in the underworld wanted him dead, which living sorcerers may have colluded with them, who are going to inherit his property and his quarrels and his obligations. All sorts of things. And the verdict is summarized in the form of a certain explanation – it was this *sonum*, who did it for this reason. But this verdict means more than it states – it's a summary of what has gone before, of the deceased person's entire biography.

For the shaman to get into a trance, she sits down – the most important ones are usually 'she', the ones who do the funerals – she sits down in a special posture, with the legs straight out instead of squatting, as people usually sit. Yes, I think you'd say she's in an altered state of consciousness, though it's rather unspectacular, visually, this kind of shamanism – they rarely dance or leap about. The really interesting part is all in the words. She does something rhythmical – banging a stick or turning the point of a knife round and round – and she sings a certain invocation. It's a song, it's got its own metre, its own tune; and in the words she describes the journey she's making to the underworld, an impossible journey, which ordinary people can't make. Well, we make it only once, with no return ticket! But shamans can come and go both ways. It's impossible precipices, huge; there's a tree linking all the levels of the cosmos they have to shin down, their soul becomes a monkey in order to do this. And it's terrifying, but they can do it, and they call upon all their predecessors – 'Be monkeys, join up your hands and your tails, help me along the ant-wide path. How could I do it without your help? I know it only because of you.' And then at some point, while singing this, suddenly her voice tails off and her body becomes locked rigid – this means her elbows, knees, have to be unclenched. And even in a frail little old woman it sometimes takes two or three strong men to unclench her, she's that rigid.

But that means her soul has reached the underworld, so her body is now vacant and free for *sonums* to speak. And then they start coming. She doesn't use different tones, no, but she does reproduce speech habits, and particularly the personal conversations and jokes of these people. But then that's part of the fading of a *sonum* – with somebody who's been dead recently there's a very strong personality which comes over absolutely, but with somebody who's been dead for ten or twenty years they become progressively more colourless, they just come along for a drink and a bit of very trivial chit-chat – just to wave the flag, really, and to underline their position in the genealogy.

But this is where I began to break up the idea of spirits and see what else was going on – what is a fifty-year-old spirit compared to a one-year-old one? It's a very attenuated, weakened idea, because it doesn't matter to people nearly as much. Yes, nobody remembers them, that's the crucial point; I think I can work out from genealogies that roughly at the time when there's nobody left alive to remember them, that's the point at which these spirits in the underworld die a second death, and turn into butterflies. Which means they have no personality, no character, their subjective consciousness perhaps continues in some sense, but . . . 'It's nothing to do with us, nothing we can do with it; we can't talk to them, they don't affect us any more.'

The afterworld is very complex, and that's what presents the problems to work out. What people who start from a Christian or even a modern rationalist viewpoint often assume is that the theology of people with a simple material culture, people who just live in mud huts, is bound to be simple. But it's very elaborate. Let's go back to the word *sonum*, which I think represents consciousness after death. It's a state of being dead but aware. There are two different kinds of *sonum*, and every dead person partakes of this double existence. On the one hand you're what they call an ancestor-*sonum*, you're an actual person with your name and your characteristics; on the other hand you have become a member of one of a range of *sonums* which are defined by the actual form of your death, so if you're killed by a leopard you become a member of the club called leopard-*sonum* and if you die by suicide, then for various reasons you go into the sun and become a part of sun-*sonum*. The reasoning is all symbolic, you see.

Now the crucial thing is, the person's death has therefore been caused by somebody who suffered from the same mode of death; so there is a continuity involved in these experiences, from one life to another, from one person to another. This kind of continuity cross-cuts the continuity of descent, of the lineage. So every diagnosis, even for an illness, let alone a death, has to combine these two. Which *sonum* is causing it? Well, it's my father, acting as a member of earth-*sonum*, or sun-*sonum*, or leopard-*sonum*, or whatever. In principle suspicion could be very wide, because even in the underworld the dead are always having a drink with one another, even marrying one another, having affairs with one another. So they move about and they make deals among themselves; so if you die coughing blood, you don't think only of people who died that way. Your death could just as well have been motivated first and foremost by somebody who died of a leopard who went along and asked somebody else who died by that other means to get you.

In Christian theology good and bad are very exclusive terms, the dualistic view of things – is God really on top or not, and was Satan a fallen angel, and so on. In Sora, and I think in many, many tribal or local religions, good and evil are not such absolute principles at all, because the realm of the transcendent is so much more human. So just as human beings are a complete mixture, and you know that you yourself, and all your friends, have good and bad attributes and you can expect some spiteful gestures and some generous gestures from them, so are the ancestors. One might say, 'What an oppressive religion – you walk around the place with all these dead people getting at you all the time.' It's not, of course, because your ancestors also love you. They put their soul-force into all the crops that grow, and into what you eat, so you are ingesting the soul-force of your ancestors with every mouthful. And, after all, nasty things do happen to us and all this *explains* them.

They're powerful, yes, and dangerous, but they also want you to prosper, because you are their descendants. In a sense you are all they've got, because life in the underworld is a very pallid replica of life above – it's certainly more fun to be alive than to be dead. So they're also jealous of the fact that you're still alive and they're not. I think there are ways in our own culture now in which we can approach and talk about this, about the ambivalence of pity, love, and fear; but not necessarily in religious idioms, in terms of spirits. Yes, I do think we still have a feeling about *de mortuis nil nisi bonum*, and haven't completely lost the sense that they may overhear and zap us – certainly part of what the Sora would think.

The funeral rite has several stages. When somebody's freshly dead you don't mention their name, you just call on 'the deceased person', until the first stage of the funeral rite is done. They're a kind of uncontrollable ghost until that point, and then they become a proper *sonum*, subject to the logic of *sonums*, when they've had a buffalo sacrifice and some blood to drink in the underworld. Buffaloes are expensive, so they're usually saved up until after the harvest, then all the funerals are staged. It's while they're not yet a proper, protective ancestor that you have to work out the cause of their death, because they are going to perpetuate that, perhaps on to you – they have the potential to cause this death in others. So once you've found out, you can try to head them off, you can try to block this perpetuation. If it's a very contagious form of death, as some of them are considered to be, you actually do a pre-emptive blocking rite to protect yourself. It's usually an actual movement, in which you lead the spirit out of the house and out of the village, and then you dismiss it into the jungle. Of course, despite the intentions, these blocking rites don't always work, because the same form of death is going to reappear – the dead keep coming back. When you're ill again, you give them what's called a banishing rite which repeats the blocking rite – 'Go back into wild space, where you belong.'

I think the whole Sora system does allow unresolved business with the dead to be worked through. Let me just show you, in that respect, this bit of dialogue involving a little girl who's just died. You see the mother is imploring her – but the child says how can she help persecuting the living, when her mother was so bad as to let her die?

The important point is that the dead person has this double aspect, as cause of illness and as protective ancestor, and immediately after the death the aggressive aspect predominates. That's the aspect which makes you weep; you think, poor thing, all the time I was having a drink there she was dying, and I didn't even know. But it's also the aspect you fear most, of course, because that's what they're going to perpetuate on to you. But what you try to do in the sequence of funeral rites is to alter the balance between these two aspects. In that dialogue with the little girl who died, on the one hand they feel sorry for her, but on the other they're saying, 'Don't perpetuate, don't propagate, don't pass it on'; and she says, 'Well, what can I do? That's the way it is – of course I'm going to pass it on.' That dialogue – it's a very cruel one, because it's aimed at that poor mother, who's so overcome she can't even talk, and the talking is done on her behalf by the grandmother. And the little girl's last remark as she goes away is, 'My mummy doesn't care enough about me.'

I think what's happening there, what you're seeing, is the psychotherapeutic side of the system – the cruelty is so like what the mother is actually feeling. Her self-reproach, as we would call it – it's reflected utterly convincingly. Now, over the next stages of the funeral rite during the next three years, the little girl is going to modify her tone, and become less and less harsh. And in three years' time she's going to be saying, 'You were an excellent mother to me, you did everything you could – you went from shaman to shaman, cure to cure.' What these people do is give a definite time-structure to this easing off of the reproaches. Your own feelings of course are not going to correspond exactly to the stages – it would be too much to hope that after the buffalo sacrifice you feel a bit better, then three years later, after the final rite, you feel completely relieved. But it *is* a structure, and they recognize that your own feelings will eddy back and forth across this structure.

In the first stage of the funeral rite you do something which is called the redemption of the dead person. When I was adopted into a lineage, I was lucky enough to become one of the people who sang this song of redemption. You fast, and you drink the alcohol; you don't actually go into trance, but you're shamans' assistants. What you're saying is, in the personae of the ancestors of that lineage, whatever the actual cause of his death: 'We shall form a war party, and we'll brandish our axes, and we'll go and rescue him, and we'll take him into the underworld, into our company, and make him a proper ancestor.' But the problem is, we redeem him today, but next week he's suddenly reverted again, because somebody's ill and he's diagnosed as the cause.

So the redemption is not effective immediately. Every time we do the cure we repeat this redemption, so to speak, by saying, 'Don't come in that form, go back to being an ancestor – what do you think you're doing?' And he says by way of excuse, 'Oh well, yes, but I felt like it, and I'm hungry' – and this, that, and the other. And we say through the shaman, 'Never mind, here's your sacrifice – now go on, buzz off where you belong.' And over the next couple of years his reversions become more and more infrequent, and less and less virulent. These reversions cut across the stages of the funeral rite, and I think they are what acknowledges that the mourners' inner feelings haven't quite followed the structure of the funeral – that there are still these unhappy memories, and at the point where these surge up, sure enough, that's when one can get attacked by the dead person. A bad person may be more dangerous; but even the purest child cannot escape this property of perpetuating her own death on to the living. And what makes it so pathetic is that she comes, there is this obviously innocent creature, and yet – 'I can't help it, I don't want to do this to you, but I'm doing it.'

Then after you've been dead a long time what happens is that you're just putting in a token appearance at these trances; and you say, 'Come on, give us a drink'; and they say, 'Who's causing the trouble? Can you give us any pointer?' And you say, 'I don't know, it's not one of my lot', or 'I didn't do it', or 'I think you'll find so-and-so's responsible, he'll be along in a moment.' That's all you have to say for yourself really. If your property has been inherited down the line, then there's no reason to retain much personality. So what happens is your subjective consciousness persists indefinitely, but it's progressively stripped of attributes, which all return to the living. Your person is made up of several strands, and the first one – onion layers, if you like – the first one to be peeled off is your actual experience of death, because within months of dying you're probably transmitting that on to someone else by causing their death or, at least, life-threatening illness. Then maybe after a while you don't even cause minor illnesses in that same idiom, and you're now a pure ancestor; you have less personality, you're a less interesting character, but your ancestorhood is still necessary because you have to oversee the continuity of your lineage and the transmission of your property. Once that's over, that side of you is stripped away – spread indefinitely among many descendants, of course – and there's one part of you then that comes back to one living descendant, and that's your name. You continue to exist for a while as another namesake, protecting the new baby from the underworld, trying to ward various other *sonums* off; but once you've given your name back to a living person, there are no functions remaining for you to perform in the realm of the living. And at some point people will ask, in the trance, 'What happened to old so-and-so?' 'Oh well, he died a second time, was cremated in the underworld, not long ago.'

Yes, they're afraid of death, I suppose. The Sora see dying as a draining, a weakening; *sonums* come and eat your soul, they just drain your soul out of you, bit by bit. Of course they're terribly aware of all the symptoms of these things because they see it all the time; it's a society with high morbidity and high mortality. Every illness can be the beginning of dying, so every recovery is a near-death experience, if you like. There's joking and teasing among the living about their move into the other world – well, you could take that as a sign of fear, or you could take it as a sign of acceptance.

I'd certainly like to think that the Sora's beliefs are very supportive to them – I'm fond of them, and fascinated by the system. But I'm not sure, objectively, how one would demonstrate that. It certainly seemed to me that it was a very robust culture, and people tramped barefoot around the jungle getting scratched and torn, and they had fights, they were quite hard-drinking; but at the same time it was a very tender culture, in which people were very alert to each other's emotions. But I'm not sure that you can ever separate interpretation from the anthropologist's own experience of being there. I had a very good time, so for me it's a wonderful culture!

The shamans start by going through initiations; they're taught in dreams from the underworld. A little girl will start to be approached in her dreams by an underworld spirit, who holds her hand and leads her down this difficult path, and there she's introduced to other spirits. And at first she's terrified, and bit by bit she gets more used to it, and then these dreams become a regular feature. At puberty she marries an underworld spirit – that's how she gets the power to go into trance; then later on, around eighteen or twenty, she will marry above ground, like everybody else. But their above-ground husbands find their wives' bigamous inner lives a strain and usually prevail upon them to give up, and they will give up until they're middle-aged or widowed. So the whole system is run by teenage girls and old ladies. I think it's to do with conserving power – it's a very Indian sort of idea really, retaining your spiritual power. But this would take some time to explain. And there is a sociological kind of explanation there which would say that in a culture where women are in a subordinate position, then of course this is a way of compensating.

Yes, I think they really do have the dream experiences. Maybe we have Freudian dreams because Freud told us to expect them! If you look at medieval and classical dreams, people dreamt what their cultures expected them to. And certainly everybody in Sora culture knows what these dreams are supposed to be like – the little girls wake up and tell Mummy and Daddy what they saw. So it's not a secret, what this kind of experience is going to be like. No, it's not impossible for a boy – it's not a culture with a rigid division of sexual roles – but the men who become shamans usually don't conduct funerals but join the lesser tradition of just healing, they usually do this as an adult. And of course it's less of a conflict for a man, between a wife in the underworld and a wife above ground, since men can have more than one wife anyway.

The *sonums* you marry in the underworld are a completely different class of *sonum*; they're actually high-caste Hindus, the ones who marry shamans and give them their powers to go into trance. Because the Sora live surrounded by Hindus, and have done for thousands of years. They have plenty of contacts, political and commercial contacts, in all of which they're at a disadvantage; they're non-literate, they live largely by selling produce in the bazaars, where they're often exploited by very shrewd buyers. So in the underworld these relations are reversed. You have these underworld *sonums* at your behest – they can come along and say, 'Whoever's causing the illness, even if it's the sun or moon or anything, I'll go and bring them along in handcuffs, I'll force them to negotiate.' There's all this imagery of power, regiments of armed attendants, people riding on elephants, bicycles, aeroplanes.

What's interesting is that the imagery is culture-specific, but the principles, I think, are universal. The rituals and the fears and so on – I suppose the way I've come to see it at the moment is that these things have not disappeared in our culture, but their idiom has been transformed, they've gone into another set of metaphors. Not just heaven and hell, though perhaps more people than we acknowledge believe in that; but there are other kinds of idioms which are now available, secular ones, which may be thoroughly materialist. A lot of the literature, or bereavement counselling as a profession – when you look at that, like so much psychotherapy it seems to be a sort of watered-down version of something derived from Freud. A lot of people want to take all that as an absolute yardstick, as the answer; but you should see it as what anthropologists call an ethnoscience, which means a local attempt at absolute knowledge. People do try to give it that absolute status – 'Those people think they're possessed by spirits but actually they're suffering from a manic-depressive something or other' – as though you've somehow explained it thereby.

Long after I'd done all the fieldwork and worked out what I understood about the Sora, I discovered a wonderful paper by Freud called 'Mourning and Melancholia'; and then later, when I looked at the thanatology literature, I found that any of those books which are sufficiently scholarly to quote sources tend to go back to that, and perhaps to nothing beyond. But the reason I like that text of Freud's is it's extremely articulate, it's extremely intelligent; whether you accept it or not, you admire the person who thought it out.

Freud's idea is that we project vengeance on to the dead, because of our anger. When I put it alongside what I found among the Sora the parallels were astonishing, the similarities. But because they were so similar that really threw into relief what the differences were; and the key difference was just in the initial presupposition about the nature of the dead. My understanding of Freud in that paper is that it's essential for him to be able to say that the dead do not exist any longer, that there is a certain essential sense in which they are now unreal, and that what he calls their 'psychic prolongation' is only in the mind of the rememberer. Put that alongside the view you get not only among the Sora but in most traditional cultures, which is that in some sense or other the dead continue to exist as autonomous sentient consciousnesses. In fact *we*'re a very peculiar and aberrant culture.

So we should be talking not only about the formal, logical framework of Freud's paper but its whole social context and implications, and there I think we'll see something very significant. What I did was to put the two ideas side by side in diagrams, which I thought I could derive from them – the Freudian model and the Sora model. Freud has a very clear dividing line between the living and the dead, and it's impermeable. The reason it's impermeable, I think, is that everything on this side, the living, is real and existent, and everything on *that* side is just unreal, is fantasy. So the impulse comes from the mourner, who has something called a libido, and expresses love and reproach and all these things he discusses, and it reaches out towards the deceased; and since this barrier is impenetrable, it can only be deflected back, bouncing off it as off a surface. It then moves in on itself; this force, this impulse of the libido, can't simply evaporate, so the self – whatever that is – has to be split up into parts so that one can attack the other, and then you get the self-reproach and so on, because there is no other partner to this dialogue. But the Sora diagram is quite different; the dialogue, the reproaches, the expressions of love, come from both sides, the mourner and the deceased.

That's why the whole thing can be read so easily in reverse, from Freud's point of view. He says that the mourner can't let go of her attachment for the dead person; the Sora say, with just the same certainty, the dead person can't bear to let go of his attachment for you. Perhaps with some curious mixture of love and hostility, as indeed you get in most close personal relations.

Freud speaks for a certain kind of professional approach – though the reason he's so attractive to read is that there's a passion in his writing too. But I don't think he speaks for everyone in our culture – someone you talk to in the street, the old lady down the road, they speak of the deceased being *with* them. And I went for a little while to a spiritualist church nearby, and there was this sort of talk all the time, very unselfconscious, not preoccupied with reading clever books to justify or explain what they said. Of course they're a minority activity here, put on the defensive – it's very different if you go to a culture in which everybody takes all this for granted.

I can't say I know what to believe myself – something makes me continue to explore the question, and the further I go the less of an answer I get. In a way I suppose I'm rather grateful for the cover which anthropology gives me. My job as an anthropologist is to work out what other people believe. A group like this, who hadn't had any contact with white people for a long time and whose dealings with other Indians were uneasy, they were very, very suspicious and cautious about any dealings with an outsider; so for weeks, months, it was such hard work just making some kind of relationship that of course an important part of it was trying to do things their way. That you're prepared to eat their food, and sleep in the hut; and part of all that is obviously that you have to start talking like them, acting *as though* you believed the same, because there's no other way of talking about these experiences. 'What happened to so-and-so?' 'He went into sun-*sonum*.' 'I was attacked yesterday by my grandfather, and I finally bought him off with two chickens.' You can't discuss human relationships except in these terms, so you have to talk like that, regardless of what you believe.

I'm not sure if I could say it changed me in terms of literal belief, that would be very specific; a bit like the reason many people give why they can't actually be Christians – they want certain parts of it, but not certain very specific mythological elements. So that would have been very difficult, especially since

I didn't have my own ancestors there! When I asked shamans to call up my ancestors they said they didn't have a direct line to them. 'We deal with the ancestors we know' and 'Your ancestors won't come to us.' But it made me realize how very hazy a concept like belief is, and how very difficult it is to know what you believe and whether you believe anything at all. So – there were times when I had initiation dreams, in that shamans' helper spirits would appear at the door of the hut with a lamp in their hands. The lamp is how you see your way down to the under-world; even when a shaman is down there, somebody's sitting by her 'empty' body, keeping a lamp burning all the time, otherwise she won't find her way. And here were these *sonums*, standing in the doorway with a lamp in their hands, and they were beckoning to me. On one occasion I sleepwalked and woke up outside, on the path outside the hut. But the dream didn't actually lead me all the way to the underworld – I woke up. In a situation like that you get so anxious to get thoroughly involved that the anxiety in itself is perhaps what generates the dream.

Sitting here now in a state of reasonable health, I feel that I'm not particularly afraid of my own death – though I'm terrified of my children's mortality. They seem so vulnerable, but for myself I think it would depend a lot on how and when death came upon me. At the moment it seems to me that if it comes in old age, and one has had a good time, I like to think that perhaps I would accept it with a good grace. To go before one's time – that is what all these cultures put such a strong emphasis on, that they're angry, there's some incompleteness about their lives.

Our own attitudes to death – well, they're very diverse, and the outcome of certain historical processes. The growth over the past few years of bereavement counselling, thanatology, and so on – that has its own awfulnesses, its smug buzz-words, but I feel on the whole it's a very positive development. And attitudes are also linked to wider cultural attitudes to other aspects of the human condition. Isn't it odd how there can be so much embarrass-ment and uncertainty about death at the same time as sex and consumerism are hyped up and made to appear so certain? Isn't there a certain emptiness to that? There's such an imbalance. With sex, it seems to be a desperate attempt to feel something;

but with death, it's an attempt to avoid feeling too *much*, to avoid rough textures – the essence of prissiness. It's part of a long historical process of de-animizing the world, it's a process which removes meaning from life. And we pay a price for this. The point about beliefs like the Sora's is that you can find a meaning for almost any event of significance – the human mind and the human emotions crave meaning. And when you're bereft of this, you feel very desolate indeed.

# NED

I'm utterly convinced now of the meaninglessness of the whole business. And as you get older and nearer to snuffing it, that strangely doesn't seem very important. I really feel that. Even when I was a Catholic I didn't believe very firmly in an afterlife, not a firm belief. Christianity isn't about that anyway – biblical evidence for it is actually extremely slender in both the Old and the New Testament. Most people who have any notion of an afterlife now, particularly those horrible born-again Christians, think you die and, whoosh, you're there. There's nothing in the Gospels to say that you're going to have that. It's much more philosophically sophisticated than that – I didn't feel at the time that I was signing on the dotted line for an afterlife. You don't sign on with a guarantee.

I don't think I did chuck the Church – it chucked me. You subordinate your own individual identity, your critical identity, at times, to what is a notion of a Church; but when the Church changes the party line overnight, and the Irish priest who was lecturing you about this and that is almost installing a condom machine because Rome has told him to – it won't wash. I mean, this ridiculous Polish Pope . . . Liberation theology, things like that . . . I can remember the very moment when I said, 'I'm packing this in.' I was in Rome, and I went to mass – a church somewhere off the Via Veneto. The rot had already set in by then, and the service was already partly in the vernacular, and I heard the familiar sort of Protestant shriek of the enthusiast, this ghastly woman at the front shrieking out, '*Sia lodato Gesú Cristo*' at every possible opportunity. And I thought, that's enough.

Mine was the religion of the Grand Inquisitor anyway. You remember in *The Brothers Karamazov*, Christ comes back, and he's causing a bit of trouble, and the Grand Inquisitor collars him and puts him in the dungeons. And he says, 'Don't come back causing trouble again; people don't want freedom.' I liked Catholicism as a great social regulator, it kept people down. And the early Church appals me, I've always said that; I'm only interested in it after the Constantinian donation, when it became the official religion of the Roman Empire. I was saying to an old friend at lunch, 'If we were four Roman gentlemen sitting about having our lunch now, and somebody said, "Excuse me, guv, there's a chap who calls himself Peter Rock hanging about outside who would like to talk to you about this amazing new religion", we'd have had him turfed out, wouldn't we? Or at least given him sixpence and told him to go away.'

Actually I wasn't brought up with any religion at all, though my parents weren't aggressive about it. I'd only been to church if friends took me. Then when I was twelve I sought baptism in the Church of England! Yes. I'd always been conscious of God, blamed him for everything, too. We had a silly perfunctory religious instruction at school, for the headmaster to sleep off a whisky or two. But Remembrance Day ... The two-minute silence on the day, the maroons going off ... That made you think. They've shoved it to Sunday now, of course. But it was very impressive on the calendar day.

I went to the local vicar – he was a hearty, extremely low-church type. So I went through all that, I was baptized, then I was confirmed – it was very low church and tedious, not at all my style, but I suppose I rather liked it. I like institutions, you know; and I suppose as an only child you're precocious, and a reader, and interested in history in a romantic way. I think all that played a big role in my deciding to be baptized. Actually I was particularly, furtively keen on Catholicism even then – it was taboo, you see. But I was twenty-six when I converted to Catholicism. I think it was – well, it would be pretentious to say intellectual arguments, but on the whole I should think it was liking for authority, for the institution. Also, it got up the nose of people like you amongst my contemporaries at that time. Well, *I* thought it did. And that was when the Catholic Church was still what it should be now. I loved it!

I don't think it necessarily took fear away from death. I did it for other reasons ... I can't understand people who have no fear

of death. It's terrifying, of course it's terrifying. I was death-
obsessed as a child. Loved playing about in cemeteries, great
haunter of tombstones. I would say it was just adolescent, only-
child morbidity. My father was permanently ill throughout my
childhood – I was terrified of his dying, constantly thinking
about death. He had chronic diabetes, with complications, so he
was away in hospital for long periods, months at a time. And I
remember, if he was late coming home – 'He's dead!' That kind
of thing. You know that poem of Philip Larkin's – 'Aubade' –
you must have read it. It's all about how religion won't help . . .
About the business of just knowing you're not going to be *there*.

And of course it was wartime when I was a child, it was the
outskirts of Birmingham – yes, of course it was bombed, we had
to go into the shelters a lot. You were frightened, you did expect
that you might be hit, because for a time there was a strong
possibility that you would be – there were people my parents
knew who were killed. And I distinctly remember bicycling
home from school when I was still a Boy Scout – it must have
been 1940, and I think the Germans had shot a lot of Boy Scouts
in Warsaw – and that immediately terrified the wits out of me,
and I went and buried my Scout uniform! And busily got an
elementary German grammar, just in case . . . My parents were
furious.

No, I honestly can't understand people who have no fear. And
once you have children, you're very conscious that they might
die – constant fear. Every sniffle. And there was polio . . . No, it
was only semi-safe when the children were small. And you're
forgetting all the nuclear stuff as well – the fifties was a great time
of fear. I certainly know that when I used to commute home to
the family, I wasn't certain I'd commute back again. Once you
have a child – instant death worries. It comes from, I suppose:
'God is going to punish you. Do not be happy. The great Bank
Manager is closing your account!'

I used to have fantasies of dying a sort of traditional French
Catholic death – surrounded by the family, the holy water, the
twig of box at the end of the bed, while I apportioned out my
possessions. What I would actually most hate would be to be
entangled in modern medical things – particularly the people

involved, that would be unspeakable. Some ghastly tattooed young doctor with an earring in one ear, and the nurse, probably indistinguishable ... I'd have to be a National Health patient because I haven't got any money, and if I go on living a bit longer the family will probably be squatting at the foot of the bed cooking a meal because there'll be no services, no nothing – we'll probably have the equivalent of barefoot doctors. And what I don't want is a load of bullshit ... Oh, you know, comfort and inspiration, and people coming and saying platitudes. I should deeply resent that, if I hadn't gone gaga. I suppose that's largely what I would feel, resentment – bitter resentment that they were going to go on enjoying the few things I do enjoy ...

Hospices – thanks very much, no. There's all that stuff about a dignified and easy way out; you see these stricken old women doing their last easel painting – 'How happy May is', you know, as she prepares to snuff it. Death is horrible. Utterly. And the way we, our society, treats it is just wrong. I mean, I've been to a funeral this week, and I actually thought of coming back and writing a codicil to my very slender will – on no account am I to have any service, music, hired preacher, appreciations, thanks-givings for life ... I'd rather have a Hindu funeral – I don't mind being burnt, but in public, not that ghastly, creaking machinery ... I would make the concession that if any of my closest would feel happier giving me an official send-off, it has to be a low mass requiem, in the Tridentine mode that I was fond of. But it won't mean anything to *me*.

I can't even rouse myself up to this 'Do not go gentle into that good night' act that many people cultivate these days. And there's another bit of bogus immortality that's popular now – that you're remembered in your friends, your children ... 'Laughter and the love of friends.' Absolute nonsense! There's a very good quotation, from 'Lines on the Death of Dean Swift', by himself – 'The Dean is dead/(And what are trumps?)'. A good corrective to all that.

I went to the funeral of a ballet critic – it was hideous, *Swan Lake* on a tape, started by some mute from the undertakers. No, they won't improve the services – there's too much money tied up in the business. A friend I hadn't seen for years had an obituary the other day, a professor of anthropology in New Zealand. And apparently they had him in some Maori longhouse and people sat up all night telling stories about him while he lay in state. That struck me as – ugh! yuk! It's like saying, 'I want my ashes scattered' . . . But you don't get the ashes anyway, they just take a handful out of the common pile and shove it in whatever container and give it to you. Of course they do! You're just part of a very large heap of grey ash. Which is a good description of the human condition.

Those memorial services, you know – 'He would have loved this,' they say, and on comes some tedious record of something he probably didn't give a toss about. I've been to enough of those occasions now, when you enter the death zone you go to them; and you think, what utter crap. What nonsense. Oh, the total unimportance of human beings; I mean, they just drop off – ants, dogs, cattle, insects, people . . . The whole thing, surely, as you get older, can only become completely meaningless. The whole endeavour. You wonder how it's all happened.

We live in a civilization that is collapsing – something else might take its place, but this certainly isn't going to continue. Of course, yes, art does mean something to me – what can you say, you're thankful of course for anything that consoles. Art having a meaning – that's too deep for me, sorry. I'd rather not think about that. '*Luchshe nye dumat*'.' That's what Turgenev says the peasants say about things; 'not to think about it'. All right, I can think the unthinkable, but I don't wish to be *compelled* to think – that's a valid part of the interview. Put it in.

I get very cross as I hang about in tube trains – I think, all this human rubbish, and I'm expected to 'care', the cant word. Of course I would rush over if someone were knocked over by a car and help them . . . It's stronger than I am. All right, I'm inconsistent. I'm good because I've inherited moral standards – I'd love to get rid of them. Nothing I'd like better. I'd love to be able to go out and blag a bank and shoot someone. But my wife dying – well, of course that would be a horror. A constant anxiety – she smokes. You do care about – yes, wife, children, a tiny handful of friends, but . . . No, I don't have any fantasies of meeting her in an afterworld. Whether it's some silly Sir Oliver Lodge spiritualism, with whiskies and sodas in the large country house – 'Where do the lower orders go?' you ask – or whether it's some heaven . . . I can imagine some terrible celestial assembly, some horrible combination of Sunday school and a synagogue, where you have to do your turn singing praises, to all eternity . . .

My mother's still alive, she's ninety – when she dies I expect I'll be very distressed, yes. And if I have to be in charge of her funeral, I don't want a hired preacher, looking to see if he's got her name right, and talking about what a good woman she was. If anybody has to make a speech about my mother's existence, I'll get up and do it to the assembled family, the virtues and faults. But I wouldn't want some jack-in-the-box . . . I'll be distressed; because I had a very happy childhood. Why am I like I am, then? Because I've *thought*.

My Romanian aunt's funeral was deeply satisfying. Unshaven priest, didn't give a toss; immensely long prayers sung by three of her aged crone contemporaries; long journey to the cemetery where most Romanians like to be buried. You don't know about Romanian Orthodox? It's rather different from Greek Orthodox. At the end, after more prayers by the graveside, one of the old crones sidled up with a string bag to the priest and produced a bottle of olive oil and a small bottle of wine. And at the very end the priest poured oil and wine on the coffin. Lovely! Libation to the chthonic gods. It's a wonderful pagan survival; but quite right, because it sticks two fingers up humanism and all that embarrassing stuff. It doesn't actually make any difference; but it is a satisfying way of seeing them off. Much better than some bleak little sub-humanist service in a crematorium chapel.

I'm sorry I shan't have the pleasure of dying a multimillionaire and watching everyone cringe and gibber . . . Keeping them on a string! One of the last pleasures, it must be. To be fair, I'd have probably given it away. Because the one thing I do not understand about people as they grow older is the way they hold on to things. My mother's very attached to trinkets, and even kitchen things, which she can't use because her hands are now crippled. No, I get very moral about that. I think you should strip off everything. I can quite see, if I live to be as old as my mother, I shall have given away all the little I have . . . I mean little treasures and pictures. Oh, yes. Strip it all off, you want to strip it all away — one iron bedstead, a chair, a table. It gets rid of humbug. It's not inconsistent with ritual — the Carthusian in his cell still went to a conventual high mass. I shall make sure I get rid of most possessions.

But I intend to do for my dog what I wouldn't want for myself. A carved headstone, with a suitable Latin inscription. You have to know how much I adore the dog! Yes, I'm much teased about my dog.

# Pat Hart

It happened in December, 18th of December last year – oh goodness, yes, I know the date, and I'm rather dreading the anniversary. Thinking, you know, that I must keep busy then. I couldn't have talked to you when you first wrote, but it's all right now. I'd always planned, you see, that Sheena and I would work together until I retired, and then she would be ready to retire at about the same time as I did, and I would give her a lovely retirement. I was very, very relieved that when Ursa came she was so different from Sheena – she's quite a different shape, and Sheena had a much, much blacker face. But even on the day of the accident, one of the trainers I spoke to on the telephone said, 'Do you want to apply for another guide dog, or do you want a breather?' And I said, 'Oh, I want another guide dog as quickly as possible, and that's not disloyalty to Sheena, it's a tribute to her.'

I first applied for a guide dog when I left university, I think, but in those days there was a very long waiting list, and I didn't pursue it. Then I had a fall – I fell into a manhole just as I was walking back from the Law Courts. I had my briefcase in my left hand and my white cane in my right hand, and unknown to me this inspection manhole was open – about fifteen feet deep, they told me afterwards. It's funny, isn't it, how things flash through your mind – I hung on to my briefcase and my stick, thinking I mustn't let the legal papers go and that my white stick might be useful at the bottom! And also I began to feel that all my friends who had little or no sight had fallen off the edge of railway platforms, and I wasn't going to let it happen to me. Yes, several have had accidents, though fortunately I only know of one blind girl who was killed in that way.

I added up the pros and cons, and then I wrote to the Guide Dogs for the Blind Association, and a few months later I was offered training at the centre at Wokingham. You live there with other students, and you train with the dog for about a month. When we got back I brought her into the office to see everybody, and so that we could sort out where Sheena was going to spend pennies and things like that. One has to remember all the time that a guide dog isn't a machine; you know, when I go to courts and tribunals, for instance, I have to think hard about how I can make sure the dog has an opportunity to relieve herself.

I ought to have brought Sheena's picture with me – she was a brindled German Shepherd, with a lovely black mask. Of course, yes, the companionship was wonderful for me. Because even losing your sight is in a way a kind of bereavement, even to a child. I remember being very angry at not being allowed to use ink – you know, in those days we used liquid ink – and I'd just got the tremendous pride of being able to use it. I'd been a very untidy writer, and it had taken a tremendous effort. When I started learning braille I remember saying, 'When can I use ink again?' and rubbing my hand across the page of a book in braille and saying, 'You can't read that.' You know, children can get very angry.

Sheena was a very independent character – for instance, Ursa likes to creep over and lie on the sheepskin rug by my bed, while Sheena would always stay in her own bed. This was partly how . . . how the accident happened, because she was so independent. I'd moved to a semi-detached house with a little private park at the back – all the back gates of the houses lead into it – and I thought, this is super, just the place for a guide dog, I can prop my back gate open and she can go in and out. I thought, she's going to spend a lot of time in the office and in tribunals and courts and so on having to be good and quiet, and she'll need this freedom. The trustees of the park said that was perfectly all right as long as she was under control, in the sense that if I called her she would come – this is one of the things that guide dogs are taught, of course, that they must answer to a call. But the awful thing was that unknown to me there was one property that had become derelict and the fences were down . . . No, I had no idea until after the accident, when I was trying to find out how she could possibly have got out. What must have happened was that she must have got out into the road, and run across into the other park at the front – she might have been chasing a squirrel or another dog.

I was getting ready to go to work, and she'd been in once, very excited; and stupidly, you know, I thought, I'll let her out again, she's going to have a long day at the office. It must have been about eight o'clock, I suppose, when I went out to call her. And normally I would hear the bell ringing as she came running, you see; and there was no sound. And I started to get rather anxious, and when one of my neighbours came out I said, 'Have you seen Sheena?' And she said, 'No, I can't see her anywhere, Pat' – and, after a moment – 'I'll go out and have a look at the front.' I waited, and then she came back to me and said, 'Pat, I think you'd better come quickly. Sheena's had an accident, and they're talking about moving her.'

I can remember saying, 'Is she dead?' and she said, 'No, but I think she's been quite seriously injured.' And these stupid things that you do – I said, 'Do you think I need to bring the harness?' You know, hoping . . . And she said, 'No, I shouldn't bother, Pat.' Fortunately I'd put on my coat and picked up my handbag and my stick, so I didn't have to come back home again – it's funny how you think of these things at the time, almost without being able to think, because you feel so shocked. And there she was on the pavement on the park side of the road, and the chap who had run her over was still there, and there was quite a group of people. Although I didn't quite realize it at the time – because, you know, really all I was concerned about was Sheena and getting her to the vet.

But there was this lovely lady there who offered to take me and Sheena to our own vet – I suppose I would have had to wait while I called a taxi otherwise, it would have been dreadful. When we got Sheena into the van the same kind lady had some old blankets, and covered her over; and I sat at the back so that I could lean over and stroke her face and talk to her, because that was what she particularly liked. And she was groaning gently most of the time; but her ears were up, you know, as though she was noticing everything. I didn't try to feel her body – I probably just had this hope that somehow everything would be all right.

Although when I had said to Monica, my neighbour, you know, 'Is she dead?' I had that awful feeling . . . You look after the body of a guide dog so carefully, you know, you groom them. It's like with children.

The lady who helped us didn't know the area, and I was so grateful I didn't lose my visual memory of where we had to go, because the one thing I was concerned about was to get there as quickly as possible. I felt she might be all right if only we could get her to the vet quickly. So we got to the vet, and the vet's receptionist recognized her immediately and said, 'Oh, it's Sheena, isn't it?' And they brought out a stretcher to put her on; and she did cry terribly then, because the vet was feeling her, and trying to . . . He said to me – and I felt he was trying to warn me – he said to me, 'What worries me is that there's no feeling in her back legs.'

I wanted to stay with her, because I thought perhaps I could comfort her; but he said no, it would be better if I went home, and they all tried to persuade me to go home. Ruth, the driver who brought us so kindly, she rang her office and said she was going to stay with me as long as I needed her. Which was so generous, because I felt so cold, you know, and this dreadful feeling of unreality.

And I said I couldn't possibly go home, I would just have walked around; so I said, 'No, no, I'll go to the office, where there will be other people, and even if I can't be terribly useful, there are one or two simple jobs I can get on with.' Fortunately I hadn't got to go to court that morning. And Ruth said she would drive me, so that I didn't have to cope with public transport. And so I had to leave Sheena; because you don't argue with professional people, do you? Then I suddenly realized I had no money, and I thought, supposing I need to come back and collect Sheena and . . . I didn't really think I would be able to, honestly. The vet sounded so grave; and somehow, right from the beginning, from the moment she'd had her accident, I had this awful feeling that that was the end of our relationship, in a way; except that I could comfort her.

The vet rang the office in the middle of the morning and said that he'd X-rayed Sheena and that her back was completely broken, that she would be in a lot of pain when the sedation wore off, and that he thought I ought to allow her to be put to sleep. And I said immediately yes. And I didn't want to ask for her body or anything of that kind, she was a very big, heavy dog – I prefer not to think, even, about that . . .

My family were all very supportive – before I knew, one of my many nieces was ringing to say, 'Do let me come over', you know, all sorts of people were offering help. I felt that the important thing was to go back home at the end of the working day, and I'd got to cope with it some time, and the sooner I did it really, the less difficult it would be. You see, I'd picked up my stick in the morning, fortunately, thinking that I might need to revert to that. Afterwards of course I had to use my long cane again; but I felt, this is a horrible instrument, and I'd so much rather have Sheena padding along the side of me, and how clever she was at guiding me past all the lampposts, and this stupid cane has to touch them before it realizes that they're there.

The only way to carry on was just to keep going – if I hadn't gone to work I probably wouldn't have been able to pick up the pieces. Other people might react differently – perhaps a rest would have done somebody else good, but for me it would have given me the opportunity to sort of relapse into myself and I would have found it very difficult to emerge again. I did find it very difficult to concentrate the first day. And I felt so dreadfully guilty that I hadn't made it impossible for this thing to happen.

I remember, the first Sunday, going to church, and feeling quite desperate about it . . . Thinking desperately, oh, what happens to the souls of animals? I just hope that there is some place . . . I hope that there is an afterlife for dogs, because it would seem so sad that such a gorgeous creature should just perish without trace. I mean, I felt so sad about her body – she had a beautiful body – but for her soul to perish as well . . . Appalling, it was too much. You just have to somehow accept, I think . . . I did feel, if only I had kept her in that morning. When she came back and was so excited, and I thought, oh yes, she must have a little bit longer, and there was still time. But I tried not to let myself think too much about that. I remember when my father died I started to say, 'Oh, I am sorry I said something or other', and my mother said, you know, 'We're not going to have any regrets'; and I thought how wise that was, because you can torture yourself quite uselessly.

It was actually about three months till they rang me up about having Ursa, the whole winter. I kept writing to them and telling them how dreadful it was, and how much worse it would be for somebody who hadn't got friends who understood; and I did all sorts of things like writing to the council saying they ought not to allow roads to be used as rat-runs, and to the Environmental Health Officer about the derelict property in the park at the back. Oh yes, I felt I needed to do things. And I did feel that I couldn't bear to speak to the man who drove that car, although he apparently got in touch with the Guide Dogs for the Blind Association afterwards and said to them, 'That poor lady, what will she do?'

I was very, very relieved that Ursa was so different from Sheena – I didn't want to feel that I was replacing Sheena. She'd gone, and I had to accept that. You see, Sheena would probably be lying with her back against the bookcase over there, because she didn't like being pent up in this corner; whereas you can see Ursa regards it as home. And it was a great help going to a different training centre with Ursa – I'd expected to have to face going to the same one where I'd trained with Sheena. I realized immediately that she was a quite different shape from Sheena, and her character is quite different.

Sheena was just a few weeks short of five years old. I love to think about her; and she had a happy life, and she was loved by lots of people – but especially by me, of course. Do you know, she'd come from a pet shop near the Mile End Road! My brother-in-law brought a lovely photo of Ursa only yesterday evening, and I've got their two photographs sitting side by side. You know, you start thinking, don't you? – you think, would Sheena be jealous? They're always telling us at the Guide Dogs for the Blind Association that dogs don't bear grudges, even when you tell them off . . . So I refused to think that, I stopped. A friend who was looking at the two photographs said, 'I expect at midnight they'll get up and play together!'

# ARCHDEACON MICHAEL PERRY

I suppose having grown up in a Christian family – not a clerical but a Christian family – I always knew that there was a thing called death and there was a place called heaven and that people went to be with Jesus. And therefore I've never been particularly concerned about imagining my own death as an end but imagining it more as a process, a continuing process. Freud says, I think quite rightly, that no one can imagine his own death, one can imagine looking down from some superluminary level and saying, 'That's what they're saying about me', but that's imagining yourself surviving. You can't imagine the complete cessation of your own being. Like everybody else I've never been able to imagine that, but I've always been able to imagine some kind of survival of death – whether it be in heaven, whether it be in purgatory, or whatever. And that kind of feeling has been refined as I've grown up, as I've thought, as my humanity has matured.

Yes, my family was C. of E., and my father was a clerk in the Coal Board and a churchwarden of his parish church; I grew up through Sunday school, choir, all the usual things. I started off as – well, I still am – a keen scientist, took my first degree in inorganic chemistry, but by that time knew that I wanted to be ordained. As soon as I finished my chemistry degree I took a second degree in theology and moved on from there; so I've always had a scientific background, a scientific cast of thought, I've always asked awkward questions. And yes, I do believe in survival of death, I do believe the Christian faith – though every now and then I get stopped in my tracks and feel, golly, isn't this incredibly unlikely! But then I think all of us from time to time . . . I mean, very often I think, isn't it unlikely that this great collection of chemical and electrical impulses can think about itself!

And so . . . every ordinary life is unlikely, and so, yes, there are times when I say to myself, 'Golly, all this is unlikely'; but they're only passing phases. Certainly all the studies I've done – I'm a council member of the Society for Psychical Research – that, together with my scientific background, has always made me doubtful about the interpretation of evidence. In other words I can say, 'Here is a piece of evidence which you can explain in terms of survival of death, or in terms of normal or abnormal psychology.' Every single piece of evidence has got more than one interpretation.

Within psychical research there seem to be no certainties – but then again, I look at my Christian faith, and in that there are no absolute certainties. It's called a faith; and not without reason is it called a faith, because you can always have alternative explanations of everything that goes on. In the end one has to take a kind of personal stance and say, 'This kind of explanation of the universe makes sense to me and the other kind of explanation of the universe makes less sense to me, therefore I go ahead' – it's like Pascal's wager; he said that if you believe in God you behave in a certain way, if you don't believe you behave in a different way, so put your wager in for God and see what kind of life that leads to. You will in fact find that it leads to a much more satisfying life in this world, so that even if there isn't a world to come, you've got a more satisfying world here – so you've won the wager either way!

I think I've always seen the possibility of alternative explanations, or perhaps of a hierarchy of explanations. In other words you can explain the human being in terms of electrochemical influences, you can explain the human being in terms of mind; those are alternative explanations, and you use the right kind of language when you're asking the right kind of question. If you're a neurophysiologist then you're asking neurophysiological questions, if you're a psychologist you ask psychological questions, if you're a student of religion you ask religious questions. You're asking them of the same whole, of the same human being, but you're asking in different universes of discourse.

Of course there's a gap, yes, between the idea of brain and the idea of mind – I puzzle away at that, I don't really see any kind of answer to it except the answer of experience. I know there is body and I know there is mind; how the hell the two are related is one of the great mysteries. You can explain the mind if you want to as an enormous kind of computer which is so complicated that it can in fact be conscious of itself; but that doesn't satisfy me, who sort of sits within that computer and sees myself as myself, and who knows that I have relations with my fellow beings and relations with my God. It's a bit like the difference between the television set and the television programme – the set is there in order to enable the programme to be sent through, but you can't explain the programme even when you've taken the set to pieces and shown how it works.

Psychical research – I got into that just out of interest; I never heard anything at all about it in my childhood, I never knew about spiritualists or spiritualist churches or psychics. It wasn't until I was about sixteen or seventeen, reading science in the sixth form . . . Members of the science sixth each had to give a paper on a particular subject of their choice to the Scientific Society, and I'd happened to pick up, a few weeks before I had to do it, a book called *The Personality of Man*, by G. N. M. Tyrrell, and it so fascinated me that I've been on to the subject ever since. Mainly because it seemed to me that here was I, with a scientific training and with a religious background, and here was someone who was trying to answer the questions of religion by the methods of science.

I don't think in fact that psychical research is going to give the answer to the questions of religion – as I thought it might over the years – because both psychical research and religion are matters of . . . you might say faith or belief. The data are there, but the interpretation depends upon the person who is interpreting the data. One of my favourite slogans is 'Experience is sacred, interpretation is free.' So nobody is going to start from psychical research and prove God.

I belong also to the Church's Fellowship for Psychical and Spiritual Studies, and there are a lot of people who belong to that because they have had psychic experiences and they are trying to make sense of them within their Christian faith. But they're finding that the majority of Christians either don't understand psychic experience, or think they understand it and disapprove of it very strongly. And this is unhappy, because if the Lord has made the world then he's made the whole world, he has made people within it with psychic capabilities and those capabilities have got to be used to the glory of God and the good of fellow men. They are faculties that have got to be hallowed and directed aright, and therefore we have got to seek to understand those faculties and make sense of them within our Christian faith if we are to remain Christian.

I don't really like the idea of arguing people into Christianity, but if someone wanted to be convinced or if somebody wanted to know – yes, I would say there is a great deal of evidence from psychical research, evidence which has more than one interpretation, but a lot of it points in the same general direction as Christian faith. That there is something to man which is more than his material frame. And you can make much easier sense of psychic experiences if you believe that something survives the death of the body. You can also make sense of those experiences if you believe that nothing does survive, but it's a very difficult sense to make. Personally, for my money, I believe that it is possible to communicate beyond death; that some – though not all, perhaps not very many – but *some* mediumistic communications really do come from a life beyond. And that when we come to die many of us may have an experience of the nearer reaches of the life to come, so that sometimes when people have a close brush with death, in that near-death experience they have already glimpsed the first few footsteps of that life and then been snatched back from it into this one.

That's my belief – it's a belief, not a proof. Because with this whole business of the near-death experience there could be more than one interpretation, we're so early on in the research at the moment. It's an exciting time for me – it's only about ten years, just over ten years, since the whole thing came out of the closet with Raymond Moody's book *Life after Life*. The visions that people have reported seeing when they were at the point of death. Until then the near-death experience was known to a very few researchers and medical people, but it was certainly not widely known and not widely studied. Since Moody's book came out, and also since resuscitation techniques have improved, it's become very widely known and the study on it is increasing. The last ten years have brought forth a number of very tantalizing pieces of research, and my guess is that in the next ten or twenty years there's going to be a tremendous increase in research.

Maybe the near-death experience is going to provide for many people the real proof that there's a life after death. Or maybe it's going to prove that we are all capable of fooling ourselves, and that there is something archetypal in the human being that when it's faced with death presents a kind of fantasy scenario which tells him that he's not going to be snuffed out. Here again I sort of stick . . . I stick so uncomfortably on the line between faith and scepticism where such evidence is concerned, I think because I say to myself, 'We are never in this life going to get proof, all we're going to get is pointers.' As I say, for me the pointers all seem to go in the same direction, but I could never stand up in a pulpit and say I have *proof* of life after death. All I could get up there and say is, 'I believe there's a life after death, I believe there is a God who made us and made us for an eternal purpose, and there are a lot of scientific findings, particularly in this generation, which point in the same direction and which make sense on that assumption – but it is still an assumption and you have got to live your life by faith.'

I think that through psychical research I have opened my mind to a lot of possibilities that I wouldn't have come across if I'd stayed completely within an orthodox or traditional Christian background, and particularly through the Church's Fellowship for Psychical and Spiritual Studies. I think I've seen that some Christians are fearfully blinkered about their ideas of the life and the world to come and fearfully blinkered about the possibility of knowing anything about it. There's the biblical story of the witch of Endor – the word 'witch', incidentally, is translated in some modern versions as 'medium', she practised divination – but if you read it in the original form in 1 Samuel rather than in the later form in 1 Chronicles you'll find there's very little moral blame attached to Saul for consulting her. The followers of Yahweh, the God of the Old Testament, were trying to keep their national religion free from practices of the local tribes, the worship of the Baal or Baalim. There's also stuff in some of the Prophets about 'Go not to the dead, why seek ye the dead?' – and that's all right if with the Old Testament you believe that the dead are cut off from the presence of Yahweh-God; because in the whole of the Old Testament Yahweh was the God of the living, not the dead – when you died you were sent into a place called Sheol where the shades lived a very grey and uninteresting existence cut off from God.

It's only through very late Judaism and in particular through Christianity that one gets the belief that God is even present in the world of the dead and that there is nowhere where God isn't. Therefore today if you are consulting a medium you're not consulting someone who is in a place cut off from God, you're consulting someone who is in a place where Jesus has already been, and where his presence and his converting power can be. That's the meaning of the phrase in the Creed, 'He descended into Hell' – not that he went to the place of the damned, but he went to the place of the departed. Jesus died as anyone else died when he died on Good Friday; he went to the place of the dead, and is present there, and he is present beyond this earth, therefore if you are dealing with a medium you are not dealing with somebody who is outside God's care, protection, or possibility.

Spiritualism as an actual religion – well, my main quarrel with that is that it takes a part of the truth and tries to turn it into the whole of a religion. Some spiritualists are very anti-Christian, some claim to be not particularly interested in Christianity, and some claim to be Christian; but on the whole spiritualism as a religion I find singularly thin and unsatisfying. It seems to be completely this-world centred in a way, although it claims to be centred entirely on the other world; it's not very helpful for mourners because it gets them stuck in a particular phase of bereavement and doesn't enable them to work through it, it seems to be self-centred in that what matters is the satisfaction of the worshipper. And, as I say, if you go to a Christian church over the years you will be challenged in all sorts of ways to change the world, to live in the world, to become a whole human being – and you will also be taught something, I hope, about the Christian hope of a world to come. But it's all set within the context, whereas there seems to be very little context within which a spiritualist belief is set. There are Christians who believe that spiritualism is dabbling with the Devil and they smell the sulphur and they go in feet first, fists flailing ... No, that wouldn't be my view of it. One does come across people – sad people – from time to time, who are completely obsessed by their psychic faculties, who almost live in a world which is not quite the world of reality; and for those people, yes, the answer is, 'Jesus Christ releases you, go and serve him, but this particular part of your life has got to be closed off because it's not for you.'

To go back to the biblical view of the afterlife – at the time of Jesus of Nazareth the whole idea of the future life was very much under discussion within the Jewish religion. In the main part of the Old Testament there seems only to have been a belief in Sheol and a belief that one lived on in one's descendants, therefore the greatest blessing from Yahweh was to have a long life and to have progeny as the sand on the sea-shore – that was the traditional kind of blessing. In the Maccabean revolution and revolt in the second century B C a very large number of Jews were slain for their adherence to the laws of Moses and people began saying, 'Look, it's not fair that these people who suffered and died for their faith should be in Sheol, surely there's something better.' And in those two centuries there was an enormous amount of speculation, theological speculation of one sort or another. Did they all go to Sheol? Was there a better place? Were they going to sleep, and was God going to raise them all from the sleep of death at the last day? If so, was he going to bring them back to this earth or was he going to bring them back to a transformed earth, or to a place called heaven?

So around the time of Jesus there was still all that kind of speculation, nothing had settled down as a standard doctrine; and so you'll read in the New Testament that the Pharisees believed in angels and a life to come, the Sadducees did not believe in angels and did not believe in a life to come. The various parties had different beliefs. Then comes Jesus of Nazareth, and in his teaching he seems to say that there will be a resurrection and that God will continue to care for his people despite and beyond death. He dies, he is seen again after his resurrection by his disciples, and all of a sudden – in the words of Christopher Evans, if I can remember them correctly – 'how amazing it is that out of a faith in which resurrection was an article of discussion there arose a faith in which resurrection was the central item in its belief'.

What can have caused that? Nothing but the teaching and the resurrection of Jesus himself. So the Christians then go into the world with the belief that God has visited his people in the Messiah, the promised Messiah, who is Jesus of Nazareth, who died, who rose again, and whose followers can join him in that resurrection life – now that's not quite the same as ideas of heaven as popularly presented today. It doesn't imply that everyone survives, and it certainly doesn't give anything in the way of details. All right, there are various stories – most of them, I think, poetic or symbolic stories – like the one that Jesus told of Dives and Lazarus, how the poor man Lazarus died and went into Abraham's bosom and how the rich man, who hadn't cared for the poor man when he was on this earth, died and was buried and went into a place of torment. So many of these depictions of life after death are in symbolic terms, very few of them have any detail in them, and very often the detail is so incongruous that I think we're meant to . . . I mean, sitting on clouds and twanging harps! That's in the Book of Revelation, the harpers harping upon their harps, but there are plenty of other things there; I think we're meant to realize that the whole thing is a vision of one person's imagination of what it might be like.

I say that there is nobody going to be more surprised at the details of the life of the world to come than those who are most sure they've got it right in detail now! I mean, most of what we say about the life of the world to come is in symbolic and poetic language. All I know is that according to my Christian belief I shall be closer to the presence of the God whom I have tried to serve in this life, that I shall be closer to the people whom I loved in this life, and that I shall find – whatever I'm doing there, whatever occupations there are – I shall find in them something of which the greatest satisfaction I can imagine in this life is only a pale imitation. But, you know, once you get into details . . . I go into my own fantasy, just as the Norse went into the fantasy of

73

Valhalla, just as the seer of the Book of Revelation went off into his fantasy of people playing harps and casting golden crowns into a sea of crystal.

I think this is probably borne out by the near-death experience itself, where the experience seems to be tinged very strongly with the religious beliefs or expectations of the person concerned – in other words, there is an experience, but it is interpreted in terms of the understanding of the person who has the experience, and you can't expect it otherwise. Whatever we experience is already filtered through our understanding – I look across at you, I see a person who is talking to me or listening to me, but that's only because I've learned to interpret visual and auditory symbols and make sense of the world with them. My pet cat has a very different kind of world and makes a very different kind of sense out of the stimuli she receives.

My own personal understanding – the sense I have made out of the New Testament and the Christian religion, and also of all the study I've done in psychical research – my belief is that all human beings, as human beings, survive death, that God has made us capable of surviving death. Without an understanding of God, and without a lively faith in Jesus, the kind of survival we come to is probably very similar to the Old Testament belief in Sheol or the Greek belief in Hades – in other words, survival into a life which is very much the same as this kind of life, in which I wouldn't have a great deal of interest because it doesn't seem to be particularly exciting.

I don't want to be in the least dogmatic about non-Christians – I've met too many serious, good agnostics and serious, good Hindus, Muslims and what have you to believe that my kind of God, my kind of understanding of God, would not want to love them and to deal with them in as understanding and helpful a way as he can. Therefore I cannot consign non-Christians to hell, I cannot believe that a God of love can consign non-Christians to hell. I believe that he may be able to open their eyes to the truth of the Christian revelation, and he may do it after this life rather than before it. But there's a very telling story right at the end of St John's Gospel where the risen Christ comes to seven of his disciples and tells Peter to feed his sheep and Peter says, 'Lord, what shall this man do?' And Jesus replies, 'What's that to you? You follow me.' And as far as I'm concerned the fate of the non-Christians I am prepared to leave with God – what is that to me? It's my business to follow him in the best way that I can and not ask too many questions about the fate of other people. In other words I'm content to leave those to God, knowing that God is a loving and understanding God – I don't believe that he's a vindictive or cruel God.

Hell – well, hell is always a possibility, it's always possible that we shall so distance ourselves from the things of goodness ... We make the bed we lie on. Hell is a possibility, hell is real; it is possible that we shall make such a mess of our lives, such a mess of ourselves, that nobody can get us out of it. That is a living and real possibility for everyone – but again that is what *I* feel, I don't think it is for me to tell you that it is your possibility. In other words, 'What is that to you? Follow thou me.' Hell is a warning to me that those who cut themselves off from goodness are in a very unhappy position, and I do not want to be one of them. But I wouldn't want to ask questions about whether there are more in heaven or more in hell; or whether there's anybody in hell in the long run. I'm a universalist – which I think a good many Christians are, but not all of them – I'm a universalist in that I believe that the power of God is so great that a person will eventually turn from the pursuit of evil to the pursuit of goodness, and that if he cannot do it in this world he's going to do it in the world to come.

Yes, there's a chance for Hitler – there's a chance for everyone. But it's not going to be a painless chance; I don't find it painless even in this life to try and turn from the things that please me but I know are not good to the things that are good. I'm quite sure that when I come to the life of the world to come and my secret thoughts are revealed and I see what kind of person I have made myself become, I cannot fool myself that I'm going to become instantly at home in the kingdom of heaven. There's going to be pain as I conform myself to the ways of goodness and as I burn out the things within me that are unworthy and evil.

Purgatory is hopeful, it's full of hope. Purgatory isn't the way to hell, purgatory is the way to heaven – it's the kind of disciplined chastening of our souls and our desires along ways that we recognize as good but we find difficult and painful. And I cannot believe that there is anybody that is so sunk in evil that God cannot redeem him in eternity if he can't redeem him in time. Therefore, as I say, hell is always a possibility, but whether it is an eternally realized possibility . . . I believe that it isn't; many Christians believe that it is. Yes. I think they believe in it because they have a high opinion of human freedom, and therefore they believe that man must in the end be free to resist God if he wants to. But I have a higher belief in the love and the power of God . . .

The problem of pre-Christians and pagans – the early Church got round that by the doctrine of the harrowing of hell. It comes in the first Epistle of Peter, where it says that Jesus went the road of departed spirits, and there are lots of superb medieval carvings of the harrowing of hell, where Jesus goes down and fetches up the good pagans who lived before his time. And this seems to me to be . . . All right, it's very artistic and poetic, but it seems to me a humane doctrine, which says that those who are looking for truth are looking for God. Those who find truth in Jesus find God in Jesus; those who look for truth and find it elsewhere, God is not going to deny them eternal salvation because they never had a chance of hearing Jesus, or because they heard in such a perverted way – I mean, there are some kinds of Christian evangelism which I find so repulsive that I cannot possibly blame people who turn away from it. The old kind of hell-fire preaching seems to me to be so terrible that I cannot blame people who say, 'I am morally revolted by it, and I'm not going to believe in a God who has that kind of attitude towards the greater part of his creation.' And therefore if a person is turned away from Christianity by that kind of teaching I cannot believe that God is going to eternally punish him for so doing.

All I can say is that I have looked into but not gone very far into some other religions and I do not find in them as satisfying a picture of God as I find in Christ. I don't want to be patronizing towards them, I don't want to say that God is certainly going to convert them to good Christians in the life of the world to come – I would rather leave the whole thing in the hands of God.

To ask questions about those who reject either Christianity or my understanding of Christianity, I leave that to God, and I do believe God is more humane and loving than a good many Christians make him out to be. Of course, some of the stuff that gets read in the first lessons at matins or evensong in Durham Cathedral . . . There's a lot of the Old Testament that leaves me intensely uncomfortable. Sometimes I say, 'I hope there isn't much of a congregation here'! And then again sometimes I say, 'Well, I hope they understand that this is a primitive society trying to make sense of its ideas of God.'

In the end, I think I believe in life after death because I am a Christian, and because I believe in the kind of God who raised Jesus from the dead, and who had so personal a care for his human creation that he would not want to see that creation come to nothing – and then I find a lot of tantalizing hints in parapsychology which make sense if I hold that belief, but which are not nearly so easy to make sense of if I believe that we are simply a material mixture of chemicals and electrical impulses which happen to be so programmed as to be conscious of themselves, but will completely come to an end. In other words I start as a Christian and then I find, as a Christian, that a lot of things point in the same direction as my belief. And then I say, because of my scientific background, 'Hold on, be critical.' I have then to examine those phenomena and make up my mind about them. A lot I find I have to put on one side as due to the will to believe or to fraud or to coincidence or what have you. But some of them I find I cannot put on one side, they do seem to me to be as genuine as anything is; and they, as I say, help to buttress my Christian belief, but they don't create it.

Perhaps if I hadn't been a Christian I would have been a parapsychologist who believed in survival. I might have come to a belief that the human spirit was indestructible but that there was no God that made it – it was just . . . it just happened that way, and it was indestructible, full stop. Which is a possible stance to take. Or limited survival for a limited number of people – there are plenty of possible scenarios. One would be that the human mind continues for a short time, maybe days, maybe months, maybe years, before it disintegrates. We tend to imagine a future world in terms of what we know about this one. Maybe in the world to come we will be only conscious of and communicating with those with whom we have some affinity, and space will not be the same as space here in any case. I don't know, it's all speculation.

It could be that though we all survive, only a very small percentage of us can communicate with this earth; possibly all want to communicate but few manage it because the conditions on this earth are not such as to enable us to. You know, there are all sorts of possibilities. Robert Thouless, for instance, produced this cipher test and said he was going to communicate it when he died, communicate the key. According to the communications from mediums now, he's finding immense difficulty in remembering the key. Whether that's simply a cop-out by the mediums who can't contact him or not is the 64,000-dollar question. But there are so many different kinds of possible scenarios that in the end I think one just has to say, 'I do not know, full stop.'

I don't necessarily dismiss those prosaic communications that come through mediums, because, you see, you have got to talk in terms which make sense to you, and if your perception is such that heaven for you is a nice semi with a decent garden, then these are the terms in which you perceive whatever experiences you're continuing to have. To some extent we make our own heaven, make our own surroundings by the use of our imagination or by the way in which we interpret the stimuli that come to us. And therefore it may not be as silly as it sounds when they describe heaven as if it might be Putney on a Sunday afternoon. For me it might be listening to Beethoven quartets and eating grapes!

I think people will be reunited with those they've lost. I've lost a father, but I haven't yet lost a wife or child or anyone as close to me as that. I mean, if I lost my wife I'd find it very difficult to imagine life without her, and I would look forward to re-meeting her – on the other hand I'm sure she would say we don't look forward to spending the whole of eternity in each other's presence and not being able to get away from each other. You will remember that story that the Sadducee asked of Jesus because he wanted to prove how silly the Pharisee's belief in life after death was; there was a woman who married the eldest of seven brothers and he died, and she married the second brother and he died, and she married the third, and so on until in the end she'd married all seven – whose wife is she going to be in the world to come? Jesus simply said, 'In the life of the world to come they neither marry nor are given in marriage, but are like the angels in heaven.' Full stop. In other words, if you ask silly questions you get silly answers.

If you ask detailed questions like that you do not know the answer and you will discover it when the time comes. But the answer may not be tolerably understandable in terms of this present space-time world where our relations are limited to the kind of relations we can have through the five senses. If the conditions of the life of the world to come don't boggle our imaginations they're probably not true. And therefore you can ask these questions but you can never answer them, and if you get stuck on the questions that's sad, because I think you're just wasting time.

I think these questions about life in the world to come need a bit of lateral thinking, and a little bit of shoving in the pending tray. There's an awful lot in my pending tray as far as questions about belief are concerned. I stick them there and I fetch them out from the pending tray and give them a dusting every now and again and generally put them back there. As long as your pending tray doesn't contain everything you ever think about, you can live life with quite a considerable pending tray. Because all the questions about life and death, you're not going to find satisfactory answers to; the main ones you're going to find provisional answers to, and you're going to hone those provisional answers as you go through life, casting some aside because they don't accord with your experience, modifying others as new bits of experience come to you. But you've still got that whacking great pending tray.

Yes, I've had experiences and feelings which have helped convince me that there is something more to life than the material and that there is a God beyond it. I've had feelings of religious experience, feelings in prayer, feelings on solitary walks, feelings sometimes as I've been talking about theology with friends, feelings as I've been enjoying myself with my wife or with my family ... It's rather like asking the verbal meaning of a Beethoven quartet – you experience it rather than encapsulate it within words. It comes, it goes; you can't force it, you can't hang on to it when you've got it, you can remember it and savour it, but you can't force it.

When I come to my own death I pray I shall come to it in complete faith and trust in God. I don't know whether I shall. In my lucid and thinking moments I know that there is nothing to be feared, either about dying or about death, for those who come to it in Christian faith and confidence. Even if I had a bad death I believe that God will see me through it – to a glorious resurrection, to a life where I shall know him better and know my fellow Christians better. But that still leaves a lot in the pending tray. And I think we'd better finish there!

# Cathy Taggart

My mother left us when I was five. No, never had a stepmother. My father brought us up on his own, my sister and me. My sister's a totally different kettle of fish from me – being married, she's more for her husband's family, if you understand me. But he was more or less all I had, and I was more or less all *he* had.

He died about three years ago. No, at the time I don't think I was cut up – I didn't understand, it just didn't hit me for about two months. When I found out that he was dead it was about twelve o'clock at night and I'd been at the hospital most of the evening, and a friend of mine came round, because I don't have a telephone, and she said, 'Your father's just passed away'; and I just said, 'Oh.' It didn't sink in, it was like somebody had said, 'It's nine o'clock', or something like that.

He'd been ill for some time and it was inevitable, we knew what was going to happen. I think he knew. When he'd had his first operation he was on a drip for about six weeks, then he came home for a while; he came to stay with me for a few weeks, they let him out. And then he gradually, you know, got sicker. And they took him back in again; they told us that they'd have to operate again and if they didn't he'd die within six weeks. They were surprised that he'd survived the first operation; he had the whole of his stomach out, one kidney, spleen, colon and part of his liver. And he still survived. But obviously, the strain of it all, he couldn't keep it up. We had to sign for the second operation – he was so out of his head on pain-killing drugs that it had to be next of kin to sign. It was a very, very big decision to make, because it would have given him maybe a few months, but he would have been in pain.

They didn't tell me that if he didn't have this second operation he was going to die, because I was pregnant at the time with my youngest one and they didn't want to upset me. But my uncle pulled me aside and he said, 'He won't have the operation, and he needs it, and the only one he'd listen to is you.' So I went to see him and I said, 'Look, you've got to have the operation.' He would die anyway, but it would give him a bit more time. And he said, you know, 'Will I be all right?' And I said, 'Of course you'll be all right.' You don't know what to say.

But it is a strange thing, I never really knew whether he realized or not. I was too frightened to say to him, 'Oh, did you know they done this and that?' We'd never speak about what happened to him. I was never told, I was always kept in the dark. It's because I was so close to my father. My sister, being the eldest, the doctors always seemed to turn to her; because I was pregnant – 'Oh, don't bother her, she'll get upset.'

After about three nights he'd been in, my sister came to the door, again at about twelve o'clock at night, and she said, 'Dad's in the operating theatre.' Straight away I said, 'It's cancer, isn't it?' She said, 'Yes.' I knew in my mind it was cancer. I knew by the colour of him. You know, he went kind of a grey colour, and that is a sign of cancer, in most cases anyway. And that was it; and he was on a life-support system and things like that. He pulled through the first operation; and after the second one, he was in Recovery, and he actually died once, but they revived him. And we had the priest in to him. No, I don't think it's right that they revived him – when he died that first time I said, 'Leave him.'

They reckoned he'd had it for about ten to fifteen years. When I was about eleven my father had a very bad accident – he was run over in Ladbroke Grove, and his legs were literally smashed to pieces and he had his spleen removed. And the doctor thinks shock can sometimes cause cancer. When he had that accident I wasn't allowed to see him for three months because he was in such a state. We went to my father's brother, and we stayed with him, and with my grandmother – we were sort of shunted about, me more, being the youngest. But we were never put into care – that wasn't allowed in our family. It's nice to be with your family, you know. We managed, and he brought us up, and we didn't do too badly.

I did see my mother when I was eighteen – I hadn't seen her since I was five. She came for my father's funeral too, but she never went. No, I didn't forget about her; I mean, there's always a maternal thing there for your mother. For me it was very upsetting when she left, because I was very anaemic as a child and when my mother left I just went to pieces because I was, you know, Mummy's girl – the youngest children normally are anyway. I wouldn't eat, and had to have injections and tablets and things like that. Being with my father, I don't think he really knew what to say to us. He thought that we knew. But I thought as a child that my mother went because I was naughty or done something wrong and she didn't love me any more. I understand the situation now, as I grow older.

My father never ever brought a woman to the house. He done his best with us, and we weren't exactly the most well-off kids in the street, but we were well fed and well cared for, you know. My father was a jack of all trades, really. He used to do window-cleaning; and he had a van, he used to pick us up from school. And we used to go to the woman next door, because where we lived the basements were joined, and she used to keep an eye on us. We were quite domesticated at five, six – you know, it was a case of wash the dishes and do this and that. I suppose you tend to get a sort of old head on young shoulders, because you have to – it's either that . . . You have to survive when you're small. I was always attached to my dad anyway, I think more so even than with my mother. Because my mother used to go to work, and when she'd go to work we'd be asleep, and when she got back we'd be asleep; so it was my father used to wash us and dress us and take us to school. So he was practically like a father and mother to us as long as I can remember.

I knew – it was sort of like an inner sense – I knew that my father had cancer. I couldn't ask the doctor, I didn't want to accept it. Even when they told me . . . I said, 'It's cancer, isn't it?' and my sister said, 'Yes.' Yet I just literally would not accept it. Because my father was indispensable . . . I think everybody thinks that about their parents – they've got to be there, always. I felt I had nobody. I felt, that's it, I've got nobody, nothing to turn to. Because my little boy's father, I'd found out he was married –

he's now gone back to America. And there was all that as well. I mean, I was broken-hearted over him. But I pushed that to one side, because I was more broken up about my father. I had nobody, all I had was my children, and I couldn't confide in them because they were too small. Me and my sister were never really close. I had one friend – she's about ten years older than me. But she's the type of person that didn't know what to say and so she never came near me. She knew how I felt, because she lost her little boy when he was two – he died a cot-death. And, you know, she said, 'I know how you feel, it's the same thing. But I don't know what to say.' That was afterwards she told me, when I said, 'You didn't come to see me or nothing.'

I coped, in a sense, I had to cope for the sake of the children. A young baby – I thought, well, I've got to. I've got three children, yes. I'd just brought a baby home from hospital, and I had my father to look after too. I wanted to do it. Because I *knew* that he was going to die. I just knew. I had a big argument with my family; I said, 'Look, I've got a right to know what's going on.' And they just wouldn't tell me, so I went to the doctor, and he told me. Because my father had told them not to upset me, because I'd get very upset if anything happened to my father. I was actually drinking quite heavily then. That was my sort of way out, of trying to block it out of my head. But it didn't work, because I'm not a drinker anyway, and I was sort of going off the rails a bit; but I had to pull myself together.

He died five days after the second operation. He was in a coma for three days, and I talked him round out of the coma – he never recognized anybody, only me. Because of the children – he was very close to them, his grandchildren. And, you know, I kept on talking about Jeannine, my daughter Jeannine. Because they say they can hear you. And I think he could hear me, because he opened his eyes and he said, 'Is she all right?' And I said, 'Who?' And he said, 'Jeannine.' He must have heard what I was saying to him. And he died the following day.

They say you get a last sort of strength before you die. And the day I was there, in the early evening, he sat up, and he was covered with wires and tubes and everything, and he pulled himself up in the bed and he said, 'Get me my stick and we'll get out of here.' You know? And I just couldn't sit there, I had to get up and walk out.

He did suffer terribly. At the end they had him on the pain-killing drugs and it used to make him hallucinate. He said there was dogs running up and down the ward, and when my daughter came in he thought it was his wife, he thought it was my mum. And he was saying, 'Is it Jeanie?' And Skippy, he was on about our old dog Skippy, and things like that. You know, it was so hard to sit there and not cry. He'd think that you'd knocked water on the bed and shout for the nurse to change the bed because it's all wet. He would have been in terrible pain, it was really a release that he did go when he did. You know? Even though I didn't want him to. But I was being selfish, because he'd have been in pain.

I don't think they should let people suffer like that. In the hospital where my father was they used to leave the window open, when he was getting worse towards the end, and I used to go and close it. And I'd say to the nurse, 'Why are you leaving the window open? – because it's cold, it's freezing in here.' And she said, 'That's to help him on his way.' He did die of pneumonia. I blamed the nurses, I said, 'You're trying to kill him.' I definitely went a bit funny. You do want to blame somebody.

I didn't want to go to the church; I thought, if there's a God, he let him die. It is weird really, I mean, at the time you blame everybody – you blame God, you blame the doctor – if he hadn't of done this it would be all right, you know. But it's not true. You do have strange ways of blocking out the pain as well. A lot of people can't handle bereavement, they never really get over it. If I hadn't had the children I think I would never have coped at all. I think what mainly kept me together was the children, plus the baby. You know, I couldn't sort of let myself down. Because it would be them that would suffer. And I suffered in my childhood, and I try my best not to let that happen to them. Because I'm all they've got, and my father was all I had. So if anything had happened to my father when I was their age I don't know what I'd have done. So I can't just turn my back on them because of the way I feel.

No, I wasn't there when he died; and that is what really . . . To this day, I will never forgive myself. I was with him that day until about eight o'clock, when I came home. And I often said, if anything happens and he gets worse, ring my friend next door so I can be there. I was the nearest relative that lived across the road, everybody else lives about a mile or two away. He died at twelve o'clock and they didn't ring till twelve-thirty. And I phoned up when my friend brought the message that he'd died. I just . . . I didn't believe it, I had to find out for myself. And they said, 'Would you like to come over and view the body?' and I said no. I couldn't, you know, I wanted to remember him the way I did before. He looked so ill – I still get flashbacks of him, sitting in bed and being lifted up like a child. Very thin, he was, like a skeleton.

I wouldn't go to the Chapel of Rest; all my family was over. And the last night when the body was in the church, I didn't want to go. The lid is lifted off the coffin and any relatives that want to take a viewing . . . They say, 'D'you want to have a viewing?' It's not a very nice word. You know, they pay their respects. It's a tradition with Irish people that close relatives come from all over. I wouldn't go in the church because I just didn't want to see my father lying in a coffin. I knew he was dead, and I knew I'd never see him again, but it just wouldn't register. The priest came out to me and he said, 'I think you'd better say goodbye to your father', and I said, 'I've said my goodbye.' I said, 'I don't want to see him in a coffin.' I was bodily dragged in to have a look, but I didn't want to. I just turned my head. Surprisingly, he looked quite well in death, he looked quite like his old self. As my uncle said, if you didn't see him you'd probably regret it for the rest of your life. But then again, I'm sorry I did see him, because I've always got that mental picture of him lying in the coffin. And lying in the hospital bed. There's one that really sticks in my mind, that's when he was being lifted out of the bed and he was practically crying. And, you know, I still remember that. And it's so upsetting.

I can feel how afraid he was of death, and knowing he was dying. I know he did. But I've never known to this day whether he knew he had cancer. I think my father was religious in his own way, because he made us have our Holy Communion when we were seven, confirmation. I've never really got into that sort of conversation about religion with him; but he asked me to get a priest for him, to confess his sins and get absolution before he died. He said he wanted to see Father Reagan, he was our parish priest, and they gave him the sacrament for the sick and things like that – they gave him a little bible. So I think in his last few months, through fear of dying ... You think there's that last shred of hope that religion can help you. It probably helps your pain, mental pain, but I don't think it can save you at all.

Obviously I don't know what it's like to be dying – I mean, obviously I've got to experience it one day. I've had sort of a similar experience when I've thought I've been dying, when I had a miscarriage, and it was an awful feeling. Like I was going down a big hole and I couldn't get up, and at the top I saw Jeannine, and I tried to pull myself up to catch her. And I was trying to pull her with me, and then screaming, 'Don't go, don't go.' I was going into this big pit. And the doctor was slapping me round the face, because I wouldn't come to. I had to have a transfusion, and I was quite ill, in hospital for a month. You know, I honestly thought I was experiencing dying. It was a horrible feeling, it was like I couldn't get back up to the light, where the children were at the top. And I was going further and further down, and trying to claw my way up and kept slipping. I felt myself slipping away, and not being able to get up.

I think it was their voices – the doctor said, you know, 'Wake up', and I came round ... I was quite ill for days after that; and I told the priest about the experience that I'd had, and he said it's not very uncommon. He said a lot of people do experience things like that, when they're between life and death, like between the two. It quite frightened me, actually.

At first, after he died ... It's strange, it's even very hard for me now to relate, because it was like I was drugged; because I was going around, I wasn't doing anything in the house, everything went to pot. And I kept saying to myself, 'Your dad is dead, your dad is dead' – I kept repeating it to myself. And then I'd cry, and then I'd, you know, start arguing with people – I fell out with all my friends, because I used to go off the handle for no reason at all, tell them to get lost.

The day of my father's funeral – it was a weird experience, because I felt like I was just going to church, I wasn't going to see my father being buried. And, you know, I just went into the church and just sat there. I couldn't hear what the priest was saying, I didn't even see he was in the church. And we went along to the grave; and I think it hit me when I saw the coffin going down. Because they were saying the Lord's Prayer, and then I realized – the words 'Our Father' in the prayer, I was thinking, well, that's my father. And, you know ... at that moment I felt that my whole world had just caved in, I thought I ought to go down there with him, I want to be with him. And I nearly fell into the grave. Because you pick up a bit of dirt and throw it in, and my father's friends were there, and he used to play pennies; and they threw in some pennies and a penny whistle and things like that. And that just broke my heart completely. It was the finality of it all, really, then ...

But I still wouldn't accept it; I accepted it I think for about an hour, crying and things like that. But then after I didn't feel any emotion at all. You know, you think to yourself, my father is dead – I should be sad. It's very weird even to think about – you just don't know, your mind is just blank, you don't know what you're thinking. And if somebody says something to you, like 'I'm sorry to hear about your father', you just say, 'Oh yeah', you know. Like they expect you to burst into tears. You just can't. I cried the day of my father's funeral, and I never cried for four months after that.

I was quite ill – I had to go to the doctor. I was on Valium for a while; I got hooked on it and stopped. I mean, I'd cry on just odd occasions. And I'd go into a shop and forget what I went in there for. I still do it now. You know, I'd be thinking of other things, daydreaming. I'd put something down and forget where it was, or forget what I was watching on the television; five minutes later I couldn't remember what I was watching. You're not taking nothing in, you're just totally blank in yourself. You don't acknowledge anything for a while. I didn't even acknowledge my children.

I had a few friends who helped me with the children, but they didn't help me with getting over my father. They'd say, 'We'll take the children and leave you to get on, we know that you're upset.' So they kept the children away from me. I think it's only the last year and a half that I've sort of straightened myself out. I haven't really got over my father yet, though. I don't think I ever will. I never will get over his death, and I never will accept it. But I'm learning to cope with it from day to day.

Oh, I know he's with me. I mean, I've experienced a few things in my other flat which I went to the parish priest about. I thought it was maybe because I was upset and my mind wasn't very stable at the time. I was at my place; and my father had a thing about pulling plugs out, and I'm absolutely terrible for leaving plugs in and switching off the appliance, I'll turn the television off and leave the plug in and my father would say, 'Always turn the plug off – causes fires.' If he stayed here, which he did quite a lot, he would always go round pulling the plugs out. And one night my friend was staying with me. We went to bed. And the next morning I got up and went round the flat and all the plugs had been pulled out. And I asked the children, and they don't touch plugs, and they said no. And then I had a kettle, electric kettle, in my other kitchen, and I had the electrician come in to check the switch because I thought it was faulty. Because when I boiled the kettle I'd leave the red switch on still, and I was in the kitchen one day and it clicked off by itself. It frightened me! And I thought, you know, if it was half on and half off it might have just done it on its own. But my friend was out there making tea and it happened to her, and she dropped the kettle on her foot! She scalded her foot quite badly because she had such a fright.

It happened a few times. My daughter heard my father coughing in the front room. And I've actually got up one night, and I've thought I've heard him coughing in the sitting-room too. And, I mean, things would happen in the house, a presence was there. Yes, I do believe he's there. Because when I get depressed and I look at his picture up there and I cry – you know how you miss somebody so much – and then I feel better, as if he's behind me. I mean, I know that he's at peace.

I do believe in God in a way, and in another way I don't. I know as a Catholic I shouldn't doubt . . . I don't go to mass; I used to, I used to be very religious. I am religious, in a sense, but you shouldn't doubt things. But I do know he's at rest. Because after the incident in my place I had the priest come over to give the house a blessing. I explained to him, you know, and he said, 'I understand how you feel.' He said, 'Would you like me to sort of . . . ?' What do they call it? Exorcize. In case he was not at rest. Yes, he did do that. Because I wasn't with my father when he died, and the last words he spoke he was asking for me. And I wasn't there.

I believe there is some kind of life after death. But it frightened me, about the plugs and that – I know I should never be scared of my father, but it really affected me for a long, long time. Because I used to have dreams as well – I'd dream of my father's old flat, where I grew up, in Bassett Road, where all my childhood memories are. I dreamt that I was back in the house. It was after my father's death – I mean, in my dream my father was dead, but I was back in that house, though my father moved into Lancaster Road when I moved into this estate. But in my dream I was back in Bassett Road and my father was there, but he was a spirit. And he come in and he said, 'Don't take my furniture, don't take my furniture', and he was all crying, and saying don't give my furniture to nobody. I think it was playing on my mind, because when my dad died all his furniture was in his flat, and I never gave a thing away. I kept it all, and after a while just gave little bits and pieces to my friends. I think that was playing on my mind.

I'd like sometime to speak to someone who really knows about those things. I think if your mind is upset you do dream a lot of warped dreams. For instance, where we used to live in a basement there'd be like a cellar door – it'd be like an ordinary door but it went to a cellar. It was pitch black and it had gas meters in there, and as a child I'd always think it was full of ghosts and devils and evil things. And I had this dream that I was sitting in the house at the age I am now, in my twenties, and my father in front of me, and this door burst open and all these things come out. In one of my dreams, it frightened me a lot, he came to me as a devil – he was dead, sitting on his chair, and when he stood up he was about eight foot tall. It was an awful . . . I don't really want to talk about that, actually.

Oh yes, I did have nicer dreams. I mean, I remember when I was really upset when I went to bed – this was not long after he died, it was after the dream about the furniture, because I was upset for days after that – and he came in my dream and just started talking to me. I don't remember what he said, apart from that he was happy and not in pain. And I think that that helped me to get over it in a sense.

Every day, or every Saturday, I'd go up to my father's place, which is up the market; I made a point of going to the corner of the street and saying, 'He's not there', walk down past his house and say, 'He's gone, he's not there.' I'd walk down and I'd stare at the house for ages. For a while I used to think too, I'll go down and see my dad – and I did walk down the road to go and see him and then think, where am I going? He's not there. You know? I've done it a few times without thinking. The word 'dead' never registered with me, it didn't mean nothing, it was just a word. I'd keep saying it in my head – 'He's dead, he's dead, he's dead.' But it didn't mean anything.

You have to leave people behind when you die, I think that's the worst part of knowing that you're dying. But we didn't talk about it. I think there was a thing between me and my father, we were so close, that he didn't want to hurt me and I didn't want to hurt him. So we both sort of knew . . . He probably knew he had cancer and was dying, and I knew he had cancer and was dying, but neither of us would tell each other. Because I loved him so much, if I'd actually heard it from him, it would have broke my heart. He loved me that much – I know he did love me – that he wouldn't tell me. You know? It's a weird situation really. Because you don't know whether knowing about it would be for the better or for the worse.

My eldest daughter – she was nine and a half, ten at the time – I told her. I brought her to the funeral because she was the eldest. She understood. She was very, very upset. Because they were very close. She said, 'You're horrible because you wouldn't let me go and see Grandad when he was dying.' I just didn't let her see him. She went over there a few times, but when he got worse the doctor said, 'I don't think it's advisable to let a child go in.' I said, 'Well, I want him to see his grandchildren.' She understood it when he died, what he died of – I explained to her. My son, he never understood. He was seven. He didn't cry – I don't think it even hit him. He loved his grandad, though. I had to explain to him . . . He used to call it the gravy yard, he says, 'Grandad gone to the gravy yard.' I said, 'He's gone to heaven now, he's looking down at you.' I said, 'He's watching you.' I took them up to the grave to try and make them understand. You don't really know what goes on in a child's mind. You know, I said, 'Grandad's buried there', and he said, 'Is he in a box under the ground?' And I said yes. What can you say to a child of that age?

It was like he was their father. Yes, I've been a one-parent family – it's been, well, relationships that didn't work out, the three children. Why I think I didn't really get on with the people was because my father was always the one I turned to. Apart from my children the most important person in my life was my father. Yes, more than my boyfriends. It sounds strange; but my father gave up a lot to look after us. My sister sort of disowned him – she only lived up the road, but she'd never go and see him. She was just ashamed of him, because he was Irish. We used to have arguments and things like that; I used to say to her that if it wasn't for Dad we'd have been put in a children's home. 'We might have had it a bit rough,' I said, 'but we're still here.' My father struggled his whole life – he never really had a good life. You know, my mother left him – he loved the ground she walked on. And the accident he had. He really had a lot thrown at him.

It was just me and my father – he was my whole family. I feel like an outsider compared to the rest of my family. They're married and got husbands – you know, I'm like the black sheep. I don't care. But my father accepted me – that's why I loved him so much. He used to help out financially, and it would be vice versa when I had a few bob, and he'd say, 'Lend me a pound', or whatever. When I was broke and I needed food he'd always turn up with a bag of shopping, things like that. I always had my dad to go to, you know. It's like someone's cut off my right arm. I've got something missing that can never be replaced. Never. No, never, I'll never get over it. The day I get over it is the day I die. It's like part of your whole life is gone. It's true. Well, I suppose really it's a case of accepting it to a point, and trying to cope with it. Which is hard.

That's why I can't go up to the cemetery – every time I went up there I'd come back and I'd get really depressed. I'd say to myself, 'I remember you, and love you', rather than going up to a clump of earth. You know? Or a stone. Because he's not there, all that's there is a shell. I go up there and I think, my father's down there; and I get so confused and I come home and I just crack up. If I'm really troubled, and things get me down, I have sometimes gone up there and started talking away to him. No, I didn't get an answer. That's when I realized that he's not there. So I find now that if I get troubled and things like that, I mean, he comes to me – I can feel him.

One thing I am glad of, that he did see the baby, my youngest. Dad got to know him for about two and a half months – the baby was just over three months old when he died. He named him, actually. He wanted me to call him Francis Aidan, which was his brother's name, but I didn't like the name Francis, so I called him Aidan Francis. And what I'm glad of is that I named my other son after my father – exactly the same, my father's name and my grandfather's name. James Daniel Patrick Joseph.

It's very hard to actually put into words – the love that my father had for me and I had for my father, I could never really give to anybody else. I suppose I have been in love when I was younger, but as I've got older I've put up a few barriers and I'm a bit wary of things. I mean, the sort of love I had for my father was different anyway, it's totally different – the same kind of love you have for your children. You know, I think because of the way I am, I'm very untrustful of men now. I jump down people's throats very quickly. I don't know, it's just the way I am. There probably are the right men around, but I haven't met any of them yet! Maybe they're extinct, like the dodo.

My main ambition now is to get the children grown up to an age when they're not so dependent on me. And then I can say, 'Well, you've done your bit, now try and make something for your own life.' You know, when you've got children, it's hard, especially when you're in circumstances where you're on the poverty line, practically. You make do as best you can and try and make ends meet; but you always have something that *you* want to do with your life, and you can't because you've got children. It's a weird situation really, because even when they drive you mad you wouldn't be without them. Even when you could bang their heads together. But then if it wasn't for them I would never have got through my father's death as well as I have.

I was heading for a breakdown, I know I was, because it was drink, drink, drink – you know, I was definitely cracking up. I had a breakdown before, so I know. It's weird, you know, I was just sitting in a friend's house one night; and from that moment on I was all right. I said, 'Right, that's it, that's enough.' I think it might have been my father. I don't know. I think he said, 'Now listen here, girl, get up and stop being stupid and look after them kids' – because he's always been like that. Sort of running around and 'Look after them kids' – that's the sort of person he was. And I was sitting there and I was thinking, you know, if he could only see me in this state now he'd probably kill me. He'd have kicked me up and down and everything. So I thought, well . . . I thought, come on, if he sees you like this . . . He wouldn't want you to be like this. So I did carry on. I remember my father crying when my mother went when I was small. And so I thought, if he coped, well, I can. I mean, I'm a lot like my father – I've got strength somewhere that makes me cope.

It's hard; but as time goes by I think you just get by as best you can. You have your ups and downs, everyone does. But even now, I think what always keeps me going is my dad. Because I know if I done something really bad, I'd be letting him down. He'd probably get me struck down by a thunderbolt! I know that sometimes I could sink . . . I feel like I'm sinking, I'm sinking sometimes. But in my subconscious I can hear him saying, 'What you doing? Get up, straighten yourself out.' Things like that. And I just think, well, get up and do it. I used to let things get on top of me at one time – bills, you know.

Oh, I do feel he's still with me. I've got a habit when I'm talking about a person . . . When I say, 'my father', I'm looking at that chair, like as if he's sitting on the chair. I mean, that's the way I think – a lot of people think I'm a bit of a crackpot! I feel him in the house. I was out one night, I left my daughter here – she's thirteen – and she said, 'Mum, when you was out I got frightened and hid under the bed. I heard someone coming up the stairs.' That is the one time when I would be afraid, if my father did appear to me. But he knows what I'm like – he wouldn't do it. I know he wouldn't want to frighten the children. No. Or me.

## YVETTE

Actually I've had two near-death experiences. When I was sixteen, that was ten years ago, I tried to commit suicide. I think at that age life sort of gets to you a bit. All through my childhood I'd sort of half wanted to live with my father and half with my mother, and then my mother's second marriage wasn't going at all well and my stepfather didn't like children. It just sort of built up and built up. And then you've got your O-levels and everything; and I used to run away quite a lot, to my grandmother – because she was super, marvellous really. And then I just decided that maybe it would be best, you know, if that was the end of that. I went out and bought aspirin, the most I could buy on my pocket-money – I slipped out during recess and bought these things, and as soon as the lunch-break arrived I went and locked myself in the toilets and took them.

I don't remember an awful lot, I don't know if I was actually dying; but as I was wheeled into the hospital I had one of these out-of-the-body experiences. I was actually aware that I was lying down, and the next thing I was floating up – up to those sort of square ceiling tiles they have in hospital, up towards the light, and looking down on them bringing the stomach pump and watching it all happening. I suppose really it's just like a few seconds of actually watching – at the time it seems the most natural thing in the world, nothing wrong with it at all.

It was, I suppose, a split second – not frightening at all, wonderful, absolutely incredible. It was quite different from a dream; sometimes I have dreams when I think, this is a dream, you know, but I was aware that it wasn't a dream. It was actually a physical removal, you could almost feel the physical removal from the body in a way I can't really describe. A feeling of total tension throughout your whole body – and then you're floating. My grandmother had the same thing happen to her when she had a hip-replacement operation about twenty years ago.

At the time I certainly didn't want to live, and if I'd known that the aspirins wouldn't have worked I'd have taken something different. But they tell you, 'Well, it was just a cry for attention'; and you start to believe them in the end, although at the time I wasn't thinking, oh, right, I'll just count out the tablets so that I don't actually die but get a lot of attention.

I remember in the ward afterwards there was this lady, she was apparently on morphine, walking around, and I woke up and she'd got her face next to mine and she was talking so loud. It was really so frightening that I remember thinking, you know, all these things I've been frightened of and yet this poor lady is obviously in a sort of hell – you could tell it in her eyes. And that actually made me realize that my own life that I thought was so awful probably wasn't so awful at all really. And there was another lady in the next bed to me who'd tried to commit suicide, and I suppose that made me feel, well, you're not on your own, not the only one.

They did refer me to a psychiatrist – they said, 'We've got someone you can talk to', and I thought, great, this is going to be somebody that understands me. And he was an Asian doctor, and I couldn't understand his speech! He was asking me questions which I couldn't understand; it was like hitting a brick wall. But what the whole experience made me decide was that it would be less drastic just to leave home; and I went to live with my grandmother. She's always had a – it's difficult to describe – a sort of sixth sense; she used to have these really deep dreams, and things would come true. Certainly everything she's ever told me has come true. No, I didn't tell her about the out-of-the-body experience; I don't even know whether she knew I'd been in hospital, I think it was kept a secret. But in a way I'm sure she knew – you know, we were really close.

That experience of floating upwards, it was constantly in my mind, yes. I thought of it as a good experience, an exciting experience. I always thought it was something unique to me at the time, though now I have heard of other people who've had these experiences. I knew it wasn't a dream, and I was dying to know – is there anyone else that's experienced this? I knew my grandmother had talked about something like that, and that was quite incredible, to think that we'd actually gone through something similar. She definitely related it to near-death, and she did have religious beliefs.

Certainly after that time I was more inclined to feel more religious, or more able to communicate; it's strange, it's as though it's a sort of step up . . . I tended to think a lot deeper, and almost be able to cope with life in a way that I hadn't before – as though there is always this release, you don't have to actually die. A safety net. I can only describe it as a sort of religious, spiritual feeling – you know, some people believe there's a God up there, whatever religion they have, and having talked to a Buddhist man I met, I know now that people in history have had these experiences. I didn't know that then, but the way I felt was that there was something . . . something taking me, and watching me; just that, the sheer feeling that within myself I had the power – from somewhere the power – to control, to cope; and that life wasn't really even that important.

I don't know whether it has helped anyone else who's been that desperate. It's just as though you reach a point where there's so much stress and despair, I suppose, that you can take an outside look at this situation and decide, you know, now what are you going to do about this? And it gives you time, a breathing-space, even just for those few seconds. It's funny, I don't think there's a day that goes by where I haven't thought about it – it's another dimension, you start to think more about life. When I was in the hospital, my aunt sent just a blank card and on it it said, 'Take every day as it comes, and strangle the living daylights out of it.' Yes, it does sound vicious! I don't know whether she's ever had an experience like mine, but that experience actually does make you get from life what you can. Because you're not here for very long, and this is the sort of bad bit, so make it as nice as you can and then go on to something much nicer afterwards. That was to do with the second experience I had as well.

My mum was very depressed when I was a child – I knew she'd had to go into a psychiatric unit, but as a child you aren't really aware, you're just aware that your mum's not happy. At the time I made the suicide attempt my mum had just had a baby, and

I was looking after it quite a lot, because she was very depressed at that time too. And my father had got remarried and they had a little girl. So I was feeling totally left out, really; it was almost as though they'd gone their separate ways and started new lives, and I felt as though I'd been a bit of a mistake, and they wanted to wipe that part of their lives out and start again with the new babies. As though my bit of life never really happened at all. And I always felt, maybe if I hadn't been born at all my mother's marriage might have been happier, because my stepfather didn't like having children intruding on their marriage. Neither did my father – I mean, I'd written to him saying, 'Please can I come and live with you?' And he wrote back and said, 'No, thank you.'

So then afterwards I went to live with my grandmother while I did my O-levels – I had more peace and quiet, because it's very difficult to revise when there's a new baby in the house. And then I met this boy, he was seventeen, who sort of cared for me, and I left and lived with him for a couple of years. It wasn't a very good relationship at all – he was quite violent – but it was the first time I'd ever really felt that anyone was really close to me, and I was a lot happier than I had been for a long, long time. People used to say, 'How can you stand it?' but I thought, well, actually I feel quite happy compared to before.

I did go home to my mum again – I've always had this pull towards my mum, I suppose it's just a craving that one day it might work – and Mum said, 'Well, all right, just for a short while', but as soon as I got back into the family again, straight away this dark cloud came down and I was as depressed as ever. So I thought the only thing was to go back to this chap; but we'd given up the flat. I was working as a dental nurse then, and the only thing I'd got was the key to the dental surgery. So we thought, well, we'll stay in the surgery; but unfortunately we overslept, and the dentist came in in the morning, and he gave me the sack. He was a marvellous chap really, but he said, 'I can't trust my employees with the key if they're going to use it to sleep the night here' – you know, there are drugs there, valuable equipment. I mean, all these things probably happen to teenagers, but you feel it's the end of the world.

So then I was really desperate. And I said to this chap Dave,

'I'm going to get on a train, and wherever it takes me, I'm going to start a life there.' I'd had my wage packet thrown at me, and I just had the clothes I was wearing. So we did go to the station, and it was a Leicester train. And we got the most terrible bedsit there, riddled with creepy-crawlies. I phoned some telephone numbers in a newspaper which I was reading on a newspaper stand, because I couldn't afford to buy it – we had hardly any food for about three weeks, and you can't get any unemployment money till six weeks. Anyway, I got a letter, it was incredible, I got this letter saying, 'Can you please phone this number about a job?' And I went to the interview still wearing the same clothes I was fired in, and I got the job!

It wasn't much of a job, it was only a clerk, but I felt as though I'd made an incredible achievement. But the relationship with this chap had really ended, so I was living back at home again, but I didn't mind travelling all the way to work every day – I had an hour to Nottingham, then change, then another hour to Leicester. I didn't mind, this was a new me – didn't need Mum, didn't need Dad! Anyway, I was coming back from work, and I was sitting in an empty carriage reading – it was one of the old trains, you know, the Agatha Christie type, you get your own compartment. I was sitting there, reading *Great Expectations*, which I'd read many times before; and I saw a chap walking past obviously looking for an empty compartment too. And I sort of looked up, and I thought . . . I felt almost as though I knew him. About five minutes later the door slid open, and it was him. He said, 'Do you mind if I leave the door open, or would you like it closed?' So I said, 'I don't really mind', and carried on looking at my book. And I started to shake all over, it was incredible, an incredible feeling.

He said afterwards that when he'd been walking down the corridor he'd thought, this is a bit pointless, because I'm going to have to go back and get to know this girl if I'm going to marry her! He was in cycling gear, and he'd got a green coat on with that club badge on – I'd noticed every single detail about him in that split second when he passed. And he said, 'Do you come on this train every day?' And I said, 'Yes.' He said, 'I usually cycle.' And we talked, and he said, 'Well I'll see you tomorrow, I'll be on the train tomorrow.' So the next day, sure enough, he was on the train. I was just nineteen, just had my nineteenth birthday. We didn't get married for nine months, because Anthony kept saying, 'We can't get married before we've got our engagement ring.' He designed my engagement ring – look. It's two otters and a diamond – he'd had a dream about two otters – and I had a friend who was a silversmith and he made it up.

We really felt as though we'd known each other all our lives, though it was after about a total of four hours that he asked me to marry him. Yes, I was glad the aspirin hadn't killed me, I definitely was, and from then on things were marvellous. When I had Becky it was fairly straightforward, and Anthony did a lot of work from home so that he could be with Becky, and then we decided we might as well have another baby straight away.

We were just pottering about at home, I was nine months pregnant, and we were going to go out for a picnic, but I said, 'I don't really feel well, actually.' It was April, just one of those first days in the year that's really quite warm. Becky was just one. So he said, 'Well, I've got a bit of work to do, how about if you have a sleep.' I'm not sure what time it was, but I woke up, and the mattress was saturated with blood, completely saturated, it was all over my face and hands. I just got up – I wasn't frightened, amazingly enough – and I walked into the next room and I just looked at him. And he was talking to someone on the phone and he said, 'I'm sorry, I have to go', and then he just picked the phone up again and phoned the hospital. So I climbed into the Land Rover; Anthony put Becky in the middle seat. There were lots of road-works, and I was bouncing around and I was still bleeding.

It was a Sunday, and I think they weren't really prepared for any sort of emergencies. Anyway, they said, 'Lie down on this bed', and then I remember the doctor coming, and I was shaking all over, almost off the bed. And they put an oxygen mask on me, and the doctor just shouted, 'Placenta praevia!' and got some blood. And I remember Anthony shouting, 'She's Rhesus negative' – he was still standing there holding Becky. And then they said, 'You're going to have to have a caesarean now'; and they were scrubbing up and everything, sort of in a panic. I hadn't had an anaesthetic yet; but I started to go out of my body, and I thought, here we go – exactly the same again. I felt, right, this time's come again. Physically I felt myself pulled from my body; and then I was watching Anthony, holding Becky, being told 'We're going to have to operate on your wife.'

This was all split second, it was so fast, but I thought, right, this is O K now. I felt really sorry for Anthony – I saw he was crying – and I was thinking, I feel so sorry for him because he's in all that turmoil that I was in a second ago. I watched him walk out of the door, holding Becky, who was just sort of wide-eyed at all this amazing machinery. And then everything went completely black – I suppose either they'd given me an anaesthetic by that stage or else I'd gone unconscious – everything was completely, completely black except that I was travelling along an artery, a vein, really, really fast, faster than you can possibly describe. I hadn't gone back into my body, and I panicked, within this dream or experience or whatever you would call it, I actually panicked and thought, I haven't gone back.

No, no, it wasn't pleasant, it was terrifying. This tunnel had sort of engulfed me, and I was travelling faster and faster down it, totally out of control, and all the time I was aware that that body was still there and I hadn't gone back. I kept thinking, I've got to come back; and then this artery branched into two, I could see it happening, almost like the heart where you've got the two arteries going in. And I could feel that I was going to have to make a decision, that there were these two branches – what's going to happen? Am I going to be torn in two, or am I going to be able to make a choice?

And then I realized that one of these two arteries – all bumpy and hilly – it was lined with what can only be described as a black coral, and you knew that if you were going that way that was going to be the rough passage, very painful, almost like being keel-hauled, that was going to be hell. But the other one was totally smooth, serene, like a still water – it's the only way I can describe it really. And with a brilliant light at the end of it that again I couldn't actually describe – a white, a really white light. And I was thinking, well, I know what decision I'm going to make, I'm going the smooth way; and half of my head was sort of tearing in two and saying, 'No, you've got to go the hard way, you must go the hard way', and I was saying, 'No, I want to go this way, I want to go the smooth way.' And all the time I was travelling so fast, thinking, well, I have to make a decision, this is it, this is the crunch, I've either got to go the smooth way, reach the bright light – which was sort of misty, a brilliant light, going round and round and literally drawing me to it . . . And then I was going down and down and down and down, and there were knives and what I can only describe as pain; but nothing actually physical, just that I knew that this was the rough, painful way, hilly way, lots of bends and corners, and you didn't know what was at the end of it.

I knew that the smooth way would be for me just to cut out of life and die, I knew that quite clearly; but I couldn't make the decision, the decision was going to be made for me. And I got to the stage where I thought, well, this decision is going to have to be made, it's out of my hands; and that's where I was sucked right into that very branch and then physically torn apart, dragged down the hell – I can't begin to describe that, I've never experienced anything like it in life. It was so awful, just completely . . . I was dragged round and over and under and scraped and butted; and at the end of it, when I was feeling about as desperate as when I'd tried to commit suicide, I opened my eyes.

And I was up on the ceiling again, watching myself, and I slowly came down, and I was within myself again. And I felt absolutely wretched, I felt absolutely awful. I'd actually come back, and I really had wanted to go the other way. I was in the recovery room – Alex had been born then. He was born within seven minutes of me arriving at the hospital. All this had happened within that time. And Anthony was saying, 'We've got a boy, we've got a boy', and apparently I smiled, but I don't remember. I suppose I was near death – I haven't confirmed it, but I know of a lot of people who have died of the same thing. Basically the placenta is attached to your own bloodstream, so if it breaks the blood just sort of pumps out. The man that did the caesarean had never done one before – what a way to do your first caesarean! There was a massive scar, and he actually came in the next day and apologized, and said, 'I'm really sorry, but it was so quick . . .' They called Alex the miracle baby in the hospital.

But at first I was really depressed – well, for a long time after having had Alex. It was post-natal depression; it took me a long time to come round to the fact that I'd actually come back. Although at the time I was so lucky in my life – I'd got beautiful babies, and a husband who I adored, and a house, and everything was perfect. But when the time came to choose between death and life, the decision still would have been death, because it was so easy and beautiful, and when I came back into my body I was cursing myself and thinking to myself, it was you that caused this by saying, 'I want to get back.' I would love to know whether Alex experienced the same thing; but I don't suppose I ever will, because he was only a new-born baby, he's not likely to be able to describe it.

Anthony was at home all the time with the children, so that was a good help; and I eventually came to terms with the fact that this had been death, that the out-of-the-body experience when I was sixteen had been like the first stage, and then I'd gone from that to this next thing, and then come back. And I – oh, I don't know, my life, my outlook on life had completely changed from that experience. I realized that you can't take anything for granted at all. Rather the way when somebody's died you realize you take people for granted – my mum was so upset when my grandmother died, she said, 'The awful thing is I took her for granted and now she isn't here.' I had this strange experience of feeling the same way about myself, that I'd taken myself for granted and everything around me. Basically I now regard it as I'm living that black coral artery, and so you've got to make it as smooth as you can – do something nice, or be helpful. It's really more of a religious view of life than I'd even had after the first experience. You know – 'Right, if this is the hell bit, the bad bit, we might as well make it as nice for everyone in it as possible.' The out-of-the-body experience was a help; but when you've been that stage further, which I feel I have, you realize that's just the sort of taster, the actual bit is really something quite special that you don't need to be frightened of at all. Because even in a situation where I was absolutely happy, not suicidal at all, even then it was so much more beautiful. Which I still find incredible.

My grandmother died three weeks ago – she was in hospital

and the doctor had said, 'I don't expect to see this lady on my rounds on Monday morning.' And Nan was praying all the time – she'd always been religious, but she'd never prayed to that degree – and I was just sitting, holding her hand, and she looked at me and she said, 'I'm at that place, and I feel that you know where I am.' Mum said, 'You're in hospital, you're in hospital.' But she said, 'No, I'm beyond that, and I think, I feel that there's only Yvette that knows where I am.' And I'd never told her about this experience that I'd had – I just felt that she knew what I was thinking, and that I knew exactly where she was. She was too ill to describe exactly the way she was feeling; but then again, you don't tend to describe it, it's rather like breathing – you don't tend to describe breathing to people. Nan said, 'I'm in this tunnel', and then she was just closing her eyes and saying, 'No, no, I've got to be forgiven first'; and Mum was saying, 'Oh, don't worry about it', and I just felt she didn't really understand.

My grandmother did go on, she had infection after infection – they get to that stage when they're just living on antibiotics. And every time I saw Nan, as soon as I walked into the room she used to say, you know, 'Oh, it's wonderful when you come, because you really understand and you know how I'm feeling.' Yes, I did want her to go really, but I couldn't say that to Mum. She was so content when I was with her; and everyone around her was willing her to live, and saying, 'Think about Christmas, think about your birthday.' I felt sorry for Mum, because I thought, well, it's her mother, and I know what it's like to have this bond; but I felt really wretched that Nan was still living. She would whisper little things to me when I went there – 'Why am I still waiting in this tunnel, why must I wait here? – it's so bright.' Then she got a chest infection, and that took her; and since then I've been trying to say to Mum, 'You know, it wasn't awful for her.' And I really feel it wasn't; but if you haven't had this experience you can't imagine it, you can't even describe it really.

No, I haven't a fear of death at all now. I think you do go through that stage, when you're a teenager, when you do fear death. I think there was a feeling, when I tried to commit suicide, of 'Let's get it over.' I wouldn't say I definitely think there is a God; but there is good, and I know that's where I went in my second experience. I do like to go and sit in a church, and think about this experience, and think about life, and beyond; I don't find churches strange places, because they've been built by somebody and they're still being painted by somebody and they're still raising money for the church roof – so I do like to go into a place where it's an open space, and it's quiet, and that feeling that other people are thinking too. But I never had done so before that second experience. I haven't actually tried meditation, it's tricky with children about – one day I will. But once you do know that feeling you can seek it, once you know what you're looking for – I suppose that is God to me. The Christian faith – well, I'm still not sure about that. I'm working on that one.

I was very depressed for quite a time, although I didn't take any tablets or anything like that. But you do become lifted from it. It makes you want to do the best you can with *this* life, especially when you've got children – you don't take any second for granted. And Anthony was absolutely marvellous when I came out of hospital. He's an angel, he really is! I've explained it to him as much as I can, but it's something you just have to experience – and he says, 'Yes, but we would have been left, I would have had two babies and no wife.'

Anthony used to have this recurring dream afterwards – he used to wake up crying for nearly a year after I'd had Alex – he used to dream that he was standing holding Becky, exactly as he had done, and they were standing outside a church, waiting for the christening, and all the relatives were there waiting. And then a hearse came, with two coffins in, the baby one and mine. And he just used to wake up crying, and he said, 'I've seen it again, I've seen it so clearly again.'

That experience I had was like being hit on the head with a hammer – it was so real, and so out of context to life as you know it, that I just felt that the shock waves from it took that long to get over. To actually accept the fact . . . I felt that I had nearly died, and you're brought up to think that that's a bad thing – and yet I'd felt it was a good thing, and so . . . Plus I'd always got the baby crying . . . It was so vivid and so recent and so clear; I felt, you know, why should I have to do this? There is that better place. And then, I don't know, I suppose once the children are about a year old, and you realize how innocent and trusting and lovely they are; and you think, OK, this is terrible, but those are little characters which we've created, and they rely totally on us. It was just that with the immediate comparison to that so much better place that you couldn't even begin to describe, it did at that time seem awful.

And then you do reach that stage where you think, there are people who are really suffering, and can I do something about it? So you turn that negative view – that *this* is awful and *that* was wonderful – and you think, well, I can't have that, yet, so I'll make the best of what I've got. So actually, although it sounds like a very negative attitude, it makes you extremely positive. It's a lifelong challenge. I tend to view life now in twos, it's really strange, in a practical and a spiritual way. The practical things are the everyday things of life which you can change, you can do something about; and my view seems to be, if it's practical and you can do something, then that's easy – just do it. The spiritual things are very difficult, because I've actually been in a state where the decision is made, it's out of your hands, so the spiritual things are really hard to come to terms with. But because it's out of your hands, that's one reason why I think I'm less likely to ever commit suicide – the decision will be made for me, there's no need to have to actually go to the trouble of even going out and buying the tablets. The life or death is just going to be decided for you; so just take every day as it comes and strangle the living daylights out of it – in a positive way!

There was something else I've just remembered, in that experience, there was a voice – it was ... I suppose you can't really describe it as a human voice, because it was just in my head. It was just saying, 'Who cares anyway? Who cares anyway?' And I could not understand why this voice was keeping on saying this. But that voice comes back, every now and then when I'm thinking really deeply, when I'm on my own. And it's all part of my outlook which has now changed; the black coral, you know, that if there's a problem there's only *you* that can do something about it. No, I wouldn't think that God would sort it out for me, no – I feel that he's given me the ability to do it ... He, it, whatever ... It's tricky really, because it's difficult to think of

God as a he, in the same way that it's difficult to imagine an experience like that if you haven't had one. There are not really enough words in the English language – whether there are in any other language, I don't know.

I know that voice sounds negative in a way – I suppose it was that which made me so depressed for a long time. But it's a very practical thing to say, really. It gives you something to get hold of, and do something with. It's a career, living is a sort of career. The whole quality, yes, that's right, of everything, absolutely everything . . . And a work career, that's just a part of it; if I have a career, that will just be one minute detail. It would never be my life like some people say, 'Oh, my work *is* my life.'

Oh yes, I am glad I've got life ahead of me – though I don't always feel twenty-six; when you've got children you sometimes feel like a hundred and one! I wouldn't sort of want to pop off tomorrow, I wouldn't go out and buy myself a box of razor-blades or something to do myself in. At the same time – well, my next-door neighbour was run over a fortnight ago and is very ill – if that happened and I knew there was nothing I could do about it, I don't think I'd be panicking and thinking, oh God, I'm going to die. I remember my grandmother saying to me as a child, 'I'm not frightened of death.' But at the same time it's not something I want – from a purely practical, selfish point of view, I wouldn't mind sticking around! I'm mastering this black coral bit quite well. It's a challenge.

I certainly wouldn't have been without these experiences – it's completely changed my outlook. I was really matter-of-fact – if you describe it as a lower plane and a higher plane, I was plodding along on this lower plane rather like a little ant. Then suddenly, there's this whole new other plane which you can't describe; but I'm not the same me, I know that, I'm not the same person I was. Of course it's only happened that once, but there are glimpses in life when you think, that's touching on it, that's going towards it; and if I can do anything to make this moment even happier than it already is . . .

I certainly think our marriage has been strengthened by my attitude – and my husband's acceptance of it too, this is quite important! I think quite a few people wouldn't have been able to.

And I haven't had any more arguments with my mother or my father or my stepfather since then. I feel you've got to cope with it; there's no point in arguing, there's never any point. I mean, it's always good to have a good go sometimes – I'm not one of these people who just sits and keeps my mouth shut, not doing anything or saying anything. I certainly say what I feel, if I can influence things in some way. But these feuds that go on for years, and unhappy, bitter feelings . . . I don't have any bitterness. When Mum phoned me after my grandmother's death and said she'd taken her for granted, that she'd never be able to stroke her forehead or change her bedclothes or look after her again, it did move me to tears, because I know how I used to feel before these experiences. But now, I feel that every single moment I'm aware of not taking things for granted. I'm always aware of it, it's the uppermost thing in my mind. It's certainly absolutely and utterly changed my life.

# James Horrigan

Ask me anything you like. The doctor asked me, she told me about you, and I said, 'Well, if it's going to help someone . . .' That's my attitude.

It started off with a headache on Boxing Day of last year. And when I went to see the doctors they told me I had an aneurysm, which is a bubble in the brain. And they took the X-rays and the scans, and it wasn't that at all. They found actually that I had a tumour on the lung. And the messages were going to the brain, but being returned to the face, and giving me constant headaches. So I had a headache for four months. I'd told them I wanted to know everything, and I wanted to know it straight down the line – you know? I think it's better, yes. So they told me I had this cancer of the lung, and I could live for seven, eight, ten, fifteen years, you know, with a bit of treatment. He just told me and I felt, well, I've got it, and that's it. There's nothing I could do about it.

So then, just after that, about a month after, I got a pain in my back, which it seemed like you'd strained yourself, you know? But it persisted, it got worse every day. So I went to my own doctor, my GP, and he said, 'Well, go and have an X-ray.' So I went and had an X-ray, and when I went back and seen him he said the doctors wanted to see me at St Thomas's. And they told me I had cancer in the spine.

Yes, that was, I must admit, that was a bit of a blow. What happened was, the way he broke it to me was that I went in to see him, and I said, 'I've been to my GP, and I understand you want to see me.' And he said, 'Yes.' And I said, 'What seems to be the problem?' And he says, 'I'm afraid I have to tell you it's much more serious than we thought.' So I said, 'Well, how serious?' So he said, 'Well, it's very serious.' And you think, well, the first time was serious; so now you're actually talking about *serious*

serious. So I said to him, 'Look,' I said, 'you just tell me what it is, and that's it.' He said, 'You have cancer of the spine – what we can do is give you radium treatments, and tablets which will curtail the pain. But,' he said, 'it's incurable, there's no control over it at all.'

I asked him how long, like, I had to live, and he said about three or four months. I thought, well, that's a bit of a blow. From quite a few years, like, they said, to, you know, a few months. He told me the truth because . . . I suppose he might be quite a long time in that business, and they get to know certain types of people. It depends on the person – sometimes it breaks them up very badly, and then others accept it. It didn't affect me mentally in any sense of the word. It affected my wife – we don't have secrets like that, it's much better that you're more open about it, you know?

To me all that I was interested in was that as long as my wife was OK, then I had no problems. I have a boy and a girl – they're both at work. We told the boy about six weeks after, and the girl in various stages – we weren't too sure of her. She's eighteen and my son is twenty-three. The boy, I think, got somewhat bitter. I think he looked around and he would see – like, the people who use drugs and things like that, and think, why doesn't it happen to them? He was very curt, very short – you'd ask him something and it was just 'Yes' or 'No', you know? And I asked him then, was he bitter about it, and he said, well, he was really. And I told him I thought bitterness was the ruination of all people. And that it will never do you any good, it will ruin you and it will ruin everyone around you.

I haven't felt it myself, thank God, no. I think that's the greatest gift I ever received. What people don't seem to realize . . . People say to you, my friends in particular, 'But you're only fifty-three.' And I say, 'But I've had fifty-three good years.' You see, I've had a good family, a good mother and father, brothers and sisters, and a wife and children. I don't think I've missed out on much. There's not a lot I'd want to change. Very little I'd want to change. You see, to me I'm just a breath away from real living. My life will start when I die. I believe I'm just . . . I'll step from there to there.

In Ireland, when I was a child, I didn't understand most of it then. Religion was just a prime subject in school, like maths, you know? And I don't quite know how to put it, but . . . If I take you back nearly thirty years ago, now I was in Cyprus. We fought the terrorists – they were shooting at us and we were shooting at them, but that didn't mean anything to me, it was a great thrill. My attitude was, I will kill them or they will kill me. It didn't bother me at the time. I lost interest in my faith completely. I came over here, I married my wife, she would go to mass and I wouldn't go. Then when my children were born and they became of school age, when it was essential that they have religious education and they were in Church of England schools rather than Catholic ones, we used to go to church. I used to go occasionally, you know, and then maybe a bit more often, later on.

Over the last six or seven years . . . For some reason I found I seemed to be getting everything my way, and not giving anything back. And it rather bothered me, I don't know why I should have suddenly felt like that. So I decided to do something about it, like I was on the Church Council Committee, and I would take the Eucharist to the sick who couldn't get out of their homes, and things like that, and I would go to the mass maybe three or four times in a week. Now that I've had to retire, I go every day – there's nothing better. You see, when you go to Jesus, you just ask him to accept everything. And of course he has all these great powers that he can accept it. So all the time I've been sick, never at any time, at any time at all, have I been disheartened.

I do at times feel somewhat down, but primarily it's because you're never free of the pain. From the time I've had it now, if it's not one pain it's another pain. My shoulder, for example, my shoulder now is very painful, and my back is very painful. They've just changed my drugs to try and sort my shoulder out. You have to accept the fact that when you have it in the spine, it affects the nervous system like hell. But I'm rather perplexed when people say, 'You are brave' or 'Have you prayed for this courage?' I really can't see where the courage or the bravery comes into it. That's what rather perplexes me at times. I mean, I'm not saying how I would be if I knew, for example, I was going to die tomorrow. I'm not altogether sure what way I would feel. Do you understand? It's no good saying, 'Oh, I would be a great big hero, I think it would be fine.' I don't know.

Ah yes, I get an answer back from my prayers. There are times I can actually just put my hand out and touch him. As close as that. And at other times I feel he's a million miles away. But I always actually find he's never many miles away – it's usually that I'm a million miles away, you know? I think it all depends on how you look at it. You see, I never go to church or pray to God for to cure me of cancer. I always ask for the strength to cope with the future, no matter what the future may be. And it doesn't matter what happens if you have the strength of the spirit, then it's of no consequence what happens to you. For example, people say to me, 'Why don't you go to Lourdes?' – well, they seem to forget that even if I went there and I got cured, for argument's sake, I've still got to die, I'm not going to live for ever.

I've had a good time – I've got no complaints at all. Oh, it was terrific as a child – yes, I had a wonderful time. There's three brothers and four sisters. My father was a huge, big, tough guy. He'd tolerate no nonsense – his attitude was, if someone hit you, you hit them back. And if they were too big he'd send a brick over! His attitude was, make sure they don't beat you up again – you know? Well, it was a tough part of Dublin. But he was very fair – you know, he would never hit you except there was a good reason. And my mother, she was great – she still is, she's eighty now – she's a little, tiny woman, though my father was big, about six foot two. She goes to mass every day, and she does a tremendous amount of work, one way and another, for people. My brothers and sisters – we've always been in the business that we're Horrigans, that they come first. No matter what it is, no matter how good or bad the thing may be.

I would say I've always been happy. I'm not really a fighting sort of person – unless someone hit me I wouldn't hit them. But if they hit me, I'd kill them. I mean, I wouldn't kill them, but they'd never want to come near me again. But they'd have to hit me first. I used to think that some of the way I carried on my life was wrong, very wrong, but you see Jesus is not interested in yesterday, he's more interested in today and tomorrow. If you go to the Eucharist he's standing there, as he was two thousand years ago, and he has his hands out, and he's asking you what you want – 'What can I do for you?' If you are sorry for what sins you have committed, and really mean your sorrow, he's the most forgiving man . . .

I do believe in hell. If people do not wish to praise God at all, if they blame God on everything, how can they ever have any hopes? Now I know a Baptist lady who believes that if she died today, she would remain in a kind of limbo until the end of the world. They believe that. Whereas my attitude is that when I die, that is my day of judgement. They do say that there is no redemption from hell. But it's never actually . . . It's never dawned on me that much. But we all have our doubts, don't we? There are times I sit here, and suddenly – I could be praying, for example – it would come into my mind: is it all worth while? Or am I going to die, and they're going to put me down some hole, and that's going to be the end of it? And there is no denying it, everybody, no matter who you are and how strong you are, everybody would have the same thoughts. You know?

Oh yes, my local priest, I can talk to him. He comes round to the house here. At times I'm not sure of things, I speak to him, and he's usually pretty good. The home support team at the hospital, they are super. And there's the local support team, nurses covering certain areas. What they do at the hospital is, they ring you up, and ask you how you are, and if you need anything. Like three or four weeks ago, just before my holidays, the pain in my shoulder was quite severe. That was on a Sunday morning. So I rang them up and paged them, and within five minutes they were on the phone and they told me what to do about upping my tablets. They're brilliant. I don't know how good they are in other hospitals, but St Thomas's is first-class.

No, I won't be going into hospital – the hospital wouldn't accept you, on the basis of you're dying. The hospital wouldn't accept you in them circumstances. You can either stay at home, and the support team will come and see you every day, or you come out to a hospice, which would be my way. But my wife wouldn't want it that way. Maybe after doing the nursing they feel happy that they've done it, and I wouldn't want to take that away . . . But then to have to see me die in a . . . It can be a very slow, lingering type of death – I'm not saying it will be, but it could quite easily be, and has every chance of being. And I wouldn't want that for her at all. It's what you would call a major problem, inasmuch as I would like to die knowing that everything was OK. I wouldn't want to go into a hospice and leave her with a doubt – 'I could have done this, I could have done that.' You know?

I have had sort of an adventurous life in one way or another – I've seen death, you know. And I like an element of devilment, if you like . . . I'm a great mischief-maker! No, but always in fun. I love playing jokes on people, and things like that. Nothing that would ever be troublesome, but ones where you could always have a good laugh. And then they'd do it on me! And I'd have to accept that as well. I mean, just an example. I went home on my holidays to my mother's house in Dublin. There is no one in the house who ever uses sugar, so I bought her a bag of sugar. Well, just before I was leaving there was this bag of sugar, still near enough intact, like, you know? I'd had a bit of it. So I said, 'You know what'll happen with that, now,' I said, 'it'll go hard and lumpy, won't it? Well,' I said, 'what you need to do is put a couple of spoons of salt in it and keep it soft.' 'Is that right?' she said. So whoever comes along will have sugar that's soft! I'm a bit . . . a bit devilish at times! I like to enjoy myself. I generally do!

I have one very bad fault – it's when I don't like someone I tell them. I find I always say my mind, and I don't care how bad it might be or anything. I tell them straight out. There is one chap in particular, which, of course, will remain nameless, and the man's never done anything to me at all. But it's nature, purely nature – I just don't like the man. And I've told him, and he feels sad about it, and I feel sad about it. But I say, 'There it is.' I get on with most, though.

I've had the normal married life – we've had our ups and downs, you know? I find over the last few years that I don't argue any more. I just think, no, don't be arguing. That doesn't mean you don't flare now and then. But I believe that there are some people that are a hell of a lot worse off than I am. I mean, I really believe that. I look at a person who lives on their own and are very ill – what have they got? Maybe they get an odd visitor here and there – but, you know, when you're very ill, they tend to shy off you. My sister-in-law, some months ago, she was talking to my wife, and my wife said, 'Would you like to speak to him?' And she said, 'What will I say to him?' I can understand it. It's understandable.

When you get very ill, you know much more about how to treat people who are ill. What I mean by that is that if you're very ill, you meet somebody and they say, 'Oh, I'm very sorry to hear that, and I hope everything is going to be OK' – well, it doesn't mean anything very deeply to you. Now when you're ill yourself, you can communicate in a very ... a very inner way, you understand? Without saying anything. You can actually communicate with them – you know? If I did have another ten years, I would like to think that in that ten years I would be able to help very sick people. Because I'd know how they feel, and I think I could do a good job in that.

I might think, why is it me, why not someone else to be ill? But that is like saying, 'Well, I shouldn't have it – *you* should have it.' And I wouldn't want to wish that on anybody. Now I was looking last night on television, it made me very sad to look at it, some children ... Paraplegics, yes. They were playing bowls, and instead of proper, big, heavy bowls they had this little, soft type of ball, held back in their hands like that, and they would throw it ... You know? And then they spoke to one lad, who spoke back with great difficulty, but you could see the intelligence behind it all. You know, I looked at him and I said to myself, 'There he is, a lovely, fine, intelligent lad, who can't control his movements or anything.' Now I look at people like that and I think if anyone has a reason to gripe, they have. And I don't have any reason to gripe.

People say, 'Well, if I was God, I wouldn't allow that' – those children I was watching. And, I mean, if you take a child, about one year old, who was very precious, an only child, say, and he gets cancer and he dies a terrible slow lingering type of death – you'd say, 'Why did you allow that?' But there is a reason. Don't ask me what the reason is, though, because I don't know. Belief is . . . Make no mistake about it, it's difficult – when you have to say to someone that you put all your trust in someone you've never seen. You get people who argue about religion, and they'll say, 'God? When did you see him, then?' I've felt him, and I know other people who are in the same position as myself. But other people, you see – 'Have you seen him?' You know – 'Did you see him on the 35 bus, standing beside you?' Something like that. But to me, at the moment, his ways are my peace of mind. That's exactly what it is. And you could argue till the cows come home, and you won't change my idea.

People do say to me, like, you know, from a religious point of view, that it's God's will that I should have this . . . And I say, 'Well, it may be a trial for someone else.' Yes, my wife, I mean, or my children. Primarily my wife – I believe young people are very resilient, they get over things much quicker. But when you're married for twenty-seven years, it's much different altogether. You know? In a financial sort of aspect there are no problems. But that's just the half – the mental part of it is much more difficult. I remember my brother saying to me at his wife's funeral – I'd said to him, 'I know how you feel, but I hope everything is all right with you' – and he said, 'You will never know how I feel.' And that's absolutely true, because it hasn't happened to me. I'm not sure how I would be, if my wife died. I can cook and I can wash and I can iron. But from a mental point of view I would find it very difficult. I might think, oh, to hell with it – that does it. You know?

I know that you're never given more than you can cope with. But one thing bothers me – I've never spoken to anyone about it . . . I think of people who commit suicide. And I often wonder, well, why do they commit suicide? If God says he will never give you more than you can deal with . . . I would like to speak to someone on that point, you know, some specialist of some sort. The priest's in the same position as us, he doesn't know. I suppose the only way, you could ask someone who's attempted suicide.

I think if I die, say, in the next couple of months, which is probably more likely than unlikely, I would think my wife would be very sad. Quite lonely up to a point. Because she's quite realistic, you see, inasmuch as she would not want the boy or the girl to stay in too much. She would say, 'You must lead a life of your own, not get tied to my apron strings.' While really underneath she might be much more depressed. There are times when you cry, as my wife does occasionally – what it is, it's something that needs to get out. I believe that every man, or every woman, has a right to cry, and that if they cry they should be allowed to cry and cry and cry, and when they've finished crying to have someone there to console them. But never to try and stop them crying. Some people have it in temper – they flare and they go to town, and it gets all out of their system. And then they say, 'Oh, I'm sorry, I didn't really mean that' – but it's all out.

Work is the thing I miss most. More than almost anything else. Oh yes, they keep in touch with me from work – funnily enough, just before you come in there was one of them on the phone. Yes, they're pretty good, you know, but you miss all the . . . And then of course, you see, no matter how well you love your missis, constantly being at home . . . I can go for walks still. Oh, you're not keeping me indoors – more than likely I would fall asleep. The drugs does that, you know. It's very tempting. The drugs and the radium treatment make you tired, very tired. No, I'm not having the chemotherapy. I mean, to me that's pointless. They said to me, 'You could have chemotherapy and that would help you along for six weeks or so.' I said no. You see, chemotherapy will always make you ill – you get physically ill, you get mentally ill, and then your hair falls out and things like that . . . And then for what? To prolong your life for five or six weeks, to me that's crazy.

I don't worry about tomorrow. And yesterday's gone, and I either enjoyed it or didn't enjoy it, which in most cases I have enjoyed it. My good days and bad days, with my pains and aches – I think at the end of the day, it hasn't been too bad. I know what it's like to be worse – when I had it originally, my back was extremely bad. And I was in quite a lot of pain, tough type of pain. I found that quite difficult. But at the same time, never depressing. Oh, it scares me at times. I don't mean, you know – 'Huh, I don't care.' No, I don't quite mean that. I mean, when the time comes, if it is one of those lingering types . . . Well, I don't know – I would just like to think it would be quicker.

I don't really know so much about death. Except I often sit and visualize what heaven's like. And I don't know! That's what. Do you know, I haven't the faintest idea!

There are times you would think, I'd have liked to have done this, maybe, or done that. But I think it was all mostly well adjusted to me – I've had nothing that I haven't been able to cope with in any sense of the word. You know, in your younger days you have your ups and downs – you make things work out. You have an attitude of: that's what you have and that's what you can do, and when you've done that – stop. But I was mischievous as well! I was always one for fun.

What I would say to people who are told for the first time that they are very ill is not to be surprised if they feel very sad or feel overcome or they get into a terrible mental state for a while. You know? But they can sit down, primarily on their own, and have a good think about the past and how they think they can cope with the future. And then that is when you call on your friends and you ask them to help you out in whatever way they can. My friends have been great, I've never had to ask. They've always been there. They ring me up and they will ask me, 'Are you going out this evening?' – for a drink or something like that. And they'll bring their car down and take me out.

I think you need always to sit and try and use as much logic as you can. You know? A lot of people talk about cancer that you must get up and fight. My way is to forget about it. That's my way of fighting it. Now, whether that's a good or bad way . . . But it seems to work OK for me. It doesn't mean that it doesn't come to my mind, but when it does I think of something else, and get rid of it that way. If it's there, it's there, and that's that. Now the doctor said I wasn't a typical patient!

There's nothing really I'd want to change in my life. I have never really had a bad time. From as far back as I can remember – a very young lad, playing football in the streets of Dublin. Nothing at all I'd want to change.

# LYDIA

The first time I ever saw a dead body must have been when I was about seven. We were still in Scotland then, in Dundee – this was in the post-Depression years. And I used to visit this tenement area – old buildings, very, very primitive inside, filled with a lot of Irish Catholic families. I used to go there from school because there was a soup-kitchen there; you could go and buy a penny bowl of soup. It was an unbelievably sordid shop, like the rest of the tenement. There was a big pot on the stove in the back room, with this thick lentil soup that glued your ribs together.

Anyway, there was this older child, Nan Gormley, who sort of befriended me. And she said, 'Would you like to see the babby?' It was on the third or fourth floor. We had to wait outside, and then slowly walked round the table where the coffin was. It was just low enough for me to see. The baby had its neck bound up, because it had died of diphtheria, I think; I just remember the head, and the waxen colour. You were supposed to say a Hail Mary or whatever it was, only I didn't as I wasn't a Catholic – Nan was saying, 'Didn't you say a prayer? Oh, you'll go to hell!' I don't know, though, whether it made a tremendous impact; it was all formally presented, you see, it wasn't like seeing someone hurt or run over, pouring blood. I think I was a bit worried that I should have said a prayer for it, but my mother – my adoptive mother – was actually rather anti-church, because she'd been brought up in a very Calvinist atmosphere and she resented the hypocrisy of it.

My adoptive mother had to work terribly hard – at that time she had a job . . . There's a word for it in Scotland which I can't remember – a sort of commercial traveller – and she used to go round for a doctor friend who had all these soaps and phar- maceutical things, taking the ferry across the Gowrie, and going to all the outlying farms. I think my aunt was possibly sending money back at this time as well; she was down in London, sort of preparing the way for us to move down there, and she worked at Rayne, the shoe shop. She was much younger than my adoptive mother, and very elegant and pretty. But I also discovered that my father did pay something towards my keep, but he died when I was seven or eight, and I don't think he left any instructions; so whatever he was contributing vanished. He was much older than my real mother. But I only found out about it much, much later.

I was told nothing about being adopted, nothing at all. There was a kind of silent embargo on the whole thing. The first time I remember consciously asking why I hadn't got a father was when I was about eleven or twelve. I must have been backward or something, I think! The answer would be just offhand, just a one-sentence reply – 'Oh, he was a businessman and he died when you were young.' Full stop. 'We don't talk about him.' And no photographs! I mean, nobody destroys photographs of their husband. Being illegitimate, that was the key – that's why they probably didn't discuss it. And then the other complication: I grew up calling my aunt my sister. I didn't call her Aunty Betty, I just called her Betty. Actually at school, at my secondary school, I was talking about 'my sister'. But then I think I must have reasoned that she couldn't be my sister. And if she was my mother's sister, why did we all have the same surname? It's a hall of mirrors, you see.

We moved to London, to get away from the background, the stigma, I think. But we were always short of money, there was always this feeling of insecurity. They were both unmarried spinsters; life was always precarious. I remember making those buttons, you know, covered with plastic thonging, that they use in the East End dress shops. The three of us used to sit there – I can feel the shape of this awful metal thing, it was very sharp on one side and your hands got sore . . . And you'd get, I don't know, a halfpenny each or something. And often they used to send them back. We always seemed to live in basements, and I always wanted to get out, up and out. I've got a great thing about light now. You know those basement flats – they're garden level at the back, but in the front they're very dark, and bars on the windows, and outside that there are railings. And all my well-to-do friends at school had homes or houses, and two parents. And there was the difference in what one would wear – there was an incredible gulf. I had a scholarship – and I was the poorest person I knew, put it that way.

I was sixteen when my aunt died – I did know she was my aunt by then, because my headmistress called me in and told me. But still nothing was discussed ... She was ill for about a year, I think; she had gallstones – she used to go out to the cinema to escape it. Then they discovered it was cancer – she was forty then. She had that awful treatment which scars, you know, burns you. I remember she was very thin and she got these terrible burns – I had to help her, because I shared a room with her. I was never actually told anything, they never said what it was. When you're sixteen I suppose you don't ... I mean, it's only when you're older that you can assess the gravity of these things. And sometimes she seemed a little better. I felt ... I was distressed. But I suppose one was trying to distance oneself, up to a point; you know – 'I am a camera.'

I'd sort of help her ... Comb her hair, wash her hair. But I think at that age ... I've got drawings I did of her when she was very ill, actually. I did a very moving sketch of my mother after my aunt's death, sitting, her figure in despair – just a very quick sketch. She must have felt desperate, but she hid it – she was amazing. I suppose she felt she had had to hide her feelings from her sister. I don't know whether my aunt knew she was dying. I don't know ... We never talked about it. No, she died in hospital, I went to visit her there. I think it was very sudden; the cancer went to her brain – she was wandering, or dreaming. I remember her telling me to take a night-dress back and take the frills off, because Sister wouldn't like it.

I was upset. But I ... I seemed to get over it very quickly. One thing I thought at the time – although she was fifteen years younger than my adoptive mother, she was quite strict with me, and I thought I might have more freedom now. So there was an element of relief ... But I felt, when she died, I wish I had sort of thanked her – we were very close, actually. While my aunt was ill my mother had to do two jobs. She used to go – she was very quick with money – she used to go to White City as a cashier. She had to be very quick – you know, two-to-one on so-and-so, three-to-four on so-and-so – giving the right change, and then paying out winnings. It's a very strenuous, demanding thing, and there she was, going off after a gruelling day's work . . . And then she had to carry on on her own, you know, while I finished art school and did my teachers' training.

Oh, I was much happier then, yes, because I was interested, and my friends were all just the same sort of people. But there was still this complete cloud . . . And the fact that one had no sort of sexual education, and no brothers or sisters – you know, an all-female household . . . No uncles, no relatives. No, I don't think there was anybody artistic in my real family, but the thing is that my aunt, my adoptive aunt, was very creative and artistic, and she had encouraged me – oh, very much – and that was why I went to art school.

My breakdown was much later. It was when I was in France, after I'd separated from my husband, and I'd gone away with the children, trying to survive on my own. I think I was ill by that time, I was down to about seven stone. I was supposed to get a sort of allowance and to live out in the country, in the sticks, you know, which was the last thing one should do – out in some dreary, far-flung corner of France. I had no money, the accommodation was totally inadequate. And it was November, and it was getting colder and colder. I kept going to the doctor and saying, 'This is getting worse and worse' – I was losing control completely. It was a sort of holiday-let place, you know, absolutely bleak – two rooms, I think, with an outside toilet. The children were about two and three, so that was a nightmare – I couldn't concentrate, I couldn't think.

So it was an SOS really. I took pills and then I went to the front door of this sort of cottage place, for someone to see me. They must have just been lots of sleeping pills. It was a small village, you see, and I think I went to the door and collapsed on the doorstep. So I think I intended to be found; because it wasn't as bad at that point as it became later.

I came to in hospital – it was so awful, just so frightening. There was no way, no reasoning, nothing could help. Sort of shut in. Going to sleep was just terrible, because I had such disturbed thoughts. Waking up was even worse. And there was this old peasant woman who kept going to and fro and saying, '*Je n'aurais jamais dû passer par la fenêtre, je n'aurais jamais dû passer par la fenêtre* . . .' I tried to slash my wrists then – it was over a wash-basin, because I didn't want to get blood all over . . . There was such a mess . . . There was still this terrible feeling, wanting to communicate one's despair. No, I didn't really think in terms of Edouard coming to fetch me. It was just a complete . . . *Néant*.

I was moved on to another place then – it was there I threw myself from the window. I thought there was this one last chance. If I didn't do it now I would go on spiralling down, I would lose the will to do anything about it. I thought, I cannot face the rest of my life like this. And I thought, I've just got to do it, like that, it's better to make the sacrifice here and now. It was the toilet window, I think, two or three floors up. When I came round – I was on the pavement – there was this rather butch matron hissing at me: 'Exhibitionist!' But she didn't realize I was actually hurt, I think. I'd broken my hip-bone.

You have to be sort of immunized to do it, you have to be beyond . . . Beyond something, a step beyond. You see, I had an awful thought . . . I really thought that it was for ever, it was for keeps, in which case I would be useless to the children. I desper-ately wanted them and needed them, but I felt it was a very selfish desire on my part, that really I shouldn't have anything to do with them – I thought, you know, I'd infect them or contaminate them. I thought I'd be a vegetable for the rest of my life. It seemed irrevocable, you know, like a cirrhosis or something – you can't undo it. I think I would have been quite happy to go at that time – to be sort of led out and shot or something. But then – I don't know if I would have done it from the thirteenth floor.

Then after that, I gave up, I suppose, the attempts . . . Knowing that when I went out of the window it was the most I could do. And I was sort of getting outside the situation – I was detaching myself from it. No, I wouldn't say I was better – not for the first three, four months. I was eventually given some medication – they did have something to pep you up, because after some months I started to talk a bit. I did have some therapy, a little, but

I didn't like the therapist – I couldn't even fantasize about him, he seemed so dreary!

I went for brief weekends home, and I went back to stay with one patient, and I got quite involved with some of the people there – one very nice girl, she'd had a dreadful time, her arm was quite carved up with suicide attempts. And there was a girl who'd had this post-natal depression, and she was so sad, missing her baby – that spurred me on to get better for the sake of the children . . . And one woman whose daughter had been murdered, though I didn't know that till later. So I got a little bit involved with other people, I got to that point; which is part of it . . . And these drugs gave me a lift that made me realize that my brain could function, wasn't permanently in that state. So gradually . . . When I went back for weekends with my mother, my adoptive mother, it must have been quite devastating for her – you know, after all this work and love and affection that she'd put into our lives. She must have had a lot of strength of character and inner resources . . . Also, I suppose she must have felt worried for the children, and felt responsible. I always remember, when I did go to pick the children up – Anna just ran from the front door with her arms out to me calling '*Maman!*' I hadn't seen them for nearly a year, you see, a long time.

I suppose I feel now that having once desperately wanted to die, that eventually when it comes it can't be as bad as all that. And that so many people have wanted to die – they're in camps, or they've been tortured, or something like that – and I sort of feel, well, I've had a second chance. Although the strain was always awful – anxiety about how to survive, how to support the children. The children did help a lot, one focused on them, but all the time in the background there was this . . . There was always the insecurity. But I never went back to that point again. In fact now, almost for the first time, I'm feeling . . . Yesterday was so nice, for instance, I mean it was quite simple – we just went into the country, a nice walk. You know, you're creating these vibes at the time which you can then plug into. And I'm doing a lot of art work now. But it's been a long tunnel!

Occasionally I might feel afraid of death, it depends – if I try to visualize this big emptiness, this nothing . . . But then, I've got sort of funny ideas I've collected, from a conglomeration of theories or ideas or philosophies – not much Christianity in it actually, all sorts of peripheral things to do with one's own intuition. Because . . . This Christian creed, you know – all this vast structure of priests and cardinals and God knows what! I think it's much bigger than that.

I think it's laws and patterns . . . The nearest I could find to what I feel is Richard Jefferies – do you know *The Story of My Heart?* – some sort of vast merging; and then ideas, or even tangible things, transmitting some sort of vibes. Like drawings have a life, or the dedications in old books, and when one likes certain objects there's a kind of emanation from them. And people . . . Oh, you know in *Huis Clos*, for instance – the idea that these dead people are in eternity, and there's a sort of screen which communicates with the real world, and when the living think of them an image flashes up on the screen. And gradually the images become less and less frequent.

You have people in your thoughts . . . And that thought can be diluted and diluted almost homoeopathically – you know the homoeopathic theory is that something is still there even if you can't actually trace it, it still works. I think the dilution of things goes on, even the dilution of a personality. Or again, put it in terms of gardening . . . I remember picking a little tiny piece of sedum – this was when I was about fifteen – and I remember planting it, and it just grew and grew and grew. And I gave bits to people, and I more or less filled people's gardens eventually. That, I suppose, is the opposite of homoeopathy in a sense, because the homoeopathic is smaller and smaller and this was growing and spreading . . . But still I feel that whatever *was* there, there are always traces and connections.

That's why I think that these vicious films they produce, for instance, all the things with violence on television, I think they not only harm people, but I've got the quaint idea that they're harming the vibes! Sort of sending out fourth-dimensional ripples. And that as a person you leave a wavelength behind you – a kind of tremor through time. Eventually perhaps it changes, from one generation to the next, and one can only feel them so far back, if you like . . . But, say, if you're walking through a country churchyard and you see the gravestone of Jemima Smith who was born in 1807, perhaps the fact that you're walking through the churchyard and looking, perhaps there's something you are plugging into. For example, I remember Jacquetta Hawkes talking about finding a piece of pottery with the potter's thumb-print in it – from two thousand years ago, it's still there. The thumb-print is always still there. I think there's a tremendous feedback from things, and from people. But what does confuse it is perhaps the amount of ugly and monstrous things that are going on. Perhaps one's idea of death is confused by these constant associations with something bad.

I keep thinking now that I must pack in as much as I can, because I find I'm feeling better about things. Now I can more often detach myself from this hurrying feeling – it's self-defeating, because the more you panic and can't settle to do things, the less you get done. I can actually enjoy doing things, I can settle. It's always been my problem – this anxiety, this haste. You know how awful it is in 'The Snow Queen' – they're lost, they can't find each other, and it's only when the roses have grown round the door and they're about eighty or ninety that they find themselves there – oh, it's dreadful.

My mother – my adoptive mother – had a very peaceful and graceful death. I still keep some of her clothes, and there were some flannelette sheets of hers – I've torn most of them up, but I've kept some bits where she embroidered her name on them; it's very neatly done, and somehow so typical of her. Again, it's this feeling I have about *things*, things holding a certain essence of people, or goodness, or something like that, which you can't measure.

I waited for a decent time to pass after my adoptive mother's death before I tried to trace my real mother, because I always felt it would be a bit churlish or ungrateful or treacherous to find out anything while she was alive, or even too soon after her death. I felt there had to be a distancing, you know? I didn't know that my real mother was alive still while I was searching, that she was just dying at that time, in fact, so I didn't see her. I believe actually, she did come to see me once, when I was about nine; I do remember a visit, but I don't remember her. If I'd been told,

'Look, this is your mother' . . . She'd obviously wanted to see me. So I discovered after that she'd married – no, she had no children, she didn't like children! Apparently she was quite a gadabout, she went all over the world – she was quite a character, very individual. If I could talk to her now? Well . . . I'd be quite interested in what she felt about me, I'd like to know what she actually did feel about me at various stages of her life. I'm *her* vibes, in a sense, I suppose; and none back.

# JOSEPH MALUAL

I came here from the Sudan as a student; I came to study electronic engineering, particularly telecommunications – that was in 1983, and my wife followed in 1984. I was a senior technician in the radio broadcasting station in the southern Sudan, and I wanted to get a further training. So actually I came for nine months or so. But 1983 – well, I left at the time when the civil war had already broken out, and the conditions in the Sudan are conditions which force you, even if you are not a politician, to involve yourself in politics at an early age. Really, to struggle for the survival of your people. So we had to be involved in the rebellion at the early stages, and my name was known at one stage to the Security in the area I come from. And when I was here in England, those who were working with me, some of them were arrested by the State Security; and I also learned that a list which contained all our names was already in the hands of the Security. And people who were caught, some of them were executed in prison. I applied here for asylum; so I'm a refugee in this country.

If things subside, of course I'll go back, yes. It is not normal, you see, for us to stay out; because normally we don't become refugees – all those years we used to fight inside there and we struggled inside there. But now, because of the kind of atrocities which are taking place, and my people, the Dinkas, being the target, that's why you can see a number of them moving out from there. If you want your children to be safe you must take them away. Because over 40,000 Dinka fellows are now in the northern provinces, and I think there are nearly one million recorded in Khartoum – these are all displaced people – and there are around 350,000 who went to Ethiopia also as refugees.

I grew up in the countryside, in the village, a small station; my father was a chief of my clan. Dinkas are one people, but there are actually tribes, there are different cultural backgrounds between them. If you consider the section I come from, the Agar tribe, we don't keep cattle in the same place we cultivate; where we cultivate we call them villages, and then we keep the cattle in the cattle-camp. Totally separate, not the way you do it here, where you have farms. Cattle are very, very valuable to the Dinkas, more than anything. If you find a Dinka fellow, you tell him that you give him one thousand pounds or cattle, he would take the cattle. Marriages are conducted in terms of cattle, and all kinds of bartering, whatever it is, payment of debts, and if you kill a person, you have to pay cattle. The impression people have about cattle is more than one can imagine, such a precious thing.

In the early fifties there were few educated Dinka fellows really, the maximum could have been ten or so in the area I come from. Actually my father didn't want me in particular to go to school – he wanted to let my elder brother go to school and I remain with him. But unfortunately he died, and that thing was reversed later on after his death; my brother came back from the town, and I went to school myself. It was a decision of my uncle; I went to school at seven. The schools then were always Christian, there were no other schools; the government schools came in later on, and there were Christian schools which were converted into government schools after nationalization.

Yes, I remember about my father's death, because he died while I was present. I think I was about four years. He was sick of pneumonia, and it was a tradition not to take people to the hospital, people used not to believe that hospital was a good thing. The elders came and made some sacrifices and all that kind of thing; this is what we do. I would not believe in sacrifices now, because people have become corrupt, there are not good believers as there used to be; that is the kind of thing which the Dinkas are experiencing now. Christianity here is also dwindling down, in a way – the British have their own tendencies of talking of certain things which are not necessarily what you would expect from priests. So I think it is everywhere; I may be wrong. But in those days, the sacrifices – people used to believe in them.

They did several sacrifices; but he died, yes. I was of course very upset, because I used to like him very much, I loved him, and stayed with him more than with my mother. My mother was the elder wife, and she was staying with the other brothers of mine. Bringing up a child in our country – a woman is not always there. There is a cattle-camp; children are always where the cattle are, and your mother might be in the village, there may be girls of your uncles who are looking after you, and sometimes your father is looking after you in the cattle-camp. If you grow up in a Dinka land you look after goats and calves, you have your own self-responsibilities, and this opens the mind of a child very early.

All the time long I was staying with him. I terribly feel a grief; because when he used to be there I used to be very, very happy. And sometimes when I'd go and play with other kids I used to be feeling relaxed, and whatever I do there I feel I do it freely, to the extent that if he left and went somewhere else and I am playing with the boys, I'd feel insecure and other boys could bully me. But if he's just there in the house, I know that he's there, and I can do wonders; and the children could be frightened of me when I was even small.

He actually died, I think, in the afternoon; I think the pain increased during the morning, and my mother and his other wife were all there before him, and I was also there. And nobody made food that day, I remember that. The time he was about to pass away, my mother had decided to go and bring some peanuts from the house, and gave them to me and asked me to burn them somewhere else outside. That, I think, was the time he was about to pass away; I heard movements, struggling with life. I came in immediately because I heard this noise; I left the ground-nuts I was burning, I left them in the fire, and I came and stood and cried before him. He opened his eyes and he asked, 'Who is this?' He asked, 'Who is this?' and then my mother told him that it was myself; so he held my hand and he told them, 'Look after him, that nothing will happen to him.' And I quite remember that, very well. He held my hand and I think he died instantly.

I was then asked to go out, taken away to the other uncle's house, and that was the time I thought that something was gone wrong, although I didn't know. I had to suspect that he must have died. I was being asked to go away from the area he was in, and he was very sick; so I began to have a feeling that he must have died – why am I being asked to go away?

So I stayed in my uncle's house, which was outside the fence of our house; I stayed there until at about eight or nine in the evening I was asked to come. But I couldn't come because I was on top of the first floor – our houses are made like that – I couldn't climb alone, to come down, unless somebody took me down. My uncle's daughters and sons were there; they jumped down to go to the burial of my father and they left me there. I tried to come, but I couldn't climb alone. So I remained there.

I was just gathering that my father was dead. It was in the following morning when they brought me down, and some other celebrations were made where he was buried – I think they brought a bull and some goats too. For sacrifices, yes, for the burial. I saw the grave. That was my first time of seeing death; you see, in Dinka areas people fear death, this kind of death in particular – to die naturally through sickness or old age. Good death is death through violence, they think; when you go to war and you die in the field, in the battle, that is honourable. It's not that there is something wrong with the death of an old man, but ordinary death through sickness and old age is the one that is feared – I don't know why, but my experience seems to show that this kind of death is feared very much, and you would find that people don't pass the grave, unless very close relatives come. Even the house the person has died in, people don't pass there.

I did see his grave, but usually graves are not made visible according to the Dinka culture. But they had a stone kind of grave which was done for him; that one is seen in the towns, but in the villages usually it used not to be practised. Because normally if you have small children or a woman alone, it would keep her in a bad condition for a long time, it will keep reminding her. If the grave is outside and you see it, even if you're talking just like we're talking now, from time to time you can see it several times in a day. And then it can remind you again, and that can be a bit bad. But there are things which are done; after a year people come back and make sacrifices, kill a number of bulls again. That one is supposed to be the final sacrifice, the one you do after a year; it is also where people change clothes, because there are clothes for mourning.

No, nobody told me my father was dead. Well, the way they

do it there is different. They do it of course when they are grieving and when they are crying, trying to remember their lost husband and this kind of thing. They talk to you indirectly, that things are now going to change. They don't tell you that your father is dead, but they will imply it in a way – things are going to be like this and this and this. If you have an elder brother, like I had, then they will address most of the issues to the elder brother. In case he is not very energetic, in case he doesn't work well in the fields, they can say, 'You are now the father, and if you don't stand on your own feet these things can be bad for you and for your brothers and everyone.'

No, the children are not helped – I think there was a tendency of children being ignored, they might not know what was happening. But of course I knew, yes. I suffered for a long time. I remember it took me several years to be normal. Because there was no attachment again; I now withdrew, and I stayed with my mother – my real mother – and there was a gulf already created and there was no proper association with her. I'd keep thinking of my father all the time round. I never talked about it, no – it's not normal that people talk about these things.

Yes, people in the villages believe that people live after death. You see, our clan in particular, we believe that there is a god of our father; but because I am another creature now, there must be a god that created me alone. And there is a special protection – like an angel; our people believe that each person has his own angel. There is one God Almighty too; *nhialic* is the word for God, and *nhial* is heaven. They are almost alike in the way you can see them written – *nhial* is the sky or heaven, and *nhialic* is supposed to be there, the father of everyone.

There are other spirits, there are angels, but it's still God Almighty is always there. And there are times when you want to make your own sacrifices – for example, your child is always sick, and you come and sit down and bring a ram, call some elder people and some spiritually possessed people. They are the ones that can convey your messages or appeal directly to God. He says, 'Now, God, we brought this ram, and it was brought by your son, so-and-so, and it is because of his sick child, and we want to appeal to you so that his child becomes well.' Or if a

man's properties are not accumulating or his cattle are not multi-
plying, all this kind of thing, so he can appeal to God and say,
'God, why are you doing this thing to me?' My father used to do
this; he would enumerate the kind of sacrifices we had done to
God, to make things go on well. Yes, I would think it helps –
although you don't know, of course, how God does it, but it
helps. Because the spiritually possessed people are not appealing
to anybody intermediate, but they are directing their appeal to
God straight away. There are families who do that and the
children just get better.

As a child I didn't look at it spiritually, I think, my father's
death. It was just my own sorrow. And of course I couldn't
imagine that there are spirits here or there who could look after
people. I only developed this idea later on. Actually there were
certain dreams – that was recently, in 1982. In Juba – that is the
capital of the southern Sudan – my second daughter passed away,
died, because of malaria. During that time my wife, who was
pregnant with my third son, used to cry all the time long. And
somebody from our clan, who was in the town, had a dream that
an old man came to him and said he should go to my house and
take a fruit – I don't know what they call them in English, they
are used for sacrifices by the Dinkas – and slice this in two in the
house, and tell my wife she should not keep crying, she will bear
a son. And he gave this child a name.

And that person did not do it – he forgot, I think, he ignored
it. He dreamt it a second time again; he told his wife the same old
man came and told me this, that you go to the house of Malual
and tell his wife this message and do this sacrifice. His wife had
known my father, and she said, 'That is the father of Malual, so
you go, since he has told you this message.' My uncle's son was
living in the same house, and he said, 'OK, I will deliver the
message'; so he started to come, but he forgot, he went his own
way. Then the third time the man dreamt: 'Since you have not
gone to do the sacrifices, you go on Friday and there will be a
ram' – he told him the colour of spots on the face, and the price,
and he should go to that place in the evening at about six and buy
the ram for fifteen pounds and slaughter it. He thought, why is
this old man coming to me three times? So he climbed his bike

and went to the place; the market was closed and there was only one ram, the same colour that he was told, and it cost fifteen pounds.

He still thought that my uncle's son had given me the message, but it was not done. Anyway, he slaughtered the ram, and the dreams stopped there. That was a punishment to him, buying the ram, for not having given the message. My wife delivered in July, and we called my son Col – that is the name of a baby that is born after the loss of another child. And one day my wife went to the house of this man to spend the day there with his daughter, and my wife called the name of my son; and the woman said, 'Why do you call him Col? What about the name given in the dream?' So my wife said, 'What dream?' – and the woman said that there was a dream that had been passed through a message. And my wife was shocked, because she would have expected the message to have been delivered to her in advance. You see, the story behind this dream is that my two elder brothers were already married, but both their wives cannot bear children – there is only me in the family that can have children. I could see the reason why the message came; the name he gave for the child means 'late', and I am the third son, the only one now who has children, continuing for the lineage.

I felt it was my father, I felt so, yes. I never dreamt about my father myself as far as I can remember. I do still call my son Col; my two elder brothers have to be informed about the dream, and my uncles, and they will want to change the name of the child from what I have given it. It doesn't matter, because he is still a little boy and it can be changed any time, but I'm having it in mind that he will have the name given to him by his grandfather. That will be as soon as things get to normal and we can go home.

We would be glad to be home; if the war comes to an end we will go straight to the village, we'll stay there for a year, even if I take up any job elsewhere again. The children have to be in the village first – here in London the environment is all different, and my children even are becoming different. It is a problem for all the Dinka fellows who are here. I do talk to my children, because these days they actually can remember a lot of things. Death is very common on the telly here. They might not digest anything out of the frequent deaths which they see on the telly, and in that case they might care even less about death, as I keep seeing in other children here. So anyway, when we go home the situation there is different; there's a lot of education that takes place in the village.

I will tell you about my daughter's death. I had to attend a seminar in Khartoum; she was sick, and she actually almost improved, I felt she had improved. She was two when she died, and she had malaria. Quinine was not there – there was some other drugs which were not very useful, couldn't cure anybody at all. It was terrible, yes. In this case you don't do a lot of sacrifices as is done in the case of big people. But nobody's forgotten in the Dinka culture, because people marry for those dead people – they have names and you marry wives for them, and the children will be called the children of that person that died. And she will continue with her lineage, or with his lineage if it's a boy.

I have another story there too, there was the same issue of dreams also coming. My wife had some dreams when she was about three months pregnant, I think, and I had gone for the seminar in Khartoum. There came a dream from my father, and he told my wife that he didn't like the idea of this little girl being brought to where he is. And then he walked away. He was having a pipe – because he used to smoke – so he was having a pipe and a stick. Now, my wife told the dream to some of my relatives who were there, and one of our clan heard the description and she said, 'That was his father.' This is the kind of imagination which is there, being reflected in a dream. So she for the first time saw the image of what my father was like. The other time she dreamt, she saw the young daughter being held by my mother, who was also dead. Now, if she dreamt what my father said before, if she could relate it to the second dream of seeing my mother carrying the child, then she almost concluded that perhaps it was my mother who wanted the child – that that was why the child died.

This is the way she can think of it. And when I also imagine . . . I mean, my daughter being taken – who wanted the child? We used to hear these stories from our elders; that among the dead people, they are alone without children, and nobody serves them, so they would like to have some people to go and serve them, especially the children. So they might, here or there, get one child or so to go and look after them. But I wouldn't say that my mother took away the child, because there is no way that I can believe it. Only, when you try to sort out problems, there is what you call solution by elimination – you eliminate other possibilities, then you remain with some . . .

The Dinkas in most cases feel that people share with God – the children are given, and always God will have one. It's a share, as a sort of sacrifice for the rest to live. But then, what about us in my family? – all of us are there, my brothers, nobody died among us. What I'm telling you is what the Dinkas feel about it. It's not what I feel about it.

Personally I don't feel so, that a spirit can do harm; the only person I feel is coming around is my father, I always feel that he's around. Always. I keep remembering when he told me, when he held my hand and said, 'Yes, look after my son well, nothing will happen to him, take care of him.' I heard that when he was dying. So I keep remembering that and all the time long, when I am in difficulties, then I keep thinking about that and things work out.

When I die – well, I would think that the same love will always be there, for my children on and also other children. I will always think so. I think I could be together with him, I do feel so, I do feel strongly about that. But that impression which my father left me, that he died at the time when I was very small – I don't like such a thing to happen again. I don't have a fear that I will die young, because I would think that God must have known the feeling I had at the time my father died, and wouldn't like my children to suffer. So that is the kind of thing I believe will not happen when I'm young. When my children are fully grown up I can die at any time – I will not mind at all. I won't be afraid. But I have a strong feeling that I don't want to leave my children young.

You see, the Dinka societies are quite established societies; the family clan is very important, and there is no question of family withering away. There is no dead Dinka – even if he's dead, he has his own family behind, whether he died as a child or not. Always, all the time long people are together, carrying on the family of everyone like that. You cannot avoid death, I say, but you can always continue with the family, family lineage and whatever. Whoever has been born in that family, to that family, there is always someone to continue it. I see that the Western cultures to some extent are losing track now, because I believe this was not the way people used to live before. And the fact that here when your children become older you begin to separate, all this kind of thing – it's definitely very strange. Also I rather believe that a child can't know much when he or she is sixteen or even eighteen – this is the time when the elders begin to feel concerned that they have an obligation to pass on to the children, now all the time long they begin to talk about the past. This is how in a Dinka society history is passed.

The thought of my father, that is one of the things which also makes my spiritual beliefs stronger too. Because all the time long anything I've thought of and I pray about, it just works in the same way I wanted it. I don't kneel down to pray and all this, but I formulate these things in my mind and I pray as if I'm addressing these issues to God.

Except that my daughter did die, yes. I didn't know my daughter was going to die, I didn't know at all. And actually, when I was leaving for Khartoum, she screamed terribly after me; she wanted me by all means, she clung to me and she caught my neck here. I think she knew she wouldn't see me again. She cried terribly, she never cried like that before, and I was even surprised. And when I was going away I was looking back, looking back at her, and I was wondering why she was screaming like that. Even my wife also later on had to tell me that she had continued crying for the whole of that evening; and it was actually the next day that she began to get ill, and the third day she died. So I also believe that if I were there, she would not have died. She was my own image, she was just like me, and I had to pray that God should bless me with somebody just like her. I got a boy instead – the boy also looks like her. A child is a gift, yes, that's right, and you have to say the gift is taken back. It has to work itself out in a way, a different way, contrary to your imaginations.

# WENDY

Wendy was aged four years when her mother died in an acute exacerbation of a chronic illness. Thereafter Wendy lived with her father and her sister, Winnie, eighteen months younger. In addition, maternal grandmother made herself responsible for the children's care whilst father was at work, and a maid who had been a daily with the family since the children were infants now became resident for five days a week. Help was given at weekends by paternal grandmother and another maid.

Much information is available about Wendy's development prior to her mother's death because for eighteen months mother had been coming for weekly professional advice of what appear to have been, in a two-and-a-half-year-old, rather minor problems. Wendy is described as wetting her bed, to have been attached to a blanket, to have had 'some typical fantasies around penis envy', and to have been unable to express her hostility in words, particularly toward her younger sister. Six months later mother was still concerned about Wendy's attachment to the blanket, her thumb sucking and her reluctance to separate from her. In other respects, however, Wendy seemed to be making good progress and began attending a nursery school.

It then transpired that Wendy's mother, now twenty-five, had had an attack of multiple sclerosis which had been in remission during the previous seven years. Apart from mother's two-hour-long daily rest periods, however, the illness made no outward difference to the family and both parents were keen to keep it dark, though not unexpectedly Wendy often resented having to keep quiet during mother's long rests. When information about the illness finally emerged the therapist felt it advisable as a

Reprinted from John Bowlby, *Attachment and Loss*, vol. III, London: Hogarth Press/Institute of Psychoanalysis, 1980.

precautionary measure for Wendy to be transferred to the clinic's therapeutic nursery school; but no one anticipated that tragedy was so close. For within four months of Wendy starting there, her mother had a fulminating flare-up of the illness, entered hospital suddenly and died within two weeks.

During the week or two prior to the acute attack mother was inclined to feel fatigued and had a pain in her shoulder. Wendy was worried and became reluctant to attend nursery school, especially when it meant father taking her there instead of mother. She was clearly worried about mother's being unwell; and her anxiety was increased by the paternal grandfather, whom they visited almost daily, being seriously ill also and not expected to live.

When mother's condition suddenly became worse and she was admitted to hospital, the therapist saw father daily to help him decide what to tell the children. On her advice the illness was explained to them as being very serious, so serious in fact that mother could not lift her head and arms or even talk, which helped Wendy understand why mother could not talk to her on the phone. The children were also told that the doctors were doing everything possible to help. During the last critical days, moreover, the therapist suggested to father that he not hide completely from them his sadness, concern and anxiety, as he had previously felt he must.

During the weeks prior to the flare-up of the illness, Wendy was expressing some hostility and rivalry towards mother and also expressed a fear on two occasions that mother might die. Basing her interventions on the theory that a child's fear of mother's death is commonly a result of an unconscious wish that she should die, the therapist encouraged the parents to reassure Wendy that her occasional angry thoughts would not affect mother's well-being. During the acute phase of mother's illness father was encouraged to continue giving such reassurances.

On the day mother died father decided to tell the children what had happened, and also that mother would be buried in the ground and that this was the end. This he did during a ride in the car. Mother had stopped breathing, he told them, she could not feel anything; she was gone for ever and would never come back.

She would be buried in the ground, protected in a box and nothing would hurt her – not the rain nor the snow (which was falling) nor the cold. Wendy asked, 'How will she breathe and who will feed her?' Father explained that when a person is dead they don't breathe any more and don't need food. There had already been general agreement that the children were too young to attend the funeral; but father showed them the cemetery, with a near-by water tower which could be seen from their window.

That evening the children seemed relatively unaffected and for a time were busy playing 'London Bridge is falling down'. Relatives, who disagreed with father's candour and preferred to tell the children stories of heaven and angels, endeavoured to stifle their sorrow and to enter gaily into the children's games.

During the days that followed Wendy invented two games to play with her father, in both of which she would twirl around and then lie down on the floor. In one she would then quickly stand up with the remark 'You thought I was dead, didn't you?' In the other, in which she was supposed to rise when father gave the proper signal (which was her mother's first name), she remained prone. There were also occasions, for example at meals, when Wendy cheerfully enacted the part of her mother with remarks such as 'Daddy, this is such a pretty tie. Where did you get it?' or 'Anything interesting happen at the office today?'

Yet sorrow was not far away. A week after mother's death the grandmother of another child became very emotional when talking about it in the car to Wendy's grandmother. Wendy paled and fell over on the seat. Grandmother comforted her, held her and they both cried. About the same time, on a visit to relatives, cousins assured Wendy her mother was an angel in heaven and then showed her her mother's picture. Wendy cried hysterically and said her mother was in the ground.

During the third week after mother's death Wendy gave evidence that she was still hoping for mother's return. Sitting on the floor with her younger sister, she chanted, 'My mommy is coming back, my mommy is coming back, I know she's coming back.' To this Winnie retorted in an adult-like monotone, 'Mommy's dead and she's not coming back. She's in the ground by the "tower water".' 'Tsh, don't say that,' retorted Wendy.

Wendy's preoccupation with her mother was shown too in a 'snowflake' song she had made up on the day after the funeral. At first it ran (probably influenced by the interpretations she had received): 'Snowflakes come and they disappear. I love my mommy and she is dead. I hate my mommy and I hope she doesn't come back. I love my mommy and I want her.' A few days later she omitted 'I hate my mommy'. By the sixth day it was in the past tense, 'I loved my mommy and want her to come back.' A fortnight later on the way to school it was 'My mommy is coming back', but whispered so low that grandmother could hardly hear it.

The same preoccupation emerged from another concern of Wendy's. Almost daily on the way to school she engaged her grandmother in conversation about the ducks on the pond: 'Are they cold? Will they freeze? Who feeds them?' At times these discussions merged into more direct questions: 'Do dead people have to be fed? Do they have any feelings?' To rebut information given by grandmother that freezing temperatures result in even thicker ice, Wendy would point hopefully to a small area over a spring; 'But, Grandma, I see a little part that is not frozen even though it is so cold.' The therapist suggested to grandmother she discuss with Wendy how very hard it is to believe that a person is dead for ever and will never return.

After one such talk Wendy decided to pretend that grandmother was mother – she would call her Mommy and grandmother was to pretend that Wendy was her own little girl. At nursery school she told another child how she had a mother for pretend – her grandmother. To this the other child remarked, 'Oh, it really isn't the same, is it?' to which Wendy assented sadly, 'No, it isn't.'

On another occasion, about four weeks after mother died, Wendy complained that no one loved her. In an attempt to reassure her, father named a long list of people who did (naming those who cared for her). On this Wendy commented aptly, 'But when my mommy wasn't dead I didn't need so many people – I needed just one.'

Four months after mother's death, when the family took a spring vacation in Florida, it was evident that Wendy's forlorn hopes of mother's return persisted. Repeating as it did an exceptionally enjoyable holiday there with mother the previous spring, Wendy was enthusiastic at the prospect and during their journey recalled with photographic accuracy every incident of the earlier one. But after arrival she was whiny, complaining and petulant. Father talked with her about the sad and happy memories the trip evoked and how very tragic it was for all of them that Mommy would never return; to which Wendy responded wistfully, 'Can't Mommy move in the grave just a little bit?'

Wendy's increasing ability to come to terms with the condition of dead people was expressed a year after mother's death when a distant relative died. In telling Wendy about it father, eager not to upset her, added that the relative would be comfortable in the ground because he would be protected by a box. Wendy replied, 'But if he's really dead, why does he have to be comfortable?'

Simultaneously with her persisting concern about her missing mother and the gradually fading hopes of her return, Wendy gave evidence of being afraid she herself might die.

The first indications were her sadness and reluctance to go to sleep during nursery school naptime. Her teacher, sensing a problem, took Wendy on her lap and encouraged her to talk. After some days Wendy explained how, when you are asleep, 'You can't get up when you want to.' Six months later she was still occupied with the distinction between sleep and death, as became plain when a dead bird was found and the children were discussing it.

Wendy's fear of suffering the same fate as her mother manifested itself also when, during the fourth week after mother's death, she insisted that she did not want to grow up and be a big lady and that, if she had to grow up, she wished to be a boy and a daddy. She also wanted to know how old one is when one dies and how one gets ill. On the therapist's encouragement father talked with Wendy about her fear that when she grew up she would die as her mother had and also reassured her that mother's illness was very rare. A few days later Wendy enquired of her grandmother, 'Grandma, are you strong?' When grandmother assured her she was, Wendy replied, 'I'm only a baby.' This provided grandmother with further opportunity to discuss Wendy's fear of the dangers of growing up.

On another occasion when Wendy was similarly afraid, the clues were at first sight so hidden that her behaviour appeared totally unreasonable. One morning during the third week after her mother's death Wendy, quite uncharacteristically, refused to put on the dress decided upon or go to school and, when the maid persisted, threw a temper tantrum. The family were puzzled, but they hit on the solution whilst discussing the incident with the therapist. Before Christmas mother had taken the children to look at the shops and in one they had seen Santa Claus attended by little angels. The angels' dresses were for sale and mother had bought one for each of the children who were delighted. It was her angel dress that Wendy had objected to wearing that morning.

A fortnight after this episode paternal grandfather died. When told, Wendy was matter-of-fact about the funeral and seemed to comprehend well the finality of death. At nursery school she was sad whilst sitting on the teacher's lap, she told about the death and cried a little; but then claimed she was only yawning. A little later, however, she commented, 'It's all right to cry if your mother and grandfather died.' Thereafter she recalled nostalgically how when first she came to nursery school her mother was not sick and would take her to and from school.

Shortly afterwards, hearing someone mention that grandfather's house would be sold, Wendy became apprehensive. She refused to go to school and, instead, stayed to check on the dishes and chairs at home. Only after it was explained that her house was not to be sold as well were her fears allayed and she was willing to go to school again.

There were many occasions when Wendy was afraid lest she lose other members of her family. For example, she was often upset and irritable at nursery school on Monday mornings. When asked what troubled her she replied that she was angry because her maternal grandmother and the maid had not been with her at the week-end. She did not want them to leave – ever. In the same way she was angry with her grandmother when, nine months after mother's death, she finally took a few days' break.

On two occasions father was away overnight on business trips. At school Wendy seemed sad and, when the teacher asked her what she would like her to write, replied, 'I miss my mommy.' On the second occasion she did not want grandmother to leave her at nursery school, got out her old blanket and sat next to the teacher. Later she cried and agreed that she missed her father and was worried lest he not return. In a similar way she was upset when the maid was away for five weeks because of a leg injury. When at last the maid returned, Wendy wanted to stay at home with her instead of going to school.

Much else in the record shows Wendy's persistent longing for mother and her constant anxiety lest she suffer some other misfortune. When a new child arrived at school Wendy would look sad as she watched the child with her mother. On one such occasion she claimed that her mother was going to wash her face because the maid had forgotten to. Any small change of routine such as her teacher being away would be met with anxiety. On such occasions instead of playing she would sit with another teacher looking sad.

At the end of twelve months Barnes reports that Wendy was progressing well but predicted that, as in the past, separations, illness, quarrels and the deaths of animals or people would continue to arouse in Wendy 'a surplus' of anxiety and sorrow.

# Assistant Divisional Officer Dick Clisby

My father was in the Fire Service before me – he was a Deputy Assistant Chief Officer, in fact he was a temporary Assistant Chief Officer. We lived all over London – whenever my father got promoted, we moved. We started off at Hammersmith, we went from there to Ealing, then Wembley, Wembley to Lambeth, Lambeth to Shoreditch . . . I didn't really worry about my father, no. I realized there was danger because I knew of firemen who'd been killed. But I didn't think of it as being a dangerous job. My mother, in fact, has always said that she never worried about my father when he was in the job, and she never even worried about my younger brother when he was in the Service, but she continually worries about me! I think in certain ways I do tend to be . . . spontaneous. I don't know if it is rash; I tend to make a decision in a short time and act on it, whatever the circumstances. So far things have worked in my favour!

When I was actually living in London I was a bit snookered – I thought, well, I'm not going to join the Fire Brigade, because of my father being in it. If I ever got on in the London Fire Brigade – and I'm quite ambitious – people would say, 'Oh yes, it's only because of his dad.' So when I got married and started working in Maidenhead I suddenly thought, the Berkshire Fire Brigade – let's go for that. In fact I stayed with Berkshire until my father died, till he'd been dead for five years, I think it was. And then I joined London, because I thought, well, if I go in there now, if I get on, people will judge me for *me*. There are still people about now, specially in the senior ranks, that remember him. But nowadays I tend to get judged on my own merits.

I think all firemen in my experience will do as much as they can – obviously it depends on the people, some people will do more than others. You know, in any system there's people who get by, people who ride the system and go about doing as little as possible. But you'll find that normally – well, in the Fire Service, with the people that have been in for a little bit, there seems to be a spirit, if you want. You know, it's hardly ever that we like to be beaten. That's why, if we lose someone, if we lose children, it hits us very badly. Firemen will go to all extremes to save people, and you've even got firemen that have thrown their lives away – not thrown their lives away, that's the wrong way of putting it – but given up their lives to save other people. What they say to you is that with the procedures that we have and with the guidelines we've got, in every situation you should be able to say, 'Right – this, this, this', like putting together a Meccano set. And then if you go past the guidelines, you're either a hero, or you're dead.

When we lose firemen we don't talk about it, no. The Fire Service is a strange brotherhood, if you like – though now it's a sisterhood as well. It's a strange organization in that we don't tend to openly discuss our grief. I'll tell you a little story . . . There was a Leading Fireman who was on the Red Watch at Paddington – that was the Watch, going back to 1974, where there was a fireman, Hamish Pettit, that was killed in a fire and a couple of others quite seriously injured. And I just happened to meet him on holiday – in Portugal! We sat in a bar having a drink and we suddenly started having a talk about people and Watches and everything else – I'd left Paddington then for Kensington. And we got talking about it, and in the end of it we both ended up in tears. Not masses of tears, wailing, but sort of tears-in-your-eye tears. And in the end he said, 'D'you know,' he said, 'I've never discussed what happened with anyone in the job.' He said, 'I've never spoken to a fireman about it – it's good to actually sit and speak to a fireman about things. Because you understand my feelings, whereas other people . . .' You can say, you know, 'Shouldn't I have done this? Could I have done that? Could I have helped in any way?' Other people don't understand it – the frustration coupled with grief.

Now that must have been twelve years after the fire. I mean, it was amazing. We had probably about a three-hour chat, sitting out in the sun, beers . . . It really was good. It was a good chat. I think my wife was there and she kept popping off, going shopping . . . I think you hide your grief and it's only on certain occasions that it comes out.

We bottle it up. You don't speak to your wife, no. One, you don't want to upset her or make her more tense when you're on duty; two, you're not too sure if she would understand your innermost feelings, your thoughts. Other times you come home and you've done something which you feel, God, I was lucky today! And you tell them about it and they don't understand it at all!

We tend to joke about death, or injuries, which is a way of alleviating it, alleviating your feelings. You know, just a way of putting a blank face on it. You tend to cover it, mask it, with humour, which helps everyone out of situations. I can think of – not thousands – but hundreds of incidents where people have been killed, members of the public, I mean, and we've joked about it. Not within the public's hearing. We joke about it because it's the only thing that can keep you sane. Something the other day: a person who jumped under a train, and, I mean, the body was so dismembered, into little bits, that you had to sit there and think, cor blimey . . . It was picking up a head here and a leg there, that type of thing. At the end you turn off, I don't know what it is, but you turn your emotions off.

When I was out in Berkshire we had a case, a bloke who drove out of a pub, went into a ditch, rolled the car over. Now, he had a broken nose and his partner had a four-by-four stake gone straight through his backbone. He was alive. He was pinned up on his seat with these massive injuries. A doctor on the way to an emergency stopped, and hit him in the leg with an injection and said that should knock him out. We got out there and we thought, Christ, how do we deal with this? A special medical unit arrived and they gave him another injection; and he just wouldn't go out. A big fellow, about nineteen stone. He was struggling a bit with his pain, and every time he did, great gashes would open up. And in the end we decided the only way to get him out was to cut the roof off the car, which we did, and climb in the car and actually cut these four-by-four stakes as close as we could to his body, and take him still in the seat to the ambulance.

A bloke who was assisting me at that time, we were working together, worked on him with handsaws, and we had to put our hands inside him and just saw off the thing. There was blood everywhere. So much so that when we got to hospital, this fireman I was working with went in with him, and the nurse come up and tried to snip his bottom button off. He said, 'What you doing?' And she said, 'Well, where is it?' There was so much blood on him, she thought he was involved in the accident. We were joking while we were working, we were saying things like 'How d'you like your steaks?' and 'Get the hacksaw, get the quick-release knife, get the mustard.' Of course, he couldn't hear us. It was the only way that you could actually get through it. The Sister said she'd never seen someone so badly injured who was still alive.

We got back to the station, we sat up in the Rec Room, and the Ambulance Station Officer came in and sat down with us. And we all sat there. And it was about half an hour, we realized no one had said anything. Everyone was just thinking about that bloke. And in the end they turned him off. They'd cut all the business out of him and put him on a machine, life-support machine. They said there was no way he would survive that much injury, he'd be a vegetable, and the decision was made to turn him off. When the Leading Fireman told me about it, I remember I was absolutely furious! That bloke, he wouldn't go under the injection because he knew that if he went under he would never come out. Which is in fact what happened. He had such a will to live.

The day after we'd worked on him I came off duty; my wife was working and I didn't want to go home, so I went out to my friend's house. And he had a bloke, Phil, staying with him who'd had his leg all pinned up. Not a fireman, just a friend. And I was telling them this story, and this bloke went, 'Oh . . .' I thought he was joking, but he was sick all over the washing-up. It was only then I realized, because he'd had this accident himself, the description I'd given him . . . You don't think about it!

No, I've never known a fireman who's fainted. You think, really, you've got a job to do, you have to do that job. If you faint, then you're not going to be able to do the job. There's also shock . . . My younger brother had a situation when a woman burned to death; and he slept on the couch, in the front room with the light on, for three days. He wouldn't go into the dark, because every time he closed his eyes he saw this woman. He was very young, and to see anyone burn to death is quite horrific. For three days, as I say, he wouldn't sleep in the dark or anything.

I suppose there might be firemen who can't take the life, but I can't think of any. The thing is that if it does affect you, there are things that you can do so that you're not up the front of it. You know, if it's a traffic accident, you can still put the bollards out and get the equipment and feed people.

I had a case of a rescue in South Kensington; that was a situation where the first appliance – that's the fire engine – that arrived was ours, and there'd only be five of us on it. Which is the officer in charge, the pump operator, who's also the driver, and three people in the back. So really there's three of you that have to be the doers, and you don't have the choice. It's like any traffic accident – someone has to get in the car with the person who is trapped or dying and speak to them. Because as they say – and I don't know who 'they' are or where they get their information from – the loneliest thing you can do is die alone. And if you've got someone holding your hand and saying, 'Don't worry' . . . I think it helps *you*, and it must help the person.

I had a case again, a traffic accident – drunk, came round the corner, hit a car, into a wall. The passenger, a woman, had just broken her nose, and she was taken out, and all she was worried about when we were taking her to the ambulance was her handbag! Her husband had taken the brunt of the impact, and I got in with him; and I was chatting to him, trying to comfort him. We were waiting for the ambulance and for the blokes to get the roof, cut the roof off and get to work. That bloke doesn't know what's going on, you know, he's worried the car's going to burst into flames, and if there's somebody with him he thinks, well, this bloke isn't mad. So it gives him comfort, having you in there with him. Also, if you can keep them from passing out, you've got more chance, because they can tell you, say, 'My chest is beginning to hurt', and you know they're having a heart attack. You can pick up things from them. 'Where's it hurt most?' and 'Can you feel your legs?' – just talking to them all the time.

This was very shortly after my father died, it must have been about '79. This bloke was quite well trapped. And, you know, I'd built up a bit of a rapport with him. And it got to the stage where we had everything off, got the whole of that side of the car off, and it was a matter of picking him up and getting him out. I then came round the back, so now I'm sitting behind him, and they were going to pick him up that side. His leg had broken in a mass of places, completely smashed all the way down. And as I reached underneath him I felt this . . . like a bag, if you want. What it was, was that his leg had completely smashed up. And as we picked him up he had a heart attack, a seizure, and died. And I remember being so angry! They'd put him on the stretcher, and the other fireman was trying to get his teeth out, because he'd just literally gone. They wanted to get his false teeth out, to resuscitate him. But they never did.

Afterwards – and it was probably because it was so close to my father dying, you associate with it in a way – the Station Officer said, 'Go and sit on the back of the appliance.' Because he saw I was upset. And I felt embarrassed – one, that he'd picked it up, and two, that I hadn't hidden it. And I said, 'Oh, I'm all right, guv'nor.' And he said, 'No, go and sit down, Dick.' And I said, 'No, come on.' Anyway, we just made all the gear up and got back on with it.

When you show your emotions, you're facing your emotions. If we faced them all the time in the depths that we go into, then I think you would end up very, very depressed and unable to do your job. You can go in, see someone completely smashed to bits, a mess, still alive, just at the end of its last few minutes, walk out and carry on with your life – you can't take it all in and absorb it, you know, you've got to pull up a barrier. You absorb what's gone on, but not the depth of feeling. We make ourselves so busy that we don't actually have time to stand there and sort of feel it all.

The only time I've ever felt ill in my life at a job . . . There was a yellow TR7, a bloke drove it off the motorway, skidded, hit a lamppost, and we got a call to 'Man trapped, car alight'. And we came down, crossed the motorway, parked up, and there was steam coming up. Anyway, it was when I'd just joined up and I got the job of holding the light for the blokes to work. They cut the car to bits from the front until they got to his legs, which was trapped. And his leg was hanging on by a little strip at the back. And I just stood there with the light, and I wasn't doing anything, and I thought, I'm going to be sick. It was because I wasn't doing anything, I was just standing there watching.

It was quite a strange story. As we got him out, I picked up a piece of his leg – bone. And right about six months later, it was Christmas, a bloke tapped me on the shoulder. He said, 'You're a fireman, aren't you, mate?' So I said, 'Yes.' He said, 'D'you remember me?' I said, 'No.' He said, 'The TR7.' And I'm thinking of the ambulance man, the policeman . . . And I said, 'I don't really . . .' He said, 'I was the one in the car!' He had a walking-stick, and I suddenly realized. I said, 'How's your leg?' Thinking, you know, that they'd have taken it off. He said, 'Oh, they've pinned it all back together', and pulled his trouser-leg up. And I had free drinks all night! As I say, a piece of bone had come out of his body, and to this day . . . I don't know what they did, they probably underpinned it or did something to it. I was absolutely amazed he was walking about. He'd obviously re-membered me because everyone else was working and I was the one he could see.

What you're doing while you work is busying your mind, you're thinking, right, now we'll do this, we'll do that. And you're working in blinkers, thinking that you're not going to worry about this bloke that could die in a couple of minutes and he's got a family and this and that. You think that this is a job and the result is getting him out. Soon as we get him out, he's off, he's gone. We do chat after sometimes – 'Oh, he's got no chance.' It's the strangest thing, people with small injuries usually are the ones that most surprise you, because they die; and yet we've had people completely laid open . . . You know, I had a woman hit by a train – I thought, crumbs . . . Her head was even a different shape. I was telling someone about it and they said, 'Oh no, she's all right.' I said, 'She must have brain damage.' They said, 'No.' She had a fractured skull and various other things; but she survived. We don't get enough news of what happens after; but then again, I don't know if feedback's too good a thing. Because what you're doing then, you're becoming too involved in it. You're there to get the person out, make it safe, get the person out with the least pain possible or, if they're dead, to get them out with dignity.

My father was at the train disaster at Moorgate. He was interviewed on telly; and what he said was, 'We're now satisfied that there's no one else who's going to be alive, now we're working to our utmost abilities to bring the dead people out – with dignity.' It's something that is important, because even though what you've got is a piece of meat, that piece of meat is someone's father, sister, girlfriend. We had an accident along Kensington Gore; there was a women in the car with a broken neck, and her son and someone else were in the front of the car with quite bad injuries, and it was a matter of getting the woman out. The woman was upside-down; and finally the doctor came up and said, 'She's dead', sort of thing. So I said, 'Let's get this woman out with dignity.' I said, 'That's a person we got there, not a lump of meat. Let's get it out, get her out, and treat her with a bit of respect. Apart from the fact that that was, up to about a half-hour ago, a living person, her family could have followed behind and been held back by the police and could be watching.'

There was a case again, very recently, of an Indian man. He either was set alight to, or committed suicide, or died and they tried to cremate him. What we had was an old man in the back garden, no source of ignition, no accelerant used – petrol or anything. Completely baffling. This body of an old man, who looked like a young man because his skin had retracted, kind of gone tight. And we were all out there looking round and everything else and thinking, what the hell! – everyone was baffled. At the end of it, as I was driving back to the station, I thought, Christ, that *was* a person. And we were treating it like an Agatha Christie puzzle. It was a person.

I think you *should* talk about it. And yet . . . You'll probably think I'm a ghoul or something; but the more horrific, or the more of a challenge, if you want, the job is, the more I enjoy it. A friend of mine's a butcher, I chat to him, and he says, 'Oh, I don't know how you could do that.' To tell you the truth, I don't know how he can cut animals up!

My father got the job – I don't know how he adopted it – of going and telling the next of kin. My mother used to go out with him, which I only found out recently. And she said, 'In the end I wouldn't go.' It was so emotionally draining, they would break down and Mum would end up getting all upset with them. And yet my dad could cut himself completely off and walk out and say, 'D'you fancy a curry tonight?' She'd be emotionally drained and have it on her mind for weeks afterwards. It did affect him, though; one of the poems he wrote was about this – 'Breaking the News', it's called.

When I went into the Service I was just twenty-three – I did know, I'd heard stories which horrified me. One specific one a friend of ours told about a fire he'd been at. About this woman who'd had petrol poured all over her and set light to. They were working away, and the woman was apparently dead, sitting in a chair with horrific burns. And the woman suddenly said, 'I'm sorry about that . . .' – I can't remember the exact words – and then fell off the chair well dead. They actually screamed when she moved.

I felt before I joined up, God, that's terrible, I can't imagine . . . Then whilst I was at Kensington, I got called up to North Kensington to a 'fire all out' – that means there'd been a fire and it had gone out. I went up there and was met by the ambulance man; he said, 'There's something dodgy here, guv'nor.' So I said, 'What's that?' and he explained the situation. I went up to the door and a woman opened it. So I said, 'Excuse me, have you had a fire here?' and she said, 'No.' I said, 'Can I come in?' She said, 'No.' I said, 'Why not?' She said, 'Well, I'm not going to let you in.' I asked the driver who was with me, I said, 'Can you see that smoke?' He said, 'Yes.' So I said to her that under the 1947 Fire Services Act I'd got the rights of entry, et cetera, et cetera, and the woman said, 'All right', and opened the door.

So I went into the house, and there's the stairs down there, and I'm looking into the kitchen, thinking, I wonder what's going on here, then. Because you walk into a place like that and you don't know, there could be a nutcase there, anything. As I walked along I stopped and there was stairs going up to the flat there. And I heard something go, 'Aah . . .', like that. And the hair at the back of my head started to rise underneath my helmet. I turned round and I looked up, and there was a woman there who'd set fire to herself. I screamed, inside. The sight of it . . . All right, I don't want to upset you. We got a burn sheet round her and tried to make her comfortable. The woman died. That was possibly the worst living burns I'd seen.

I wouldn't say that nothing could get to me now. Children. Children is something that you'd even find – I don't really mean that to be *even* – but you'd find firemen crying if a child's burnt or if you lose a child. Really, for kids, you'd find that we'd do anything. Most people would do anything anyway, but if it's children involved people would sacrifice their own lives. There was a bloke, George Frederick Davis, who was a fireman – he got a posthumous George Cross. He went into a room that was badly alight, saved two children, then he was so alight himself he actually dived out the window. He died, anyway. I don't know if the kids died or not. You've got to save any form of life, no matter how injured it is, how hurt it is, you've got to try your best with it. Because as I say, the strangest things happen. People who you think can't survive, survive. I don't know. Life is very strange! Death is stranger.

I'll tell you about the South Kensington fire I mentioned. I'd been off ill for ten weeks with a torn muscle, which I did at a job at Shepherd's Bush. And I went back and I thought, I'm going to fiddle it. What I'm going to do – if we go in between eight and nine o'clock we can relieve our opposite number – so I went in early and relieved the sub-officer who was on the Watch, so I was then on duty. They'd have stuck me on light duties, stuck me in an office for months and then sent me to the doctor. No, it wouldn't be nice! We like to be operational. I got on duty, on the basis that once I'm on, it's difficult to get me off. Anyway, at about half past eight we got a call to Queensgate. It's on the border between Kensington and Chelsea; they tried to contact Chelsea en route, couldn't contact them, so they got in touch with me on the radio with a priority.

They said, 'We've received multiple calls to this and we've received information that persons are trapped at the back.' So as we pulled up I met Station Officer Hughes, who's on the Green

Watch at Chelsea. We were old fireground buddies, if you want, sparring partners – we work as a good team. Graham said, 'I've asked for six appliances.' I said to him, 'I've just got a message over the radio that persons are trapped at the back. I'll go and suss that out.' He said, 'I'll deal with the front.' I said, 'All right.' So I went through the basement with Kensington's crew, got up at the back of the building, walked up, and there's about seven Indians on the flat roof about three floors up. I said to the blokes, 'Get a ladder up and make sure that they're all right.' They're on a flat roof, coming out from the building, so they've got radiated heat but they're in no immediate danger.

I walked on, looked up, and up on the fourth or fifth floor there was a Chinese person – looked like a Chinese person, but in fact he was a Vietnamese person – holding a little girl out the window, and going to throw her at me. Smoke was coming out above him. Most people in fact die of smoke inhalation and then are burnt at a later date – it is better, because you go out coughing rather than with the actual burning. So I said to him, 'Stay there, stay there, I'll come and get you.' I didn't want to get into a position where he'd throw the child, because there was no way I could have caught it – I'd have tried, and it would probably have broken my back and the girl would have died afterwards. No, they don't hold out a sheet. A sheet wouldn't stop you – it would break your fall, but it would still kill you.

So I rushed out, rushed round to the front of the building, and I ran to the appliances trying to find a rescue line, a specially tested line. I couldn't find one, all I could find was an ordinary general-purpose line. So I pulled it out, said to Rosie Lee, who was operator of the turntable ladder – that's the big one – I said, 'Get us up on to the roof, Rosie', and he said yes. He said, 'OK, then, Dick.' Anyway, I got up there, climbed up there, he had to break through a branch of a tree to get me close enough. I said, 'Whatever you do, get me some men up here as soon as the additional appliances arrive – I need help.' Because everyone else was inside the building working on the people at the back, so I was up there on my own.

So I looked at the bloke and said, 'Stay in, stay in, stay where you are.' And I tied this general-purpose line off against the fire escape, and as I pulled it, it actually sort of bent with me. I thought, I don't know if this is going to take my weight. And I laid across the front of the parapet, and what I was going to do was go down into the building, sort of abseil a little bit down and go through the window. And I remember sitting on there thinking, Jesus! And something was coming up, my son's birthday or something, and I thought, this is something that I could actually regret doing. Someone shouted up, 'Be careful, Dick', or something like that.

I thought, my God, what shall I do, what shall I do? And I was just going over the parapet; because the options, to me, were: yes, yes, no, can't do that, right, that's the only course available for me. Go over there and get the family out. And just as I'm going over I saw Tom Sawyer, who was the next rank up from me, Assistant Divisional Officer, he's a massive man. I said, 'Thank God you're here!' He says, 'Dick Clisby?' I says, 'Yes, how are you, guv'nor?' So we had a conversation, and as he said afterwards, it was like having a conversation with someone in an office – it was completely cool, rational . . . 'What you going to do?' 'Doing this – family in there – I know there's two in there – there's a woman in there as well . . .' He said, 'You're not doing it that way, that's unsafe.' And I said, 'Hold the line, then, while I go down.' He said, 'No.' He said, 'Try and go through the roof, I'll get you some more help.'

And with that he disappeared, and Leading Fireman Corbin arrived. He come across to me and we said, 'Right, we'll get through.' So in the end we opened up a skylight, smashed through the roof; then there was a big drop. So I thought, right, here I go. So I jumped down into it, and I said, 'You get that line and wait there for instructions.' So I went in with them, and by this time the back half of the building was well alight. And that's the only way out. I went up to these people and I said, 'Stay calm.' There were four of them, a Vietnamese family, male, female, two young kids, and I said, 'Stay calm.' The lines I had weren't long enough to lower them to the ground; the firemen were on the flat roof by now, so I said, 'Get a ladder up to us, we'll come out and join you on the flat roof.' They started doing it, and I heard the firemen coming up the stairs with the hoses. I thought, great! So I said, 'Don't worry.' I said, 'I can hear the BA crews' – breathing apparatus crews – 'we're safe.' Then Corbin said, 'It's getting very dodgy up here, guv'nor. Can we get them out?' I said, 'No, I can't have them coming out through that smoke and heat barrier' – because there's a chance that they would panic, and five floors up you don't need someone running about.

So I said, 'Right, we'll wait.' In fact I got a carton of Ribena and opened it, and we all just sat drinking Ribena. I was leaning out the window, you know, calling to the crews. There was a song, 'Always look on the bright side of life', which was in one of the Monty Python films, and I was sitting there, thinking this in my mind! Suddenly, there was one hell of a 'pschoo' below, and they were just putting the ladder from the flat roof to us. It suddenly went bang, and it blew the flat below out. Suddenly they jumped off, and the ladder started to burn. With this I thought, ah well, that's that option been closed down. Now it was Corbin or the BA crews getting us out through the roof.

The bloke was looking round and I said, 'No need to panic, no need to panic'; and this time the smoke was coming through the floor. I said, 'This is standard Fire Brigade procedure, what we're doing is ventilating.' I said, 'They've got the fire under control.' Suddenly I heard all the shouting outside, saying, 'It's getting bloody hot' – the BA crews were coming up the stairs. And I said, 'Go back down downstairs, it's behind you.' Because it was catching this room, and they'd gone above it and they were getting all the heat from it, and I could hear them shouting – you know, 'Get out, get back.' They went back down to fight the fire. I says to Ian Corbin, 'How's everything up there?' He said, 'The roof's bad behind us.' I said, 'Where the effing hell are the rest of the men? Let's get some water on it.' Things were starting to get a bit hot.

So I went back into the room that looked down on the flat roof, and that was well smoke-logged so I closed the door up and put a bit of towelling down so that we didn't have excess smoke coming through to us. I said to the bloke, 'Don't panic, don't panic'; and with that – there was a small kitchen down there, and the next-door was going like anything – and suddenly 'pschoo', it came through the wall. And so suddenly we had flames. I looked round at the bloke and – I didn't say it – but in my eyes I said yes, this is where we panic. He said, 'What we do now?' I called up and I said, 'Ian, we have to go *now*.' I said, 'Have you got anyone up there to help?'

So Ian Corbin let the line down, which I tied round the youngest kid. Got the first kid out, got the second kid out; and by the time the second kid got out, it was hysterical, because of the heat and smoke and everything else. And so I said, 'Right, let's get the father out' – because the father was light, very skinny, and he could move one of the kids off the roof. Ian Corbin had got one of the kids across to the crews – who didn't come on to the flat roof, because one side was so badly burnt and the other side was unstable. So Corbin's got the father out, and the father's helping one of the kids to get across into safety, over the party wall.

Things down my end are suddenly getting very bad. The woman who was now left – like it always is – she was very big, and very hysterical. I tied the rope round her, but she just wouldn't go. Ian Corbin by now was looking into a chimney. About eighteen stone, six foot three, massive, ideal; and he's a smoker, which helps. And we're struggling with this woman and I'm thinking, for God's sake, something's going to happen, you know. This bloke we'd got out said there was a family next door; I thought, oh, I can't think about them now. So anyway, finally we got the woman out; and I thought, well, I'll check to see the situation, see if there's anything I can do. And I opened the door, and it was like a blowtorch there. Then it come up through the kitchen, and the whole place was smoking. So I slammed the door, had a quick check round, and I said, 'Right, Ian. Now.'

And he said, 'Guv'nor,' he said, 'I haven't got any strength left at all.' He said, 'I can't do it, I can't pull your weight.' I could tell by his voice that, you know, there was nothing there left. So I said, 'Ian. I've got nowhere else to go.' I said, 'You've got to get me out.' He said, 'I don't know how we're going to do it.' So I ran and got a chair, and from a bunk-bed that I'd seen before there was a little stepladder; I put the stepladder across in the hallway, climbed up with it, and then he let his hands down. And

I jumped up and then caught his hand, and we struggled out. I was coughing and retching.

There was a story at Westminster, they were talking about it afterwards – and they thought that Ian Corbin had collapsed, because he had his head right in the hole. They said they didn't know what he was doing in the first place, until the family started arriving out. And they said – because there was now a bit of flame coming out and heat and everything else – it seemed inconceivable that anything else living was coming out of this house. Then they suddenly saw this white helmet come struggling out, and realized there was a fireman in trouble. By that time it was too late to do anything because they couldn't get across, they couldn't get water to keep the fire off of us that side.

Anyway, we got out, and by this time I was coughing and coughing and coughing, I couldn't see a thing because of the smoke. And I heard someone say, 'Dick, Dick, over here.' And I thought, no. Because the radiated heat here was so severe. I said, 'Let's get over this roof and then climb along that way', which is what we did. Suddenly there was a cool breeze, blowing against the heat. And we got round over the party wall and sat there and just literally started to throw up. Anyway, the crew came up and said, 'Are you all right?' and all that stuff, and I said, 'Just leave us, leave us. For a bit.'

We got the other family out in the end, they were all right. Everyone was saved. Now the story which unravels is, the next day I'd gone back to get details because I had to do a report. And that Vietnamese bloke had gone back, you know, to see if there was anything to salvage. I said, 'Oh, I don't suppose you remember me' – because now I'd got my best bib and tucker on. He said, 'I remember you, I remember you.' I said, 'Whereabouts are you from?' – thinking it was China still – and he said, 'Oh, I'm Vietnamese.' I said, 'I'm very sorry about this. Have you got somewhere to go?' He said, 'Yes, they rehouse me.' Excuse my funny accent! I said, 'Oh, blimey.' 'Yes,' he said, 'very bad news. I come here,' he said, 'and boat sink. I get put into hotel in Hammersmith' – I don't know if you know the Fremantle Hotel, that burnt out – 'and they rehouse me here and look!' I said, 'Cor blimey, sod your luck – if I was you I'd go back!' He said, 'No, lot better here, lot better here!' I thought, well, you don't know what it's like the other end.

I suppose I could have sent someone else up to do the job. But then again, that would have meant two things: one, I'd have to have found someone to do it, because the other appliances hadn't arrived yet; and two, then I'd have had to live with myself afterwards. And if, say, the bloke threw the child, or the family died, or anything, I'd have had to live with that. Someone said about it, 'Well, that was amazing.' I said, 'No, because everything I did was choice, an option.' This is what has to be done. Am I going to do it? No. Who's going to do it? No one. So it's me. Ian Corbin is one of the few people who could have done what he did, because he's as strong as an ox and he smokes, so his lungs wouldn't suffer so much. Well, yes, I did see my own death. When it came through the wall, the fire, and I looked at the Vietnamese bloke and we said nothing . . .

The very next day I got some silly letter from my bank manager, and I just felt like tearing it up. After that everything else can seem so petty. Which is what I say, you like the fires. The senior officer that came up when I was first up there, we were just chatting about it and he said, 'Yeah, the thing is, I love them. I love the fires.' We all love it. But that was one . . . When I look back now, I think that when I was just about to go over that parapet, tied on to a dodgy line, and it was five floors down and then through a conservatory before I hit ground, I was actually scared. Scared. But I thought, I haven't got a choice. Or I didn't have a choice I could live with.

If you can get in there with people, and say, 'Calm down. Let's sit on the floor, so we're below the smoke level, open the windows so the smoke goes out, and just sit' – then there's a good chance you'll get people out of it, because sooner or later we'll get enough people there to put the fire out and get to you. If you jump, it doesn't matter how many people, how many doctors, how many nurses get there – that's it. No one can help you. I'd rather be overcome by smoke, because if my colleagues find me there's a chance they can resuscitate me. If I jump, no one can.

I love being operational. Last year I spent seven months doing

a desk job at Wembley. And every time Wembley went out . . .!
And Kensington, whenever they were on, I'd monitor it – and
they'd have a four pump fire or something like that, and I'd go
up and I'd read the messages as they came in, and I would know
who would be there and I would imagine it.

I think people get into the spirit of the Fire Service somehow –
we always say it's not a job, we don't do a job, we're in the Fire
Service. It's a way of life; people get taken up in that way of life
and it alters them, the job changes the person. There's a fireman
who was with me at Queensgate who they call 'the thug'! And he
has thug-pellet cigars, and he's always smoking, and he once had
an argument with someone when he was riding an emergency
tender – so the story goes – and he leaned across and stuck an axe
through the top of the bloke's car. And he's got cuts all over him,
and he used to work as a bouncer, and everything else. A real
rough diamond! And at that job, when I was trapped in the roof,
he was one of the BA men and he went out and changed his
cylinder, put it back on to go in, came out, did the same again . . .
He was one of those that you knew would actually get you out of
the building; he's like a Staffordshire bull-terrier – you don't call
him off, he does the job.

We have the rules and regulations, but there are times when
firemen need to bend them. King's Cross, now, was what you call
a snatch rescue. Townsley – the man we lost – rushed into the
thing without breathing apparatus and without his equipment,
because he didn't have time. What the books would say is, he
should always put his set on, go to BA control board when it's
set up, say, 'I'm Station Officer Townsley.' 'How much pressure
you got?' You say, 'Here's my tally.' 'Fine, we'll put your name
on the board – where you going?' Put a little note on location of
team – 'Right, off you go.' Five minutes have gone past; another
ten people have died. So what Townsley does is, he rushes in,
thinks, let's get some of them out while the rest of them are
getting their gear on, and of course . . . We've had discussions at
work about what Townsley did, comparing it with what we
would do, with the best of our knowledge. And I would say in
that situation I would do exactly the same thing as what he did.

But again, with King's Cross, I was sent up to our Ops Room

and then across to London Transport Control, and I was sitting on the end of a radio, stewing ... Oh, I'd have given six months' pay, or a year's pay, to have been there! They were all colleagues – I knew all the Red Watch, I knew most of the people involved. It's like your friends fighting a battle and you can't, you know, take part in it. Literally I was that close – I said to the Division Officer who was there with me, 'I'm going to the loo, then', and give him a wink to see what he would do; because I'd have jumped out, got in my car, and shot across there ... He said, 'Dick, stay here.' He said, 'There'll be plenty of people there, I need you here.' Oh, I was so frustrated at the end of it – you know, I was wasting my time passing messages across when I wanted to be down there actually fighting the fires.

Yes, there is a frightening part, if you were ... I've seen people, firemen, who've had very bad burns. There's a thing, the itch, if you've got bad burns and you suddenly start itching – it's where you've got an infection which means you've probably got three days at best to live, it goes so fast. That is something that would frighten me. But my father wrote me a letter just before he died and he put something like, 'You'll make good in the Fire Brigade, stay with it, because if I know anything, I know firemen' – I think he knew I had the temperament, and would enjoy it. There's a photo I'll show you afterwards, up on my wall, which really sums it up; it was after a fire, and it was all out, and we were going to the canteen van, and you can see the enjoyment! But then if you lose someone, everybody's a bit subdued; and it's not because there's a body there, and someone has died, it's because we let them die. We get frustrated – 'Could we have done that? Is there something we could have done?'

No, I'm not religious at all. I don't believe that there is a God at all, a superior being or anything. I believe that people turn to God – I've had many arguments with vicars, priests, after weddings! – people turn to religion if they're old, sick, dying, or they have a need which religion satisfies. I think that when you die, that is the end of it. In 1976 I dived into the Thames and I ripped all the muscles out of the back of my neck and stopped breathing, heart stopped. I was pulled out by some friends of mine, put on to the side, and the next thing I remember was having a pain in my chest. Dave was giving me a heart massage and mouth-to-mouth; and I came to, and all I heard was someone saying 'I can see his brain'! And, 'He's going to bleed to death if the ambulance doesn't arrive'! Death seemed just like going to sleep, and in fact I was in a lot of pain and it was a release. I'm glad I did come back. But it didn't make any difference to me at the time whether I did.

I was brought up as a Catholic, and if you know Catholics . . . Well, I could do the catechism backwards now probably. The only time that I *would* worry is if someone said to me, 'You've got cancer now, there's absolutely no chance of you living.' I think I would commit suicide about half-way through that time. I think I'm a realist – I would say one day, now was the time. I would rather die at a fire than die at home with a heart attack.

If I had to have an operation I'd be terrified, and in fact I have been terrified, having two wisdom teeth out! I had two days in hospital having my wisdom teeth out, and three days with shock afterwards! Then that woman's body I handled – well, she had hepatitis B, and I had to have a course of injections, they had to put the needle in two inches deep. The first one that they gave me I nearly fainted, and after the second one I had to lay down. The nurse was ribbing me, and saying, 'How can you be a fireman?' And I said, 'I've had a broken leg, and if you give me the choice now between a needle and breaking that leg, you can have that leg.'

I suffer from nerves for ridiculous things like needles, and dentists. I've been rejected by a dentist, he's actually stopped and said, 'I can't continue with this, because you're either going to pass out or have a heart attack.' He said, 'Either way, I won't get that tooth out.' And that's why I had to go into hospital for it. And when I stood up that time my back, all the way down my shirt, was absolutely soaked with sweat!

But I always think I've seen so much of life . . . I've got a friend at the moment who's going bankrupt, very worried about it, and I've said, 'There's nothing in this life that's worth worrying about like that.' People say I'm the eternal optimist. My wife's sometimes nagged me a bit about my attitude to life. And I've said to her, 'I'm only here for possibly another thirty-five years, if

I live to seventy.' I said, 'That's the end of it – and you're dead for so long.' You've got to say, 'Well, I've got thirty-five years and I want to do as much with it as I can.' The job – that makes it worth while, that gives you the feeling that you're here, doing something that's good. And you enjoy it. I think a lot about when I'm dead how I would like to be either buried or cremated, and I think my decision is I'd like to be cremated. Because it would be nice at the end of it to say, 'I've fought you all my life, now you can have me!'

# CHRISTINE

I'll talk to you about it, but I think you'll find it . . . well, quite scary. I'd like to tell you how horrible, how scary, how black, I find the idea of death, but perhaps your readers won't like it. Perhaps death-fear is something you should just have secretly at home, not out in the street and frightening the horses.

The street . . . It's quite a good place to start. I'm not agoraphobic, but one of my bad places, *deadly* places, is out on the street, one stranger after another pushing past you, and even those rows and rows of shoes and the underwear in Dorothy Perkins' windows and the Marks and Spencer's plastic bags and the punks and the bus queue – it's because it's all uncaring and jostling and interminable and a kind of limbo. Because when I'm talking about death I don't just mean the ending of my life – I don't actually believe that's possible somehow – but the way that that ending, ending-to-be, seeps into life. Deathliness is what I mean. It's being in a strange place, where you can't find anything you know. To me fear of death means fear of loneliness, being left alone, fear of a sort of dreadful indifference. It means having an operation when I was a child and someone holding a mask over my face until I had to stop struggling, sort of give in and stop being me. Me, myself – at that point it was forcibly taken away, that's what I feel.

Me-ness, you see – it's something I've always felt was extremely fragile, it's as though I have to carefully piece it together every day. I've been working on it for all these years, trying to get it to hang together, sticking it together, holding it together , like one of those little delicate kids' models you make with balsa-wood and Araldite. And then in the end the whole thing is just going to be swept away. And there's a kind of fear that you'll die without having ever really got the show on the road.

Somebody or other said the big question was, is the universe friendly? User-friendly, you might say today. Is it! It's not friendly, it's not even cruel really – it's just totally indifferent. It doesn't hear you, it doesn't know you're there. The mask is put down over your face whatever you feel, whoever you are. It doesn't hear you, it doesn't care, it always wins.

I'm amazed when I find people who say they don't feel like that about it, or anyway say they don't. Woody Allen does, so I can't be the only one. I liked that bit in one of his films where he goes to see the Marx brothers – it's the scene where everyone's singing 'Hail Freedonia' – and he thinks life might be worth living after all, in spite of death. Maybe he's right – maybe seeing Harpo playing the harp does make it all worth while!

You feel that people like Woody Allen and Philip Larkin, for instance, who've come right forward and said they're afraid, you feel they should somehow be let off a horrid end. But no, Philip Larkin gets throat cancer. I don't know exactly what that involves and I don't want anyone to tell me. And I expect Woody Allen would like to go out to the sound of some jazz trumpet being played, but he'll probably be this old, old creature hooked up to tubes in a white hospital cell on the eighteenth floor.

This thing about dying alone on the ward with all the gadgetry round you is the special modern kind of horror. I hate hospitals, I dread them. If my daughters could be with me, if I could be at home with the dog on the bed, it might seem all a bit different. Because death to me is *separation*. But if they could be there with you, if they could be holding your hands . . . Would you feel it? I do think I would. You read, you know, he died in so-and-so's arms, and I've often wondered what that meant – did the person get into bed with him? It would be difficult to get your arms around otherwise. If someone was in bed with you when you die – that would be quite nice.

In the old days, at any rate, they didn't have that hospital horror, I suppose. Doctor Johnson, for instance – he was one of the great death-fearers, like Woody Allen, and me, but as far as I remember his deathbed was not that bad, he sang hymns and read prayers and that sort of thing. Dying people now feel ashamed of themselves, they feel they're embarrassing everybody. They apologize for being such a nuisance – I've seen it. My father was being polite only about an hour before he died, and I thought, strange, you go on being polite even then.

Doctor Johnson was really afraid of being judged and sent to hell, of course, and you could say that at least we don't have that fear any more. In a way we don't, I suppose. But . . . I can only talk about myself – I think I do have a fear of hell, but it's a sort of before-death hell rather than after. The whole procedure, from the morning you get the letter asking you to come back to the hospital for tests . . . Sometimes I feel that every millimetre of my skin, just all over me, is one millimetre of total vulnerability, that I'm a construction built for feeling every kind of dreadfulness and unprotected from anything doctors and surgeons decide to do. You see, there still is the idea of hell around, I think.

There's a Simone de Beauvoir novel where someone is about to commit suicide and then she realizes that she'll leave behind a body, an object, for people to look at and handle and do what they like with, and that stops her from actually going through with it. That's another horror – it's the left-over body . . . If only people could just vanish instead. We're sort of grotesquely stuck with this body's fate.

There's another side to my ideas about death that sounds a bit nicer – it's that swoony death, it's Keats saying, 'Now more than ever seems it rich to die/To cease upon the midnight with no pain.' Of course how he *did* die was far away from home and spitting up blood and thinking about how he'd never even slept with his fiancée. But there is that idea, of ceasing upon the midnight . . . One gets tired by life, life is a tiring thing, and you lie down and you feel, I'll just rest. And rest. And rest. Goodbye, life. But then of course you get up to make a cup of tea eventually, so I don't know whether the real thing is ever actually like that.

I know some people do have a sort of suicide fantasy which is swoony and consoling – you know, 'Nothing can really get me, because I've got that bottle of pills hidden away. I've got sixty-six pills, I've got my emergency exit, so I'm safe, it's under control.' But could there be anything more *lonely* than actually committing suicide? I think that's why people hardly ever do it. As you peg out in hospital you at least have a chance of a nurse being there changing your pillowcase or something. But with suicide . . . I mean, I suppose when you've swallowed the pills you have to just sit there for about five minutes while you wait for *it* to start. I don't think my sense of *me* is strong enough for me to deliberately dismantle it.

I've read a lot about life after death, pro and con, whether there's any reliable evidence. But then, would one want to go on and on and on? Being afraid of losing your self is one thing, wanting to trudge with it through eternity is another – it's quite a tiring thought. But timelessness isn't possible for us to imagine. Or one only gets the very, very faintest glimpse of it . . . Actually, yes, I *can* imagine 'heaven', in quotes, in a way, I think I can imagine bliss. But I'm not going to talk about that, sorry.

But when I read the arguments about survival after death, I'm thinking about my parents really – yes, they're both dead. In some strange way I think one can have a whole fantasy set-up that one's totally unaware of. In some way I've assumed – but, I mean, unaware – that although my parents are dead now they've always been sort of hovering up above watching me. Mostly criticizing, as usual, but . . . Then I've tried saying, 'They *are* completely dead, they died, they were burned'; but then the feeling is – impossible! I don't quite want them to be alive – God, no; but I don't want them to be *dead*. Maybe sort of kept on ice somewhere. I do feel – maybe I'm getting into psychological clichés – that if I let *them* go off and be quite dead, I'd be less clutched by death myself. Actually, when my mother died, I felt nothing. But it was a very spooky nothing.

I have had sort of glimmerings . . . A bit of moral uplift here! I had a very serious illness, and at the time I had a dream about a nice big dog that I thought was mine, but I had to give it over and was somehow being told, 'Oh no, we only lent it to you and we want it back now.' In the dream I was terribly taken aback and upset, but it was good for me to think about it when I was awake. I felt that it meant that the animal body I live in was only lent, and could be demanded back. I do sometimes get a glimmering that one could just let things take their course and be quite patient with it and be part of it. A leaf – well, it's a bit of a cliché – doesn't make a fuss about falling off a tree and turning into leaf-mould and all that. One isn't a leaf, that's the trouble – perhaps leaves are more suitable for death than people. Heaven might be surviving on long enough to reach that point where you quite willingly give up – just donate your life back, perhaps.

And on the other hand there's my hell – it's that jostling through crowds of people you don't know in the street, and it's hospitals . . . And a kind of dark space you fall into just before you get to sleep where everything is grotesque and unrecognizable. It's nobody being there with you – that's death, for me. That film *Shoah*, you know, about the extermination camps – the film-maker said the point of the film was that by seeing it we could go through the prisoners' deaths *with* them. Obviously in a way that can't make sense, but in a way, I don't know . . .

If it's true that every separate thumb-print is different – can that be true, actually? – if it is true, what's the point of creating a one-off person each time and then wasting them? Why are they – you know, *they* – so indifferent to us? How do we reconcile our me-ness with the indifference? In some way perhaps we have to supply the whatever it is, the opposite to indifference, ourselves, because it's nowhere else in the universe.

Actually I feel quite cheerful after telling you all that. But it may just be because I don't know whether I do believe that I shall die. I'm not sure that I believe it at all.

# ROSEMARY GORDON

It seems such a paradox, in our own world, that we're trying to forget death, shove it out of sight, and on the other hand we're creating atomic bombs to destroy everything we've got. There's been a late showing of Bergman films; they showed *The Seventh Veil* – the pervasiveness of death there! Admittedly it was about the Black Death, but apparently he made the film under the influence of this terror of the nuclear age. And then there's the AIDS situation, and the present violence that's about. I think if I had had children I might have gone off to Australia to be out of the way of the bomb. But fear of nuclear war doesn't *specifically* come up much in my consulting room as an analyst. There are so many other ways of living out fears.

Of course people who haven't had enough time, or feel they've wasted time, will be the ones who feel sad and apprehensive that they have left their life unlived. The Ibos of Nigeria have different rites for different kinds of death, and the best death is what they call 'the death of the gods', which is when you're old and you've fulfilled your life and are ready to go. But then, if you think of some of the great people who died early, like Mozart – how much he'd done in that time! I'd certainly like to think that people die when they want to, or need to; but I doubt it. Other factors come in. I knew a man – I can talk about him now because he's dead – who didn't believe in death, he thought it was an inefficiency. He had the idea that you could go on for ever, without limit. But he died relatively early, of cancer – which is in its way a growth without limit.

There has to be a balance between the life and death forces in us – Eros and Thanatos, yes. They have to be in balance. When Jung talks about fighting against a wish for death, that means a regressive kind of wish; getting out of this awful life, these terrible problems – 'Let me die, so that I don't have to bother with it.' You can see it in mentally ill people, who withdraw into their illness, as it were, as a way of not being available. They don't have a consciousness and identity available to die, they stay within a dream world, so they have nothing to lose, in a way. But if you do that, you're in a sense already dead. You can have a deadness of all sorts; people who are very rigid, who resist change, are dead in some ways. They get fossilized, won't go along with what's happening – that's basically a sort of death. If you're not there, nobody can hurt you.

Some people don't know how dead they are, but you feel dead in their presence. It's a terrible feeling. Or they can have a pseudo-aliveness – I met someone recently who talked and talked and talked, yet I felt more and more . . . The eyes were kind of dead, there was no real aliveness in that exchange. There are masses of possible reasons. It could be because of not having separated, within themselves, from a dead parent. I had a patient whose mother died when he was three or four, and he wasn't told about it, not for weeks, until one day somebody said, 'Oh, your mother's not coming back, she's gone to heaven' – and that was that. There was no photograph of her, nothing. And he was a half-alive person, not really there at all. Till one day, what was it? – yes, he took his wife to his mother's grave, and he suddenly dissolved into tears. He'd never done that, never cried. And then he came to a session and said, 'I've been in a fog all my life – I've just come out.' And he started being alive, started asserting himself, all sorts of things happened. I thought of him as the man who lived in his mother's shroud.

That's not even a healthy death, because in a healthy death you disintegrate and something new happens. I remember, at college, a thing that really intrigued me was the nitrogen cycle – you die, you disintegrate, it goes into plants and the plants go into animals and the animals into us. That's the other side of it; so I think we have both to surrender and to fight. That's very much my belief: that in order to be able to create or to die, you have to be able to do both. Even with people who have, say, cancer – they may rage against it, but their rage may take away the energy that might be used to heal the cancer, you can misdirect your energy. There needs to be something in us that is ready to die if necessary, a capacity to envisage death; if you can't let go, you can't transform. We are handicapped if we have only the life-wish.

This comes into every kind of creativity. Gardeners – look how they have to prune to get something to grow. If you want to make a sculpture, a stone sculpture, you have to destroy the stone to make something new. If you're a writer you have a blank page – Colette talks about the terror of the blank page – and the white page has to be scribbled over. The nice stone is suddenly hacked into, the white canvas is suddenly smeared with paint. If you were very inhibited and couldn't face that kind of destruction, you couldn't create. You take a risk – very frightened people can't take the risk of putting anything down on paper. If you freeze, you hope to hold off death; you know, in France they have a saying that if a man finishes his house, he dies.

Within therapy we find often a struggle with a death-wish, again with Thanatos, if you like, rather than this openness to death. People come into therapy because they find that something obstructs their aliveness, their capacity to move on, to develop. Some are actively self-destructive – they always break up relationships, or they fall in love with people who will be sadistic towards them. One will have to find out then what it is they're destroying, which bit of self. Perhaps they are destructive because they can't let go of the old; they always destroy the new, or if they see a change they break it in the middle, as it were, and go back to where they were. Or they're held back by fantasies that they have destroyed their mother or father in some omnipotent way. And then a very important factor in not getting better may be because we won't give the therapist the pleasure of *giving* something. There are people who try to remain sick just to spite their parents – 'See what you've done to me – I won't let you off the hook.'

People who are actually destructive to others . . . There can be a sense then of: 'I'm identified with the death-giver, I've bought myself a little extra life, killing you; I'll feel safe, because I'm on the aggressor's side.' People who actually murder and destroy must feel very powerful at the time. It *is* mad, inasmuch as they actually do what ordinary people might be dreaming of; it might come to us in a dream, or even a waking dream, but on the whole we don't do it. But of course a whole country, or a war, may push you towards it. I suppose Freud invented, or discovered, Thanatos immediately after the First World War – people having done unspeakable things, and Freud wondering how on earth this could be. I think that is what brought him to the concept of Thanatos.

The fear of death, and therefore the identification with death, the winning side – that has something to do with this capacity for cruelty. This is where I blame the bad side of imagination; because if we have imagination, we can imagine the horrible things that the other person experiences, and we make *them* experience it rather than let it happen to us. In many primitive societies, for instance, the name people give themselves is the word 'men' – the others, the other tribe, are not men. You break the common identification. If you say all men are human, then we all belong together; but if you want to fight a war, or attack somebody, you can say, 'Well, they're not human' or 'They don't feel like us.' And often you humiliate them first so that they almost themselves forget their own humanity – it can be a caricature of the child–adult relationship.

A lot of it has to do with man's need to be in control, powerful, not see himself pushed under. A young man I knew, for instance, who felt himself very teased and bullied because he was weaker than his school friends, he became very intellectually haughty – by being sarcastic he could make people feel awful. Certainly many exhibitionists and paedophiles are men who are not very sure of their potency, but they can impress and frighten children. In order to die – or to create – we have to allow that it won't all be under our control.

Many people find it intolerable to think they can't control how and when they will die, though actually it's amazing how few people take an overdose when they're seriously ill; there's a fantasy that you keep back a bottle of pills for an easy way out. But there isn't really an easy way out. With some patients a fear of death emerges, and not with others. I think it depends on how they imagine dying, whether they've had an experience . . . I had one patient who was afraid of dying to the extent that she couldn't go to sleep – it was as if she had to stand guard to see that she'd go on breathing. But she had once as a child nearly drowned, so there was that experience of a near-drowning state ... But again, it depends on how old you are when that happens, because I met a man recently who'd had a terrible fall in the mountains, and it hadn't affected him that much – but he was an adult. And then I think that some people almost don't want to stay in this world, and then their fear of death has to do with fear of their own inner wish to die, fear that their own inner longing for death will defeat life forces. They don't trust their life forces well enough, they don't trust their bodies well enough. I mean, this person who couldn't sleep, obviously she didn't trust that her body would carry on, she felt she had to watch it or else it would let her down.

Even birth itself is an uncontrolled event; people who are asthmatic, or claustrophobics – one wonders if there has actually been some experience there ... There could well be a connection between how easily you got out and how easily you get out the second time. People born by caesarean section have a sudden transition; but they often have a feeling that they're not good fighters. Of course the human mind is so complex, we can never get to a single factor. Maybe in two or three hundred years, when we have lots of cases and methods of investigation, we may find out more – for the time being we're just going to say there was somebody who had this experience and now is such-and-such a person.

Bereavement also is often a part of my patients' experience, yes – and any kind of loss can be a bereavement, losing your job, your marriage. And of course losing someone you love – or hate. If there's been a lot of hate it seems it's almost harder to take, the mourning can become more pathological – you expect to be punished, you expect the dead person to avenge themselves, to haunt you in some way. But perhaps also there may be a wish there to make it up in some way, otherwise the hatred lives on. Therapy, hopefully, will create a situation where the person can mourn, overcome their fear of revenge, and in a way turn from pathological mourning to real honest sadness. Otherwise there can be a kind of pull from the dead. I've read about a Pacific Ocean people, some island, where when somebody dies, the chief calls every member of that family to come and present themselves to him because he wants to know that they haven't escaped with the dead.

I just don't know about survival of death. There's that law in physics – 'Nothing goes to nothing.' There are out-of-the-body experiences, people who feel themselves to be up on the ceiling looking down on what's happening to their bodies – that seems to be a very common experience. But of course there still is a body there; so what happens when the body really disintegrates ... Modern physicists seem to be going so far ahead now – there's David Bohm, who feels that both mind and matter are one and the same in a sense, just different movements, different formations. But I don't think I do believe in individual survival, and I don't think I particularly want to believe. Although I must say I had the feeling that when my father died after my mother – about two years after, just a day's difference – I had a sudden fantasy that she'd been waiting for him, and they'd just hopped off together. Just a fantasy; who knows where it came from – is it my culture, is it my unconscious, you know?

I think I'm quite happy not to know the answer. Death doesn't frighten me. Dying might – one doesn't want to die in great pain. But change, process, is always painful, it's no good saying it isn't – that's why psychoanalysis is painful, or having a baby. Once you get to the other side, there may be a development continuing on and on. I've never been worried about death. I've been very influenced by Eastern philosophies, and I've always found it quite easy, the nirvana concept, the merging with the rest of the world, or in Christianity the unification with God. I think the people who find death very difficult are the ones who are very attached to their own personalities. It's very much a Western problem. In the East I think you feel part of the whole; but where you feel attached to your own identity, you don't want to lose that which you know, and then death becomes harder. In Western religion the whole idea is that you stay yourself, even though in God's world; but I think in the East people may be quite happy to be part of this bigger thing – that's where the cultural emphasis is.

Jung said a long time ago – he was very intuitive – he said that a year or more before death, when there may be no sign of any dying, people may be already changing. Helene Deutsch also, she talks about good dying involving changes – decrease in aggression, decrease of attachment. And I've done some research with Rorschach tests – the ink-blot tests – with people who didn't know they were dying, and I found that they see very interesting images, sea journeys at night, things being reborn, plants dying and growing ... Some of the results were extraordinary, quite different from the usual ones.

It's really a question of whether we can live, make life meaningful, in spite of the fact that we're going to die. We do manage to live with it, that's the point; we haven't gone mad, although we know it's going to happen. And even the death factors in us, these can be transformed, and have potential.

# Edward Blishen

It's the envelope that's such a nuisance, I think – the body. I mean, I feel like most people – ageing people, and I'm nearly seventy so I am definitely ageing – I feel that as far as the spirit is concerned I have a lot left in me, a lot of whatever it is, puff, left in me; but I know the envelope is wearing out very fast indeed. It seems to me it's a very bad model in which the spirit is so sturdy, but the body . . . Oh, I feel it very strongly. Sulkily I think, oh, those people look at me and they think . . . I have a friend – he's now in his seventies – he says sometimes he's getting on extraordinarily nicely with a young woman in some crowded room somewhere, he's getting on very nicely, and then he catches sight of his face in a mirror . . .

I remember my father, who lived to be eighty, had that kind of terror that something is going on *inside*, which will result in something abominable. This sense of the worm at the core I think is very powerful – well, naturally, because . . . I mean, the human frame is such an extraordinary thing. We're given it; it's not serviced; we have no handbook; most of us know disastrously little about it. It's the most complicated machine we're ever likely to be in charge of. And we're not in charge of it, in fact.

I always remember, when my mother was in a home towards the end of her life, what an elderly woman said to me, in the midst of these broken creatures . . . An old man, inching his way down a corridor, looking like a broken spider insect, you know, and he'd worked out a whole series of jokes about his own impotence – they have tremendous resources of comedy, many people, but it's such a terrible comedy, I think, a sad comedy that people have to embark on . . . But this elderly woman said to me, you know, 'I just wish so often that people could see us as we were in our prime!'

I can see it would be awfully nice to make a case for age being rather a sort of hidden advantage; but I find that very difficult, really. Clearly it is a loss that our skin shrivels ... One of my grandsons said to my wife some time ago – he saw her hand lying on a sheet – and he said, 'Your hand is ... old!' It was so much the *mot juste*, so much the surprising word. And of course it was a term used by someone who loves somebody to a person he loves. But nevertheless in our terms a devastatingly cool term: old.

The serenity of old age! I find the very reverse. I find parts of myself which are recognizable – they've always been there, I regard them as less desirable parts of myself – I find them becoming more prominent than they were. No, I'm not nasty! Oh, I would love to have had a real shot at nastiness! No, I've suffered all my life from being nice – it's very unpleasant! An awful drawback, a great handicap. But in everybody there are – even in those who are involuntarily rather good-natured and mild – nevertheless there are qualities that are much darker and I think are fiercer. I don't think in me they've had any chance of becoming very active. But I can feel them moving about, inside me. I mean inward failures of tolerance, I mean even inward sort of little violences and aggressions ...

Oh well, they may have been there before, but of course life's been so busy that they didn't have a chance. The arena is different now. The arena is quite different. I do have this very strong sense that for a long time life is enormously busy – I mean, you are in the middle of doing everything that you're going to do, and you have a family, and everything is going on, an enormous racket and noise. And subliminally you have a feeling that this is all rather hard but in the end it will stop and you'll discover that you're enormously wise and pure. And then you reach the bit where it stops and the arena does get more empty – I mean, they've all gone. And you have this feeling – good Lord! You suddenly realize that far from being wise and mature, you're exactly as you were when you were eighteen or nineteen. Only an elderly fool instead of a young fool!

Yes, there have been satisfactions in being a writer. But in so far as this is of any importance at all, I think I shall never quite recover from the great snubbing I had from my father. I mean, this is not a complaint against the poor man; but I do find that difficult to get rid of. But certainly I've been helped by being a writer. I remember Beryl Bainbridge being interviewed once on television, and the interviewer – I can't remember who it was – was being curiously obtuse; he kept saying how extraordinarily unhappy her life had been and he couldn't understand how she could ever be happy. And she was trying to say her life had been extremely uncomfortable and distressing at moments, but that in fact her ability to be perfectly happy about it was her ability to write about it – she was able to transform it and make use of it. In my own case too, again for what it's worth, I always had the prospect, as it were, of being able to make use of experience.

As a writer you just write; you keep notebooks, diaries, I write hundreds of letters, and so on. It's all just a continuous process of attempting to say things about things – any occasion will do, in a sense. I think the pattern-making desire is very strong; to see the pattern, to put it down in terms of the pattern. I remember talking to whoever it was who did that great standard edition of Pepys, and his saying that Pepys quite clearly was a man who wanted to have it twice – to live, and then to have the second life that came from recording that life. And I think the urgency wouldn't be present for writers if there weren't going to be a final moment; a great deal of human excitement and tension seems to me to result from the fact that it's a finite experience. Now Boswell – oh, there's a man who really couldn't bear to lose a bit of his life, could he, he had this enormous greed for life and for himself. I find it an enormously invigorating thing. And yet – you're right, he was suicidal too. Drink, sexual folly at a time when it could be fatal. One of the great sexual fools of history!

I love the ordinary, you see; I can't think of anything more magnificent or extraordinary or sensational or melodramatic or more science fiction, if it comes to that, than ordinary life. This is why I quarrel with my Buddhist cousin; he says how marvellous it would be if you meditated, because then you would be elevated above all these daily anxieties and inadequacies and puerilities. But it's the daily anxieties and inadequacies and puerilities that I love, actually. I don't think that the ordinary minutiae of life, the little details, are unelevated – it's all tremendously elevated! In fact, I have an arrogant view about this, I think only if you appreciate the beauty of the tiniest things and the most ordinary things have you any hope of appreciating the huger, extraordinary ones.

I don't think I see writing as defeating death. I get no consolation from the thought that a book of mine might survive – I'm rather doubtful whether they will, for any length of time – I've no great feelings of that sort. But when I'm talking to children in schools about writing, trying to say why people write and why I write, I think I have a sort of curiously holy view of the thing; I believe life is a tremendous gift, an amazing gift, an astonishing gift, and that it seems simply curmudgeonly not to make a response. And for me the response is writing down what I experience; otherwise it looks as though I've been given all this, all this daily experience, and I don't do anything about it. So for me it's a doing something about it – which, as I said, I think is really related to the fact that one knows that it's a finite experience, that it's coming to an end.

I feel angry about death. Yes. But when I saw my mother-in-law die, I thought it the most . . . I was quite astonished by how beautiful it seemed to be. It seemed to me possible, watching her die, to understand all those images in which people used to think about death, like the spirit leaving the body; there was this sense of the body being left totally vacant. I've never known such a sensation of vacancy as when my mother-in-law died or as when I saw my mother dead. The sense of the empty body which had been left by something was so immensely strong. I also had when my mother-in-law died this tremendous sense of, as it were, someone opening the camera and taking the film out and holding the film up to the light, and everything had gone off the film. And that is – well, it's awe-inspiring . . . It also seems to me quite dreadful.

I think for me, I would say, ultimately, the destruction of this elaborate individual life, with all its great experience, its longings, its hopes – the destruction of every human life is incomprehensible, ultimately incomprehensible. It's impossible really to understand. So impossible to understand that we don't even believe that we're going to die. Because it is quite impossible to believe . . . I mean, at the age of nearly seventy . . . In the last two or three days, walking out in this rather unusual spring sunshine, I have had the inevitable thoughts of an ageing person – gosh, supposing this is the last time . . . Or the spring just faintly reminds me of what sort of hopes and thoughts and urgencies spring set going thirty or forty years ago. I think about death an enormous amount, and I believe I have a great and rather macabre imagination, but I know fundamentally – it amuses me as well as saddens me in some ways – that I cannot really believe in my own death.

Certainly you have these thoughts when you're young too, there's no doubt about that. I remember the first death that I ever had experience of – a school friend who got cancer and died at the age of just fourteen. I was just a little younger than he was, I was about twelve. An older boy at school, he'd lived just round the corner from me. For a year or so afterwards I couldn't even pass the house where he'd lived . . . I don't think I've ever recovered from that death, the first death. I couldn't believe it, I mean I really could not believe it. He had been teaching me to play chess – his death is the reason why I've never played chess. Even today I have this feeling about chess which is the result of the fact that incomprehensibly, savagely, my relationship with the boy who was teaching me chess was destroyed by his death at fourteen. Fourteen is very difficult to understand . . .

I didn't have any particular religious belief – I'd found the homilies at our Sunday school even at thirteen or fourteen impossible not to laugh at. The leader was a famous expert on railways, and the metaphors were all drawn from railways – you know, we were all thundering along the track towards the great buffers, and we must be awfully careful to keep our brakes shining and oiled . . . No, I didn't imagine my school friend Kenneth Hockett hanging around at all. What I recall as having been filled with was a sense of his absence – I mean, the fact that it was possible for someone to be . . . obliterated. I think I found it unforgivable, in a way. Of course at the age of thirteen or fourteen there's the sense that life is life and there's nothing else at all – life exists in order for one to be alive. And the discovery that it also exists for one to be dead, or to die . . .

I think the feelings that children have about death are immensely complex, they're extraordinarily complex. I'm sure you need all kinds of – however foolish and sentimental and romantic – intermediate explanations in order to defer the moment when we have to come to terms . . . As we never do, in fact! Oh, what nonsense I'm talking – I've never come to terms with it! I provide myself with all sorts of splendid reasons for not believing that it's really going to happen, or not believing that the story is really as it appears to be. At the same time we make predispositions of which we're hardly aware – sorting things out in one way or another, moving towards it. There's no doubt about it, the human consciousness is always rearranging itself because it's going to occur. But . . . No! Nobody believes it.

What has often struck me – it's an absurd thought and it strikes me again and again – is how ridiculous it is that all the people who have filled history have imagined they were alive, whereas in fact for most of the time they have been dead, the most obvious and long-lasting fact about them is that they're dead. When I read a biography, and I think of that belief in one's being alive that possesses the person; and you know of course that on page 352, if he's Matthew Arnold, he's going to leap over a five-barred gate and drop dead! Kingsley Amis put a poem of mine in the *Oxford Book of Light Verse*, and it says, 'Edward Blishen, 1922 to – dash'!

I remember as a child having this very strong feeling about writers, that one sort of professional hazard of being a writer was that you were dead. You know – Charles Dickens, 1812 to 1870 . . . You sort of have a sense of the Hall of Literature, full of tombstones. And I have a very strong sense of the pathos of people while they're alive, even myself – well, I am alive, immensely briefly. That the fact of our being dead will be the main fact about us.

When I say life is a gift, I have no impression of an actual donor in any recognizable sense; but nevertheless . . . And I'm not sure of the justice I'm appealing for; I don't know that I'm appealing to any recognizable justice. And clearly it's not the sort of world that I think it is anyway. I mean, human beings make themselves at home here – heaven knows it's a very valiant act on our part – we do somehow make ourselves at home in a place which is totally terrifying. I do believe there's something in us that prevents us from observing how incredibly terrifying it is.

We aren't aware of death in the way people were in the past; that's obviously a major change in human consciousness. I mean, the fact that I can say that in the course of nearly seventy years I've only seen death in action once, seen dead people twice – how extraordinary that would have seemed a hundred years ago. It seems to me there's a very strong argument, though I don't know what one could do about it, that our condition is extremely unhealthy, in the sense that we know so little about it, the sheer physical fact of death.

Let me tell you a story about that. My father died; I'd gone to the hospital one morning to be told that he had died half an hour before I arrived. I think it was one of the greatest shocks I've ever had – he was eighty, I know, I know, but at the bottom of your soul is the belief that fathers don't die. And then the nurse said, when I was in this state of shock, 'Would you like to see him?' And I said, 'Yes'; and she said, 'Well, I would advise you not to – remember him as you knew him.' And I was so . . . I was so unlike myself that I agreed with her; so I didn't see him. And ever since, I've had immense regret about that. I realized it too late, that I had a great sense that I had a duty to see him, that he would have wanted me to; that it was necessary for me, somebody who knew him and was close to him, to be there and to acknowledge his death. I feel that so strongly that I've asked my elder son to be sure to come and see me when I'm dead. No, for my sake as much as his, for both our sakes. It's a totally irrational thing, of course, and yet it's very strongly based on . . . I suppose, in a sense, the duty you owe to a relationship. I certainly have no rational views on death!

But I can't even begin to think in terms of an illimited existence, it doesn't work at all; everything we do and are clearly springs from our knowledge of a limited existence. And here's another point of view, you see; I'm reminded of that excellent quotation – who was it who said it? – that 'I'm very glad to make room for someone else, as someone made room for me.' In a sense I also have, alongside this sense of the unforgivable nature of death, a sense of the perfectly good order which it imposes. Alongside resentment there's also a sense that it is rather beautiful in itself. I feel this very strongly about having grandchildren; when I had my first grandchild my thought was, this is the nicest possible way of beginning to die.

I'm sure that willingness to let go is possible, a perfectly serene acceptance – I'm sure that it's possible. And I think in my own case that the existence of children and grandchildren will make the possibility of accepting death infinitely greater. The satisfaction of leaving behind parts of yourself, other existences for which you're responsible, will be balanced by a regret that you won't see what will remain of them. But I still think if one tried to imagine much longer, to be in a position where one would accept having to go with a sense of satisfaction, the existence of children and grandchildren I must say would play a part in that. I do much admire the Buddhist's belief that you should teach yourself to have a proper view of the unimportance, or lessening importance, of individual satisfactions, to be less excited about them. It's a very proper view that it would be extremely sensible, in a world in which everything dies and decays, to accept, bit by bit, the decay of yourself and your personal experience. Oh yes, yes. I wish I were capable of that. I'm not sure that I am.

It would be absurd to be over-simple about it; because I can see that in fact you could still hang on to things and have your pleasure in them, as it were, alongside a feeling, a very proper feeling, that it's a dying thing. A graceful acceptance of the fact that every moment of pleasure contains within itself its own death, and so on. I'm not sure that it might not be something that you learned as you got very old. I suppose if I had to think of a desirable state of mind for myself as I get older it would be something I'll probably never attain – that is, to feel at one and the same time pleasure in being alive combined with readiness to go. I suspect that some people may come pretty close to it. How they achieve it, I'm not sure.

The more I talk about it, the more I see that I have in myself what is probably quite a characteristic muddle – a strong objection to death, a completely irrational sense of awe in the face of it, an experience once or twice of its great beauty, which has made it possible to understand almost all the mysterious and mystical ways it's been described in, together with an everyday sense of abhorrence.

I remember interviewing a nice young novelist called E. M. Lamming, who'd written a novel about an old man which I liked very much. And she said, 'When I was young I always wondered why the old were not running around in a panic.' And I said to her, 'That's what the old wonder too'! Why am I not running around in a panic? Now that the *Guardian* has this rather pretentious obituaries page I've become very much aware that my own age-group is in the frontline, and I do have this feeling of satisfaction that at least they're not taking us alphabetically!

When you're older, certainly your expectations have been reduced ... There have always been teenage suicides. Well, what kills young teenagers ... Adolescence is the period when you have the most magnificent ideas about the potentiality of living creatures, together with an extraordinary sense of your own littleness and foolishness and confusedness and unimportance. And if you're a writer – for example, I look back at the notebooks I wrote at that time, and it's really quite good writing, but it's full of a sense of rage and impotence, because I didn't know anything. At that time you've no idea what to do with experience. But I can't remember a time when I wasn't excited and thrilled by words. That's how it began – the thrilling business of putting words together, and that was always associated with the sense of being able to re-create life. It is the signal that you are alive. It is the most splendid thing you can do to show you're alive.

There are people – back to Boswell, for instance – whose appetite for life is so intense ... I think of Proust, because Boswell's feeling about life was almost as though it was something to eat, and actually as you know the major image of Proust's is the madeleine; it all begins with this sense of something delicious to eat. And I think that sense of life as something to consume ... I mean, writing, or any art, I suppose, is not only a re-creation of life, giving a bit back, but it's also a consuming of it. Sometimes over-having it. I remember saying to a novelist friend of mine, I remember us both agreeing in a rather sad and surprised way that one way of looking back over what we'd written was with regret – because in a way we had taken our lives and used them and laid them waste. The dissatisfaction that the writer has is that it never has the immediacy, the thrill . . . I look back to my own childhood as I described it in one of my books, and I see that in a sense I replaced it with the book. What any artist does, I suspect, is to replace the experience of life with some artefact. I don't see it only as a re-creation.

Re-creating death – yes, I think it can be done, I think Beckett does it. 'The dwindling of the words' . . . Oh, he's a heroic figure, I think. He *is* terribly frightening. But again, in certain circumstances extreme difficulties actually feed a writing gift. You know, he had this curious relationship with his mother – when he went home to Ireland and was with his mother, he used to go to bed and draw the blankets up over himself, and never come out. He was reducing himself . . . Death to him is a dark, black womb, isn't it, a return. But then again . . . Part of what people must quite commonly feel about death is that there's a relationship between the beginning and the end, that one is the experience of coming out of a kind of darkness into life, and the other is going out of life into a kind of darkness. I do think it's true that Beckett's deaths are always terribly like births.

I think birth experience can affect feelings about death, I think it's very possible. I have a nightmare, which I've had most of my life – it takes one of various forms. A characteristic form is that I'm buried in the earth, and everybody I've ever known is buried in the earth, but all at intervals from each other. It's a sense of being in a deep burial of darkness and entombment, and of everything which we do that is life immediately turning into death. And when I wake up I have this dreadful sense that – in fact it is true – the death of life occurs at every moment of life, that the moment of one moment ago is already a form of death. I do feel that this dream is related in some way to a memory of birth.

Actually this nightmare is so terrible that when I wake up, even if I come down here and put the light on, it's no better, the sense of silence and separation is so deep and dark. I sit – I read if I possibly can – until the feeling has gone. But it's an actual feeling so plausible, so oppressive, so strong, so clear, of it being possible to see that life dies at every second. Very often it starts by my thinking, probably the evening before, of someone I haven't seen for ages – sometimes dead, more often alive but out of touch with my life. It has the sense that in fact the persons we used to be are dead anyway. That the past is a great grave. It doesn't allow any consolation.

But as we talk I realize that almost everything I say about my feelings about death has two sides – a perfect sunless case, and a perfect sunlit case. My father, for instance . . . I think quite a lot about him – he was a powerful man and very difficult to forget – and I do have a sense of my father *in* me, a very strong sense. Physically, as I get older I look more like him, and sometimes I even hear myself speaking in his tones. This feeling of being inhabited by the ancestor . . . Though I have absolutely no rational conception of a continuing life, immortality, survival, and so on, nevertheless I cannot regard my father as an extinct person. I think he remains – this is as far as I can rationalize it – that he couldn't really cease to exist while I remember him. He may even wish that I didn't remember him; I'm talking in terms that I don't quite adhere to, but . . . Actually, I think there is some anxiety in all of us to be remembered.

There are two graves I often go and visit in our local graveyard, merely because they're literary graves. One of them's the grave of Anthony Trollope's sister – the Trollopes lived up at Hadley Green – and Anthony's sister died when she was about eighteen. She's buried in the corner of the churchyard. And I go there because I very distinctly have a feeling that nobody else bothers about her. I feel I have a duty. D. J. Enright said one of the nicest things anybody's ever said about me in a review, that I'm a very good obituarist of ordinary people. I have this strong feeling . . . Especially about people who would otherwise not be remembered, like old teachers of mine; I have this strong feeling that there's something quite dreadful about people going and nobody ever, ever, making any comment on their existences. So I suppose I do have a mysterious sense that in fact there is a kind of duty involved, there is a duty to preserve, there is a duty to remember. Round the corner, not far from Miss Trollope, there is William Makepeace Thackeray – not the author, but his grandfather. And I go round for the sake of his grandson, you see!

When I walk round that churchyard – it's a very old churchyard, a beautiful church – I do have this strong feeling of
sorrow, that here lie people of whom nothing is remembered
any more.

I called my book about my childhood *Sorry, Dad*; after my
father died, whenever I said something that I knew when he was
alive he would have rubbished – 'Total rubbish!' – I would look
up, or down, I would look up and say, 'Sorry, Dad'! And so I
thought, well, let's make a book about my childhood and my
relationship with my father and make that the title. What I missed
as much as anything – I mean, I didn't miss it in the sense that I
regretted it, but I missed it because it was no longer there and it
had been there for such a long time: his voice growling at me and
putting me down! So I think I do have this sense of him . . . I
have this ridiculous joke that I know when I get to the other side
he'll be standing there with all my books under his arm and
looking frightfully angry!

My mother – oh, I loved my mother enormously, and I think of
her even more. She had no desire to die, you see, Mum was very
opposed to it – she thought it was a foolish thing, totally silly. She
was so amazed by and interested in life, she had no desire whatever . . . She was probably the only thing that made it possible to
live with my father. She loved my father, you see, very much; and
at the same time she deplored him. After his death she spoke in a
double language, without any sense of the contradictoriness of it;
she spoke a language of tremendous and genuine grief, and a
language of tremendous and genuine relief. The two things went
side by side.

When he was dead she asked my sister how he would be, now
that he was dead and in his coffin, what he would be wearing; my
poor sister was somewhat thrown by this question, and gave
some sort of answer. And my mother said, 'Well, as long as he's
comfortable.' And it seemed to me one of the most extraordinary
things I ever heard anybody say. But she meant it absolutely. For
over fifty years his comfort had been her absolutely prime con-
sideration – and even, grotesquely, in his coffin. I think one of
her greatest griefs was that at this vital moment when she should
really have been in charge of his clothes, should have been

responsible for everything he wore and so on, that she was not, that she was displaced. I think that hurt her as much as anything.

I hope to go out, as it were, vanishing into a kind of Charles Chaplin iris. The iris was the term for the camera shot, you know. At the end of a silent film you would see the tramp, you would see Charlie Chaplin walking ... I had this very strong feeling when I watched silent films as a child – I was always at the cinema. The final shot dwindling to that little iris and then vanishing. Charlie Chaplin walking along the road, and the camera eye would begin to close in; walking away, down a road, twirling his stick, getting smaller and smaller. And then slowly it would go absolutely dark.

# PETER

Gay people tended to hear about AIDS sooner – it was about four years ago, I think, that the first information came, and I remember having a discussion with some straight people and looking at an article which merely pooh-poohed it and said it was just a small incident. Straight people were completely uninterested in it, but I'd been aware of discussions and the fact that in America it was serious and that people were dying. At that point, before the various types of medication had come into use, people died a lot quicker. I knew through friends of friends about people who would come down with pneumonia and die a couple of weeks later, as opposed to now when it can be held off for longer. I don't know whether that's better or not. The man I've been looking after had a lot of radiotherapy and chemotherapy – it was his decision. There was a lot of thinking along the lines of 'Why is he doing it?' – I thought that often, and a lot of other people thought it. 'Why bother, why keep going?' But unless you're actually the patient there's absolutely no way ... You can't judge, or make anybody's decisions for them.

People then thought that it was specifically the problem of very, very promiscuous people, or they didn't believe it, or it was an American thing. I'd been sort of aware that you can have sex with people in this country, but don't have it in America, which now seems ridiculous. That's how I felt – the attitude that it was something that was happening over there. The reason that I got involved working with the London Lighthouse in the first place was that I'd been relatively promiscuous over the years – not so much recently; and I was consistently having kitchen conversations with a lot of friends of mine who were all HIV positive. And I had this increasing awareness of what would happen if all my friends died and I was still alive – what would that mean?

I'd actually got quite sick, through being overworked, and I went into a panic and I had some allergy attacks and I thought, oh, my God, I'm dying. And I went and got tested and they said I was negative. I felt guilty that I wasn't sick, wasn't positive. The thing about the HIV test is that now I know in retrospect that nobody should really be tested unless they're actually genuinely ill, because it's like carrying a time bomb around with you and it radically affects your life. The doctors don't really know ... That's what's scary. A lot of the people who might be dying now might have picked up the virus six or seven years ago, so there's lots of people who look very fine and healthy now who might die in ten years, whatever. Just the don't-know factor is devastating.

My initial reaction was that I had to do something about this. And I heard about the Lighthouse very vaguely – they had this volunteer training programme for community help. It's a group of people who say AIDS is a challenge, and it's also in many ways a gift for the gay community and the public at large. What can happen is that people who are sick, who may be HIV positive, who aren't in immediate danger of dying, have to take control of their lives. They have to re-establish what's good and what's bad in their lives. The disease is immuno-suppressive, which means that every aspect of your life which is in any way endangering your immune system is relevant – drinking, smoking, your personal relationships, relationships with your family; the way – specifically for gay people – the way in every day of your life you're oppressed in one way or another. All these things and issues, however small or however big. Instead of ignoring AIDS, you say, 'Well, I have a potentially fatal disease, what can I do in my life that I've never done before that can make it right now?'

But what the Lighthouse is saying also, which is why I've become so completely involved in it, is, why bother to wait until you've got a potentially fatal disease to do all these things? Everybody involved around the issue – the doctors, the nurses, the social workers, families, friends – one way or another they can actually question what's good, what's bad, what they can do in their lives to make it what it always should have been.

I've had a history of drug abuse and drinking and casual sex and endless relationships that don't particularly go anywhere; and

I ran a business and earned a lot of money and partied a lot and flew around – and I was very, very unhappy. I'm not unhappy now, my life's completely changed. I *was* unhappy when Andrew died – the man I've been looking after – but the overall feeling I've had since he's gone is that my life's never been better, because I've had this incredible experience.

I have very, very good friends, instead of having transitory relationships with people whom you've known for years but don't really get very close to, lots of very, very close friends. I've managed to re-establish what was really good in the relationships, and it's actually been very easy for me, I'm very committed to it. The friends who've known me for a long time, from what I was to what I am now, can see I'm a more capable and caring person, because I've managed to deal with a whole load of upsets that have been troubling me all my life. It's not something I'm going to go out and preach to someone else, though.

You can take all the tragedy and all that's terrible about the disease and use it to make you live better. I'm much closer to my parents. The man I've been looking after, he had this extraordinary relationship with his mother. There are gay men who don't tell their parents they're gay until they've developed the disease and they might be dying. The Lighthouse does workshops, for instance, and on numerous occasions mums go with their children to the workshops, parents go with their children, and see them operating in an environment with predominantly gay people, maybe, and women, and social workers and doctors, and everyone's loving and kind. And all of a sudden all the fears and horrors that the parents have had about, you know, 'My son's gay, therefore he must be promiscuous, therefore he's degenerate' – all this stuff is dispelled, and they can come to terms with it. It doesn't just have to stop at people with AIDS, it can get bigger and bigger – the knock-on effect is wonderful. You have some committed people who make a major effort to do what they can themselves, without preaching or being too grand about it, and the knock-on effect into society could be huge. It might not be a huge movement in six months or a year, but just to present a sort of loving community out of a disaster, which it is, is a contradiction for everybody.

There's no doubt, gay people are being prejudiced against every day. You're a woman and you know that in one way or another women are being prejudiced against all the time, black people are being prejudiced against every day of their lives, without question. It's just a fact. I know two gay men who died in New York, both of whom weren't promiscuous, who caught it probably from their lovers being promiscuous, but the initial reaction is, 'Oh, they've been promiscuous, they deserved to die.' It's just dreadful, it shouldn't happen; there should be no blame, no guilt. And it's very important that everybody does a lot of work on themselves and their own prejudices, and what's happened to them, and how they've been hurt, so that people are more open and honest. You don't blame people for this kind of thing.

What's important to remember, for the gay community specifically – and other communities as well, but it's my group of people so I'm very aware of it – is that it's an immuno-suppressive disease, and if you don't treat yourself well you'll die quicker. So if you're conditioned to think of yourself as worthless – which is what a lot of gay people feel, which is why there's so much drug-taking and so much alcoholism and so much sexual abuse going on in the gay community, you know, 'Oh, my God, I'm worthless, I deserve to die' – that will kill people off. It's quite obvious from what I've seen with a lot of people who have the virus that when they do a lot of work on themselves and their own pride and their own worth, and deal with issues that have been flung at us as long as we can remember – because most gay people know they're gay from very, very early on, and they've had to walk around suppressing and hiding and cheating – well, if you can chuck off those issues, you live longer.

There's a lot of work done with counselling at the Lighthouse to enable people to re-establish their worth and who they are and what they want and what they need, and to make plans for themselves and treat themselves better. What happened when I first got involved with this, what I realized was that if I'm going to do this work, which I want to do and would be beneficial to other people, then the better I felt about myself, the more beneficial I could be to other people. And the initial reaction was to be very evangelical about it; but what you realize after a bit is that, with this genuine feeling of well-being and worth and that the abuse and oppression can cease, you can't actually preach it, but you can model it. So I found myself getting much quieter about it, and the anger I feel sometimes with people who don't listen . . . You just have to accept what you can do, think about what you can do, and try and model the principles in your everyday life.

I knew I was gay by about thirteen. I've got a gay brother, an older brother, who told my parents when he was twenty-one, and I sort of managed to avoid the issue until a few years ago. Half out of cowardice and half out of attempting to protect my parents' feelings, that they've got three sons and two of them are gay. My initial reaction with my parents when I started doing this work – well, I realized that any kind of feelings they may have about me being gay or working with people with AIDS or anything like that is their problem; it shouldn't be my problem, I shouldn't have to carry it around with me all the time. And all the protecting I've done of their feelings had actually made me more and more miserable and more and more incapable of dealing with my own feelings. The more honest I've become over the last months, the better their relationship is with me, and the more truth that's spoken, instead of half-truths and semi-lies, the better it gets. It's just terribly important that I keep doing the work, so I don't lie to people and I tell the truth and present myself for what I am.

I worked in London in the art world and the design world for about ten years. So far as my friends were concerned I didn't have to pretend not to be gay. Well, I'm not earning a living now, I'm hardly living off anything. I hope at some point to re-establish some kind of proper salary. What happened was that I was doing some volunteer work in the Lighthouse offices, and doing volunteer training and counselling courses, and I got to know this man Andrew, who was quite ill at the time, and they thought he was going to be ill for about a month, and I agreed to be involved full-time with him.

If I hadn't had the counselling facility available to me, I don't know what would have happened to me. I can be with the person who's sick, and sometimes take a lot of abuse, and sometimes take a lot of sorrow, a lot of crying, and not dump it back on him. Because the sick person doesn't want to hear my feelings or see my reactions, but instead of bottling all that up for month after month after month, there are always people that you can counsel with. You can say, 'I've just had a bad day, I've just had a deeply distressing experience. Something that Andrew said has really upset me', and sit down and be listened to for fifteen minutes or half an hour. I'd phone somebody up in the evening and say, 'You've just got to listen to me for five minutes' – it's like having a release valve all the time, which is why we can do it.

What I've come to know is that the closer I got to Andrew . . . It happens in all relationships, but this was a slightly strange set-up; the closer you get to somebody, often the more abusive they can be to you, because what happens is that you've created a certain amount of safety. I actually spent probably more time with him in the last six months than anybody else he knew. He'd be with me all day maybe, and a friend would come over in the evening; he could vent all his anger and whatever he was feeling, his frustration, on me during the day, and then when the friend arrived in the evening it was all smiles. And what I learned from the counselling was that the abuse that was coming at me, or any kind of anger or frustration or whatever it was, had nothing to do with me whatsoever.

It was all stuff that . . . For instance, if I'd sometimes run up the stairs, he'd get upset, because he couldn't run up the stairs. But it was quite good for him to get upset to see me running up the stairs, because actually . . . Instead of pretending that everything was fine and all right a lot of the time, he actually had to sit and think about 'What's happening to me?' and 'I'm dying', and come to terms with some of those things. I'm not saying that, you know, people should be bullied and bludgeoned with the truth, but there were lots of occasions when it was very important for him to realize that he was a dying man, and what it meant, and to cry and let go. A friend of mine went to see a doctor the other day, and the tests weren't very good, and tears started coming up in the office; and the doctor said, 'Take a deep breath, take a deep breath', and he did, he automatically took a deep breath and stopped from crying. And he went out of the office and thought, you bastard, I was actually going to let out a little bit of emotion, make myself feel a little bit better. Children do it, little babies do it – they get hurt, they cry, the hurt goes away and then they're healed again.

Andrew had been diagnosed about a year before, but he'd got seriously ill a couple of months previously. His father was dead, his mother was a bit freaked out, his brother wasn't particularly involved – he'd sort of handed himself over to the Lighthouse community rather than his family. Which is very normal for gay people, it's very common for them to adopt their families rather than go back to their own. It depends on the individual – I mean, I know what would happen if I was ill, my family would be there in a minute, they'd all be standing round me all the time. In the last few months his mother got very, very close, and was around a lot. Somebody was going to have to be around Andrew most of the day, all the time, and I took it on. The deal was that I'd be responsible for his needs during the day, week-times, and some-body else would deal with the evenings and weekends.

People with AIDS tend to go in and out of hospital; they get bad and need blood transfusions, they might need various kinds of therapy, radiotherapy, chemotherapy. Often pneumonia is quite common, which can either kill you or just hospitalize you for a week. It affects all aspects of people's health; there are some people who get dementia, which means that although they don't really need to be hospitalized they can't look after themselves, and there's also . . . You know, people might have chronic diar-rhoea, or might fall over a lot, or it can be any kind of combination of dozens of different aspects. What can happen is people staying at home who are lonely, and dying, their friends are frightened; but they might think, I don't want any of those born-again people preaching at me. But all that we've been taught to do is to sit with people and be with people without dumping our rubbish on them. In hospital they don't have the same kind of care, and also we're all geared up to thinking that people are going to die and that that's OK. In hospitals doctors and nurses are geared up to people getting better.

The wonderful thing I had with Andrew is that he died at

home surrounded by me, and his friends, and his family. The reason I got involved is that we organize a home support system, which is all over London – people are split up into groups of carers, and the idea is that bit by bit we take on more and more clients, in varying stages. It might just require a trip to the hospital, or to sit with them when they get some results so that they're not on their own – it's predominantly to break isolation, to stop people from being on their own. With Andrew it was one to one because I'd got to know him, and he was living nearby, and it just became apparent that somebody really had to be about during the day.

Initially we thought he was only going to be alive for about a month at this point, then he got a bit better; he died about four weeks ago, so it would have been six months. He could get out, and sometimes we went into the country, and one week he needed to go to hospital every day, so, you know, it just varied from week to week. A lot of the time it involved literally doing nothing, which is what I think most people find hard. And sometimes he'd cry, and I had to be there. Sometimes he'd talk and I had to be there. And sometimes he just wanted to go to Marks and Spencer's – he was badly marked on his face so, you know, he didn't want to be out on his own.

He was in his late thirties. He varied from being completely accepting to furious, absolutely furious. Most of the time he was very furious, very angry. He was very beautiful, had a very good career. The main advantage that *I* got out of it was that I was spending all this time with a man who was terminally ill; he was coming to terms with all the things that had been right and wrong in his life, and what was good about relationships and what was bad, and what could be achieved and what couldn't be achieved. And I watched him struggling quite horrifically with a lot of moral dilemmas that came up every day. I resolved, the more time I spent with him, to make absolutely sure that all this stuff that was coming out from him was going to be dealt with by me in my life. People kept on saying, 'Isn't it depressing, isn't it horrific?' and 'How can you deal with it?' My attitude was that this was just the best opportunity I've ever had.

A lot of the time he was quite vicious and sort of cutting, not very nice, which initially I thought was to do with the disease, then I worked out that actually quite a lot of it was to do with what he was like before he was ill. But working on the principle that everybody is basically a nice person and that if they're vicious and cutting there's a reason for it, that that was part of the way he'd been hurt when he was younger and little, then I didn't have to say, 'Well, I'll put up with this because he's sick and I won't put up with that because that's what he's like.' You have to accept the whole thing. Oh yes, I used to spit vitriol, but I'd go and do it at the counselling sessions, you see; I could say, 'That fucking bastard', you know.

In the last month I nearly gave up. He was getting more and more difficult and more and more frustrated. And the more bedridden he got, and the more going up and down stairs became a complete nightmare, and the more isolated he was getting and angry he was getting, the harder it got for me. And we used to have fights. And then what I learned was, 'I'm not going to take all this abuse, I'm going to fight back, and it's his decision to deal with it, because he requires my support and he has to come to terms with the fact that he requires my support.' But at the same time I knew all along what he was going through and how difficult it was. But it got really confusing for me, because I thought, well, this is actually what I've decided to do, and I want to be of help, and I want to be of assistance, but at what level am I taking care of him and at what level am I allowing myself to be abused? I was actually getting terribly upset. But I know, for instance, that he'd have a bad day with me and then tell his mum how much he appreciated what I was doing – but not tell *me* about it.

He stopped seeing a lot of people. He actually got more isolated towards the end. He didn't look good – black marks over his face. He saw fewer and fewer people. But I was lucky from the point of view that he'd done some counselling, got rid of, you know, 'It's my own fault', and all that business. The actual nursing is quite minimal as far as that's concerned, because he wasn't taking any medication – just yanking him in and out of bed and dressing him and all that sort of thing. He went to hospital for radiotherapy for a while. But there weren't a lot of things to do apart from day to day just being there. I know that what happened with a lot of volunteers was that they'd come in and tell jokes and be terribly busy and make dinner and 'Let me make the bed and clean the bath' and all that sort of stuff – but a lot of people had terrible trouble just sitting down and not saying anything for hours!

What he liked was just, if he was watching television, he liked not to be alone; and sometimes he'd cry, I'd hold him, hold his hand. Sometimes he'd get angry because I didn't react, and sometimes he'd be pleased because I didn't react. Sometimes he'd cry in order to get somebody else going, and then he could stop! It was a very stable relationship, but it got sort of iffy quite a lot of the time. The last month . . .

What happened is that we had a bad week before he died – he'd really been rather bitchy. And I actually had the Friday off for some reason on a day he had to go to the hospital; I said, 'I'm having the day off, doing something else.' When I went in on Monday we barely spoke all day. And on the Tuesday something just shifted completely. He'd had this conversation with his sister-in-law about Christmas, which completely freaked him out; I think he didn't know whether he'd live till Christmas. I wasn't really entirely sure what the conversation was about, but there was definitely a sort of element of despair. And he burst into tears, and that day we re-established the relationship that had gone a bit wonky over the previous months. He cried a lot, and he fell asleep – it was a good thing, it changed, all that day.

On the Wednesday when I went in he was quite clearly seriously ill, much more so than he had been. He was taking a lot of morphine because of the pain – the Kaposi's, the skin cancer, it goes right through you as well. There was this constant pain, and he was very thin, and he wasn't eating, couldn't swallow much. The moving was very hard, he was very weak. I don't understand the entire medical thing, but various other organs started packing up towards the end. He was going vague, the morphine made him a bit doolally all the time. I tried giving him a bath, and it was really a nightmare, really hard. And I was aware, I think, on the Thursday . . . I hadn't actually admitted it to myself, but it became completely apparent to me, not knowing anything about it and not having seen it before, that he was dying. His mum was staying there, and I would leave in the evening and she'd take over, or somebody else, and I think they called the doctor.

On Thursday he just deteriorated quite terribly, and on Friday it was obvious that he was going to die any minute. He was sort of very hazy, couldn't remember things, and he was hearing banging sounds. And I didn't really . . . I don't think I really felt anything! I was shutting down. Until the Friday evening. He died about five o'clock in the morning, Saturday morning. There was me, and close friends of his, and the nurse, and his mother. I don't know how much he knew what was going on at that point, I think he was definitely aware that there were people about, but he wasn't communicating really from Thursday onwards. There was definitely an atmosphere in the house that he wasn't alone, and he was dying surrounded by people who loved him, who were constantly there.

The weirdest thing, that I haven't really quite come to terms with yet, is that . . . I all of a sudden realized about nine o'clock on Friday evening that the guy was going to die, and I got really upset and started crying quite a lot; but I kept on thinking to myself, well, if I'd met this person before he got sick I'd never have become friends with him, so what's my role here? But it was quite clear that we got very, very, very close to each other; and what kept me going was the feeling of what I'd achieved over the six months and the amount of effort and time I'd put in. Yes, there was relief – oh, there'd often been occasions when I thought, my God, this has got to finish soon, I can't stand this.

It wasn't sad that he was dying – he died completely surrounded by people who totally adored him and who gave him the best possible death he could possibly have, in his own home. It was the first time I'd been with anybody who was dying or dead; the overall feeling afterwards was one of joy, really, it was like: death is *not* frightening, it doesn't need to be horrific, it doesn't need to be cold and hideous. And after he died, the laying out, which I'd never done before – it just wasn't horrid, all the myth of the fear and disgustingness just wasn't there. And you think, well, you know, I've been misinformed.

You know, everybody has this horror around death . . . You

see, the fear of a lot of gay people – it's a society which is very much geared up to what's beautiful and youth and health, and keeping all that is what makes life worth while – it's not the fear of death, it's the fear of losing everything in that way, that's what's horrific about it. It was awful, a lot of it was terribly sad and really dreadful. But I really felt, when it was over, I had just been on this most extraordinary . . . I've been given the privilege of this extraordinary experience, and seen it right through from the early stages to the finish; and I'll do it again, and I've learned so much. It's changed me for the better to such an extent that I can't even begin to describe it, and the people around me have seen me change. And what I did was consummately worth while. My mum said something quite funny the other day, she said, 'I don't want you becoming one of those old men that are obsessed by death' – I'd talked about it quite a lot to her. I said, 'No, the fact of the matter is, I have a greater sense of self-worth now, this week in my life, than from anything I've ever done.' And her reaction was, 'Oh, it's all very well, but . . . You can say that to me and your dad and maybe a few other people, but you shouldn't go around saying that in public'! And I was thinking, this is just completely insane, I mean, you get an experience and you actually genuinely feel this, after years of putting yourself down . . . Being gay, you know, means you're worthless; you can exist in this society, but behave yourself.

I don't have any fear of AIDS myself. The fact of the matter is that apparently about five per cent of the people who test HIV negative actually have the virus anyway. And there's the possibility I might have the virus, I might not have the virus. I have a relationship with somebody. I might get sick, I might not. The virus is very hard to catch, it's not like hepatitis or anything. No, the subject of sex didn't come up with Andrew, perhaps it was mentioned once in the entire time. After all, it doesn't, I think, under those circumstances. I'd do it all again, oh yes – but not this week! I've been doing office work for them for the last few weeks – there's a rota. What I've learned is that when you earn money, and you're on the roller-coaster, and earning more and more to keep going, it's very hard to get off. And I got off, and it was very bumpy to start with – I got very worried and very scared and didn't know how to deal with it – but now as long as I can eat, and I'm warm, it's actually all that I want.

The week after his funeral – it was a very good funeral, about two hundred people there – a week after that I felt really odd, because my routine had just got completely shattered and there was nothing to do. After he'd died I'd said to someone, 'God, it's such a relief really, isn't it?' And he said, 'Yes. And then . . . And then . . . And then . . .' So it sort of comes in waves. But I really don't need to bash myself over the head or feel guilty about not doing much for a month. It can be worked out – I might have to move, or get a smaller place, or whatever.

If you think about it, basically it means that every day you clear up all the issues that might be disturbing you; so you don't have to all of a sudden start throwing all of this rubbish on to someone, saying, 'Oh, just before you die, I want you to know this, this, this . . .' And you do it with your friends, and everybody around you. For instance, I've got a friend who died in a car crash three years ago, who I hadn't really grieved over – he was living in America and got killed without my having spoken to him for about three or four months. I didn't really feel anything for a long time; and since Andrew's died I think about him constantly. There were so many things that I hadn't finished, and hadn't said, and I just never want that to happen again with anybody I know. Without beating myself over the head about it, I would seriously make a conscious effort to say all the things to all the people that I know *when* they happen, or to clear up all the bad feeling. Sometimes it doesn't always work, but . . .

The great fear of death is usually the fact that you haven't lived your life properly. Right up to about a year ago, when I was particularly unhappy and living in a not very good way, if I'd had to die I'd have felt, what a waste of life. This year I don't feel that. The feeling would be that if I got run over, or whatever happened, it would be much easier for me to die, I'd know how to die. There'd be fear and stuff coming up all the time, but I wouldn't have that thing of, 'Oh, my God, I should have done this' or 'I've always wanted to do that.' And I just feel like the whole of 1987 has been like a foundation-stone to what's going to happen for the rest of my life.

# Dr Roy Porter

I've been looking at the letters and diaries and journals and wills and remains of people in Britain from about the
mid-seventeenth century to about the mid-nineteenth, attempting
to see how they coped with being sick, having diseases, trying to
become cured, to heal themselves, to cope with doctors – and
then finally to come to terms with dying. To some extent it's a
culture which is very death and decay oriented, because of the
sheer fact that life expectancy is low, that medicine can't actually
do very much to cure many people most of the time – individual
people's experience might be of being in pain a great deal of their
lives, or of suddenly losing their nearest and dearest ones because
of a terrible epidemic.

It's really within our own lifetime that the enormous transform-
ation has taken place, and that applies to the liability to get
serious diseases, their seriousness, and above all to the way in
which one copes with death all round. My father, for instance,
had rheumatic fever when he was fourteen and spent a year and
a half in bed; nowadays if you get rheumatic fever it's nothing.
Over the period I'm talking about I don't think there's a vast
amount of change, medically. What one has in regard to people's
confrontations with disease and death is more a variety of possible
reactions – in 1600, in 1700, in 1800. Sterilization – yes, that helps
if you're having a surgical operation on an operating table, sure;
but in terms of the likelihood of you dying of measles as a two-
year-old in 1920 as opposed to in 1820, it doesn't really make much
difference. It's quite recently that there's a real decline in people's
liability to die of terrible epidemic diseases.

The plague of Pepys's time was the last plague and it was the
most horrific epidemic disease for a couple of centuries, in the
sense that it killed off more people more quickly, more certainly,
and more gruesomely than any disease in the eighteenth century.

People were dying like flies. And through the eighteenth century people are dying in comparable numbers, of measles and influenza and diphtheria, but it's not really until cholera comes along that you get as gruesome a death as death from plague. Cholera is a horrible way to go – it's equally fast and you really do disintegrate within twenty-four or forty-eight hours from catching it to dying. It strikes Europe between about the 1830s and 1880s. What happens roughly is that it's endemic in India and as a result of imperialism, to use a shorthand, there's so much trade and traffic between India and Europe that it actually gets here for the first time. Public health measures then overcome it. But the reaction to cholera is much the same sort of reaction as to plague – the prophecies of doom, the sense that this is God's punishment for a wicked society, the sense that it's the conspiracy of one group in society against another, you know – the rich trying to kill off the poor, or the dirty poor infecting the rich.

The plague is worse among the poor, not least because it's the rich who can flee; if you were a rich Londoner you got out pretty niftily, and the poor basically had to stay behind. And it's roughly like that with cholera as well – it's more likely to be the poor who drink infected water, who can't boil their water up and so on. But don't forget, Prince Albert dies of typhoid; and so in some sense death and disease are the great levellers in the nineteenth century.

With the plague, you might well get half the people in a street dying within a week – the visible impact is enormous. The basic religious explanation that you get in England is that this is providential, that there are hidden meanings to it which we can't necessarily understand; it's all part of some sort of divine test that's going on, God's way of seeing how Christian people will respond to adversity. Therefore it's important that people should be generous to sufferers – yes, the world as moral gymnasium. That was very powerful. There was a minority view amongst Christians that because the plague and so on were God's judgements, it was therefore not proper to seek medical aid, because in some sense that would be contrary to the will of God. And, you know, that's the theory that remains very powerful in Islam, this sense that it is actually God picking out individual people, and that's why public health measures never got anywhere in the

East. Christ healed people, yes, and that's what most Christians said, but there were small sects ... For instance, this comes out very nicely in the eighteenth century when you get small-pox inoculation coming along; basically, most Anglicans and most Protestant dissenters say, 'Great – God helps those who help themselves', but you do get old Calvinist preachers or Presbyterians who will not have inoculations going on in their parishes.

During the plague you get a certain sort of powerful altruistic social response among some groups of people; people do stay behind, and other groups flee and are like the rats abandoning a sinking ship. Most of the wealthy physicians in London flee – they rationalize fleeing from London on the grounds that their rich patients have already fled and they have to serve these patients. But you do find a substantial number of doctors and clergymen and aldermen staying; and there are wise women, helpers, nurses, midwives ... I think they have a primitive notion of their own invulnerability, in a way; you know, they've been exposed to it for so long that they just stick it out. And some of them survived and some of them died.

They thought at the time that it was probably airborne but that by following certain precautions, like covering yourself with vinegar, you could ward it off. We know now it's passed by flea-bites and suchlike, but they didn't know that at the time, nobody understood the role of the flea in passing it on. Even rich people did have fleas, you know, there's plenty of evidence of rich people with lousy clothes and hair and all the rest of it at this time. Just look at all the reports of travellers going to inns in the eighteenth century; couldn't sleep because of the bugs in the bed, et cetera. It's a dirty society by our standards.

It was a disease that spread mighty quickly and which killed mighty quickly as well. I mean, if you became tubercular you probably knew you'd got five or ten years, at least you had time to sort your life out, whereas you could catch the plague at breakfast and be dead by dinner-time. In a Catholic society it's crucially important that you should have the sacraments. But in a Protestant society there is a very strong sense that that is mere superstition and that so long as your spirit is right it doesn't really matter whether you have a priest there or not. So far as I'm aware – and it's a very difficult subject to do proper historical research on – I don't think it was the rule for people to attempt to have a priest by them when they were dying; it was much more important to people that their family should be surrounding them than that they should actually have a clergyman in. In all the documents I've come across which actually picture historical deathbed scenes in England in the eighteenth and nineteenth centuries in particular, the clergyman is not an essential part.

It is an important, a very important difference historically, because it makes it a great deal easier for death to become secularized within Protestant culture, in the sense that there is nothing special of a religious nature for the priest to be doing at the deathbed. It seems to me that there's a sort of model of the good death which you get among English Protestants of the time – Addison, for instance, asking people to come and see how well a Christian can die. What he's doing is *he*'s putting on the show; it's not 'See how I submit to my clergyman', it's 'See how I die in peace.' It's a good example of the tranquil death. Just before Addison, in a more dissenting culture, then it's not the tranquillity of death that counts, but a sense of encountering death, struggling, triumphing over fear. You triumph over the *world* – you actually exit from it with confidence that you are going to be saved, that you're about to meet your Maker, and with a certain sort of joy.

Roughly speaking, I think that what was normal in the seventeenth century, shall we say, is that people died in this way, died conscious; and then what happens during the eighteenth and nineteenth centuries is the invention of the sedative. Opium becomes available in large quantities from the early eighteenth century onwards, and you can show that doctors increasingly are administering large doses of opium and similar mixtures, in order that people should pass away, as it were, into a sleep. And this becomes the norm of an easy death. When you come across the word 'euthanasia' in the eighteenth and nineteenth centuries, it's the idea of an easy death – doctors can induce unconsciousness so that the death should actually be painless. And this becomes a fashionable way for many people to die in the early eighteenth and nineteenth centuries.

Before, it was a question of this act of dying bravely, as a way of coping with the pain and the fear. Well into the seventeenth and eighteenth centuries you get it in English books that tell you how to die – there's Jeremy Taylor, *Holy Living and Holy Dying*, and there are quite a lot of tracts being issued to people on how to die the good death. But it seems to me that increasingly, in a fashionable society at least, the performance and palaver, the public spectacle of being a dying person, making it right with one's Maker, making it up with one's family, give way to a much more private notion of just being quiet and peaceful and, as it were, slipping away to nothingness. That's present from probably about the middle of the eighteenth century onwards. The family would be present, of course, but it was no longer meant to be quite a public occasion, where all the neighbours came, and there was food and drink and in some sense a sort of show.

The idea of death as a challenge, to see how well you can deal with it – I do believe, sociologically and psychologically, it's the thing to do. Roughly speaking, you can say that in the seventeenth and much of the eighteenth century it's the done thing, with the dying, to tell them they're dying and tell them this is everybody's lot and they've got to prepare for it. And then increasingly in the second half of the eighteenth century and through the nineteenth you get more the feeling of euphemism or the feeling of holding back, more the belief that it is actually courteous and comforting to the dying person not to force upon him or her the stark truth of it. Because it's unnecessary pain, you know – bad enough to die without having the assurance that you're going to.

I think eventually the overcoming of a terribly high rate of mortality means that in the end death becomes a less frequent and less familiar event, and so in some sense its terrors get doubled and have to be concealed more. But that doesn't really happen on a large scale until probably about the second half of the nineteenth century. I think one of the reasons for the more private death is that traditional Christianity, the Christianity of the sixteenth and seventeenth centuries, had presented this absolutely stark picture of sinful man, of a jealous God and a powerful Satan, a vision of absolute conflict in which the reward is heaven and the punishment is hell, so in some sense things like physical pain are of very little consequence *sub specie aeternitatis*. Whereas later on you get a much more comforting, rosy vision of religion – you know, Christianity's a nice cosy sort of thing and hell is not real after all – everything gets sentimentalized in a way. You know that Isobel who is dying is going to go to heaven, and so it's sad that she's parting from us – but the Last Judgement, all that has disappeared. People formally believe in them, but they've stopped being present in the way that they were.

There's a sort of sense that God can't be a nasty God who would send most people to hell, and a feeling that what is terrible about death is the grief and the parting and all the rest of it, rather than that somebody's really going to be punished everlastingly. I think, you know, your average educated gentleman or lady in, say, 1780 probably does not believe in a literal hell, whereas his or her great-grandfather certainly had. They're as Christian, but it's a very modified view of what Christianity means. So there's more a feeling of loss of life, and less a fear of what's going to happen afterwards; so people can die sort of tranquillized, and they don't have to demonstrate to their Maker in their last moments their sincerity as truly faithful.

The thing we've got to explain is why we've all become so squeamish about death in the twentieth century, why and how that happened – was it mainly because of medical changes, the development of the terminal ward and all of that, or is it mainly because of the demise of Christianity? I mean, there's a sense in which, you know, nobody had to be ashamed about death – it's not pornographic in an age where religion is true. But if this life is all you've got, then it's somehow unfaceable. So some people obviously say that it's the secularization that has actually made us incapable of coping with death, rather than medical developments. It's appallingly hard to say. There may be a sort of fantasy, as you say, that medicine can keep us all alive, but it's based on the fact that most people succeed in living on much longer than they did. Though the incidence of men dying in their fifties is still quite high; and I think it's accepted that cancer has increased considerably as a disease over the last century.

It's hard to be sure about, because bureaucracy and the medical regulations have taken over, and clearly most people die in hospital. I agree that can be barbaric. I think a lot of people who are terminally ill just find themselves the victims of a bureaucratic system – they don't want to upset the nurses and the doctors and the whole system, because they're all doing their best, and they know best, and all the rest of it. I don't know that it means that everyone's attitude has changed that much – it would interest me to know what ordinary people do feel. We sort of assume that the Victorians were very loquacious about death and that nowadays we're all embarrassed, that death is now the unspeakable thing. It actually may not be true.

There may be doctors who in some sense are actually hiding death from themselves – that would be really worrying. Colluding in an illusion with the sick people and their families, who really do believe that the next machine will keep their loved ones alive, against all hope. Doctors are obviously put in an extraordinarily difficult position in that it seems like a dereliction of their responsibilities if they don't make every effort to keep as many people alive as possible. The level of communicativeness from doctors to patients in this country is very low, too – people who've done surveys of cancer treatment in England have found this – but if you contrast with America you get an opposite picture there. Patients there have actually become very assertive of their rights, and it's been shown that it's the norm rather than the exception for physicians in America to give a full account to their patients of their condition and prognosis – partly because they actually risk being sued if they withhold information. There's certainly more openness on this in America than in England. I know this because every year we teach American students who come across and do a summer school here, and they spend some time in University College Hospital, and they're quite shocked by the incommunicativeness of the doctors and the lack of curiosity among the patients. There is a happy conspiracy of silence in England, whereas the norm in America, they find, is maximizing information. England is a great place of embarrassment; not just death but *everything* is more embarrassing in England than anywhere else.

Yes, they embalm the dead in America, too – I imagine it's a sort of combination of religion and capitalism that makes more of a scene of all these things there. Jeremy Bentham – do you know about him, the great Utilitarian? – insisted on not only being embalmed, but that his corpse should actually be prominently put in a public place. This was in 1832. It actually is on show! His idea was that on the one hand it was a good anti-religious device and it was also a way of showing that one didn't fear death. He said it was in fact an economy measure, because it would save having statues, and save wasting land on cemeteries. He's in the main hall of University College, London – there he is in a kind of sentry-box, behind glass. His body has survived actually very well.

But in general there was always a very powerful sense of almost the sacredness of the physical corpse that partly goes back to the Christian belief in the resurrection of the body. There was a great deal of public hostility to messing around with people's corpses, and obviously that's one of the reasons why body-snatchers and people like that were treated with such hostility. Anatomists and dissectionists, you know, regularly got their premises smashed up by the people. So you get societies formed in Victorian England actually for people to leave their bones to the anatomists as a public service – John Stuart Mill did. It was to show that there's no fear, there's no belief in the real resurrection of the body and so on. I imagine that most of the people who made a show of donating their bodies to scientific research were atheists, though clearly one could be a Victorian Christian and think that what happened to your body is neither here nor there.

I have very little sense of mystery personally and, you know, if somebody wants to amputate my arm, then my arm gets amputated and that's that. Once you take away the original metaphysics of it, the Christian resurrection, then it becomes a matter of sentiment. I feel blank about it, but that may be because I've never actually witnessed the death of anybody I've been really close to. So in some sense I've escaped the whole culture of death just by being forty; that's one of the privileges of living in the 1980s – one can feel blank about it because one never had to encounter it. I was originally interested in the history of science, and then found a lot of scientists were doctors and got fascinated by the history of medicine. Then more and more I got intrigued by the doctor himself, and that led me on to an interest in the doctor's patient and what it was like to be sick in history, and then on to dying and the death rituals. I just have a historical fascination with everything people have done and felt, and because death has been the great mystery, people have needed to demystify it or to create myths about it, more than anything else.

But actually . . . Let's leave it as the great mystery. I mean, I have no idea what's going to happen, and I think it will be . . . You know, I think it will be interesting to be conscious as one dies, because one must undergo the most extraordinary changes. Thinking, I'm dying now. Historically people in the seventeenth and eighteenth centuries say, 'I'm dying now' – suddenly something or other has come over them which enables them to be confident, and they're usually right. And, you know, loads of people have thought they were dying and have had death experiences, and then in some sense have been revived and have lived to recall the strangeness.

I think I'd like to be fully conscious of it all. Because, you know, you'd just be missing out on something otherwise. Clearly one doesn't want to be in excruciating pain and all the rest of it. But I think one would want to be with the people who mattered to one. Being fully conscious and reasonably free from pain and having everybody there – that would be the best thing, because that's as near to what is nice about living as possible.

I do think we are cheated of a good death today. Hospices clearly have been a step in the right direction; and I think in its macabre way the coming of AIDS will help. Because for the first time we may well have around us people in their twenties and thirties and forties dying prematurely, knowing from four years beforehand that they're going to die, and developing around them support communities who are used to being with people who are dying. In the last forty years, since the end of the Second World War, we've lived in a society where relatively few people die prematurely – visibly, at any rate. One of the things that will happen with AIDS is that because it has received so much public attention, and it's such a visible problem, heroic efforts will actually be made to make sure there will be enough community support and support of friends, so the dying-alone syndrome won't be universal there.

Something good may come of it in the sense that the ease with which the old in our society can be pushed out of sight will not apply to youngish people dying of AIDS. It's a bizarre thing to say, but there's something peculiarly unfortunate about the fact that it's the old who die in our society – because the old get a raw deal in every possible way. Ours is the most appallingly ageist society in reverse. And, I mean, the thought of dying doesn't worry me, but the thought of being senile perturbs me a great deal.

I hope we don't have to go back to a society where people are dying like flies to get back to that sense of dying as something where you show your mettle. You actually first have to go back to a society where you treat old people well, and if you start doing that, then treating the dying and death well is no problem. But at the moment we treat old people in a totally appalling way. It's partly a fantasy that we're all sort of young and healthy and go jogging and all the rest of it – that's the only thing that it's good to be nowadays. But it's also that it is a unique phenomenon of our society which nobody has really made much effort to come to terms with, which is that we are increasingly living in a society where the normal age is about sixty-six.

You don't see them, no – the old are out of sight. It's the young who are, you know, throbbing down the Euston Road and jostling on the tube and so on. We live in a society where old people have become extraordinarily invisible, because they're not powerful in the way they often used to be. There's no general place for them, they're not productive, they're not repositories of wisdom. It's a society where there are just simply so many more old people around than ever there used to be. If you'd tried to set up lots of Victorian old people's homes you wouldn't have been able to fill them – though there was the obscenity of the work-house, of course.

There are desirable patterns of life which are held out to us in which basically we're all masters of our own time and consumers of our own pleasures; and children and old people get in the way of that, and death negates it all. I think we all want our own way a lot more then people ever used to think was possible. And anything which gets in the way is treated with cruelty.

## Tom Lee

I am a Romany, though I've got fair hair – I was the
only one this colour out of nine. My grandmother, she was Irish,
like a ginger colour, and they reckon I take after her. All the rest
of my family are dark, very dark. You see my brothers in the
photo there – boxing, yes – they're dark. Now, when we was
hop-picking in Kent a few years ago, we worked right through the
hop season; and my sister and my elder brother came down to see
us, very smart, had a nice car and everything – and they walked
into the pub and they got refused. I said, 'What's the idea of that,
then? You've been serving me all the time.' I don't look like a
gypsy, you see. He said, 'I do not serve gypsies, just get out.'
People think we're sort of animals, and things like that. But today
he's not allowed to do that; when we went to the High Court in
London, the judges said the gypsies are an ethnic minority, and
all the pubs have took the signs down now.

This site used to be my grandfather's slaughter-yard, you
know – they used to shunt the cattle through the railway, round
the back here – and he used to make the wagons just up here. It's
my land now – not just this yard, there's seven and a quarter
acres. There's been gypsies here years, hundreds of years – it was
a winter stopping place when they weren't travelling. It's a well-
known name among gypsy people, my grandfather's – Jimmy
Lee. He was a wagon-maker. My wife's a Cooper, her people
travel in Buckinghamshire. No matter where you go, you'll find
the true Romanies like ourselves all related. It's some years since
you've seen those painted wagons, I'd say about the beginning of
the sixties. My father had one, but we burned it.

I was brought up in one of those. You could have as many as
nine in one of them; you see, you could sleep two in the bottom
bunk, and then another four or five in the top bunk, and then
you could put another mattress on the floor. People don't under-

stand ... I mean, people will have gypsies move into houses, they come to me themselves, begging me to get them into a place; and after a fortnight they're back out again. They come back – 'Ah, Tom, where can I buy an old trailer? I can't stand it.' Look at me, I can't stop in a house for about two minutes – I've got to get out, you know.

My parents travelled all over – Kent, Essex, Sussex, all over the place, really. We did field work mostly. Us boys used to lead the horses up and down, you know, ploughing – we used to get half a crown a week. I've got some of the old tally cards – it's where you get paid, from the farmer. Seven pounds a week, for nine of us, and that's from seven o'clock in the morning to six o'clock at night. It was a hard life, very hard. But it was a sort of free life, you know, you're not tied down.

No, I didn't get any schooling – I learned to read and write in the army. Actually they kidnapped us off the field, picked about six of us up. Because we was working in the fields all day, and used to have old caps on, so I suppose we did look older than we were. The farmer didn't know, he said, 'Yes, they're about twenty year old, mate, I'm paying them men's wages.' They swore we was eighteen, but we wasn't; but birth certificates, we had nothing like that. I knew there was a war on, but I never took much notice of it. Until I was in the potato field one morning, in the mud, and the police came and just said, 'You, you, and you', and that was it, we was taken away, still smothered in mud. We was crying our eyes out – never been away from home, had we, didn't know what it was like to be away.

Actually I got on well in the army – they always used to ask for me on patrol. Because we was patrolling through the woods, looking for mines and that, you know, and I happened to say, 'Well, there's nothing been through here, because I can tell from the rabbit runs. When I was a boy I used to set snares in these runs to catch rabbits.' I said, 'There's foxes been there too, there's droppings there. If there was mines, they'd have let them off.' The officer said, 'My God, I've never thought about that.' So after that on every patrol – 'I'll take Lee with me', you know. I had a very good record.

When I come out of the army, I accused the police and the

council of murder, for harassing my father – they harassed him and pushed him about, wouldn't let him stop nowhere, and the old man just gave up in the end. They took him into custody for stopping on the highway as a gypsy, put him in a cell – he'd never been in a cell in his life. And when I come I looked through the door; he was crying, he was just a little old man. After he died I went straight to the local authority and I said, 'You murdered my father.' I said, 'You killed him.' I sent my war medals back in protest over it, I said, 'I'm returning these for what you done to my father.' And I said then, 'It will never happen to another gypsy as long as I'm around.'

When my father died we burned his wagon – it was like that one in the picture, one of the old ones. They said, 'You can't burn it there, Mr Lee'; but I said I was going to, I'd have the Fire Brigade, and they said, 'All right, as long as it's controlled.' So we set fire to it there and then, on the bomb site. It would be worth a fortune today – when I think about it, it makes me feel bad, because today I don't suppose you'd buy it for three or four thousand pounds. The police said, 'Don't burn it, Mr Lee, don't burn a thing like that', because, you know, it was all lovely paint, a beautiful thing. I said, 'No, it's got to be burned, that's the way he wanted it.' There were blankets in there never been out of the cellophane packet – brand spanking new. The only thing I got was the four wheel-caps – I've got two and my sister's got two.

I don't know why – it's just the custom with us, you know. I wouldn't like to see the wagon change hands and go. I would say fifty per cent of the wagons, about, are destroyed nowadays. Well, it is thousands of pounds, but if you love a person you don't worry about money, do you? It's the custom, that's the way it is. I've even seen horses shot, there and then, in the field. Beautiful horses, beautiful horses. There was a case when a man was dying of cancer, and he had a palomino horse, a big 'un, and he made a tractor dig a hole in the field, and he shot it just before he died. The week after that he was dead, and then I tried to buy the horse-box back for a keepsake, because he was a very good friend of mine; and his boy wouldn't sell it to me. He said, 'I don't want to sell it, Tom'; and it's still there today.

The first funeral I remember, it was my grandfather really. I was about thirteen, I think. He was one of the best wagon-makers – cut all the carving out, the scallops and the butterflies. And he used to have a boxing booth here for years, my grandfather – there used to be a lot of people, like Freddy Mills, all started there. He was a well-respected man. A well-loved man. His grave's just down the road here – we buried him in Canning Town in the cemetery there, there's loads of gypsies buried down there. I would say, living round Canning Town, Poplar and Stepney Green, there's more descendants of gypsies living in houses than anywhere else in Europe; because years ago, at Barking Banks, there was as many as four hundred gypsy wagons on there. I remember all the cars and the horses at my grandfather's funeral – they must have stretched for half a mile, and they took him all round the streets, Canning Town, all round. It was a very big turn-out.

When you go to a non-gypsy funeral, then you find they've got a sheet to them, up to here, and you just see their face; but at our sort of funerals you see the whole lot, you're dressed nice, because people come to see, don't they? Even when my brother was dead, we bought a new suit, new shoes, new socks for him. He'd have his waistcoat on and his coat and a handkerchief in his top pocket and perhaps a pen. In my grandfather's time it was corduroy trousers. Same thing with women – the chains, jewel-lery, a lot of it's buried with them. I don't think it looks right with just a sheet across. And most likely they put a shoe in the coffin for luck, something like that, and they might lay a whip in there.

The old customs, the old gypsy burials – no, I wouldn't say they've changed. All my family has had lovely funerals. There's a lot of talk about it afterwards and all – 'Did you see the cars, Tom? Ah, look at the flowers!' Do you know what I mean? The last one I went to must have cost a fortune, because they had a marquee there, a massive marquee, and the food – oh dear, there was tables and tables of it, you know. And they sat for three nights; when they're going to bury someone, say next Wednesday, they sit up Monday night, Tuesday night . . . The body is either in the caravan or sometimes they put a little tent up; they've fetched it home from the undertakers. They take big urns of tea, and the women will fetch the grub round, you know – 'Come and help yourself' – and they sit there eating their sandwiches and all that. And you see them going in and out, in and out of the tent. You get people come there and they just get up, you know, and they say, 'Oh, he's in there, all right', and they go in, and come out, come out and have a cup of tea. They light a big bonfire, don't they, all sitting round the fire. They generally find somewhere for it, a site, you know – you see fires out in the field here.

I would say they're some of the biggest funerals that go on in the country, gypsy funerals. I would say the biggest, actually. And they dress up – the jewellery comes out, and the gold sovereigns. Some gypsies have got their own undertakers, they know exactly what they want – horses and carriages, you know, and so many cars. There's a glass hearse, the way they used to have years ago, and you have the four horses in front, with the plumes up. All black horses. It costs you . . . How far was it for my brother? I suppose half a mile – that was nearly six hundred pound. And you have to have a big do afterwards, don't you, with catering and all that sort of stuff; and then you've got cars, and then you've got the vicar to pay, and then you have to buy the ground, don't you, and flowers, they're very expensive. I suppose for my brother it was, say, two or three thousand pounds. Oh yes, if a gypsy hasn't got the money he'll sell stuff to get it – if you don't, you show yourself up among other gypsies, don't you?

They'll come from miles for the funeral – the gypsy grapevine is better than any telephone in the country. The news just travels – zoom, zoom, zoom, it's gone! They come from miles, miles. There's a saying among gypsies that the only time they see each other is at funerals and weddings. My mate, he died, and he wanted all the gypsy trades following him. So we had horseboxes, we had lorries loaded up with scrap iron, we had builders' lorries, we had jack of all trades following that man, and that stretched for nearly quarter of a mile. The flowers, they were out of this world – you never seen so many flowers in your life, lorryloads of them. Don't know where to put them sometimes. Oh, you don't think about money.

We have a service in church, yes – Romany people are Catholic, though quite a number will have C. of E. funerals. I don't know if I was baptized and confirmed, no. Then we generally buy our own ground for burial, you know – I've just bought a bit down there, actually. My father's there and my cousin's there, and my aunts, and grandfather and all. On my father's gravestone, he's got a boxing booth on top, all made of brass and little buckets in the corner and all that, and it's got on the top, 'The fighting Lee brothers from Canning Town'. And when I went down there, I wanted a bit of ground for my brother, and Stan – he's the cemetery superintendent – he said, 'Well, I can't find a bit, Tom.' Argue, argue, argue, we was. And eventually he found me a bit right behind my grandma. I wanted my brother there, you know what I mean? Didn't want him buried away from the family.

We don't have cremations, no – very rare. It's like going to hell, when you have them burned, isn't it? I wouldn't like none of my family cremated. I mean, I seen them in the church, a little vase like that, you know, stuck up against a tree, it's not really . . . We like to have nice tombstones, and flowers and that sort of thing. You sit there and say a little prayer for them, don't you? I went round the other day. I can't ever remember going to a cremation of a gypsy, and there's not many gypsy funerals I miss.

I do myself believe a person goes to heaven, yes – I always say my prayers every morning and every night, and for my dead family and all. I don't go to church very often, no, but I'm still religious in a way, you know. And I bring up the grandchildren in the same way. Because my great-uncle, he was a gypsy evangelist. He's buried in Epping Forest – the only gypsy buried in Epping Forest. Buried where his wagon was – his tombstone's still there.

When my brother died, we found these old certificates, insurance certificates – I've never seen anything like it in my life, they were that long and that wide, parchments actually. It was tuppence a week towards your burial, one for all of us – even mine, when I was two year old. I said to my sister, 'Sarah, whatever you do, don't part with these', and she said, 'Tom, I've never touched these since mother died, she gave them to me and she said, "Whatever you do, look after these."' She said, 'There's yours, look, yours is tuppence, here's mine and that's fourpence, and Jimmy's, his is tuppence, and George's tuppence.' When we unrolled them I couldn't believe it.

I would say gypsies is superstitious, yes. About their trailers and things like that – they don't like to keep them around afterwards, do they? I'd never buy anything off a dead . . . off a person that's been dying. Or if I did it would never leave me, put it that way. Yes, I would get rid of everything, myself. I would, personally – yes, jewellery, everything. There are only certain keeper things, what you call keeper stuff, you know. Like rings, and the old red-gold chains, and sovereigns. We burned all my brother's stuff, we broke his wagon up and burned everything. The only thing I saved from him, I think, was his tobacco box and his cigarette-lighter.

I like to see a bloke have a good send-off, you know. Because sometimes . . . You can't believe it, can you? One day you met them, like three weeks ago, and they've been fit people, you know. And it's hard to believe, really. Some people say, 'Well, Tom, we've all got to go, mate' – they look at it like that.

Very rare, missing a funeral – nine times out of ten I know the person anyway. If I didn't go they'd most likely say, 'I never seen you there, Tom.' My grandfather was the same, he'd walk for miles and miles to a gypsy funeral. Miles and miles and miles. You see people there you've not seen for years. I see boys now, they're about six foot, and I knew them when they was just as big as that. They say, 'Hullo, Uncle Tom', and I say, 'Hullo, son, who are you, then?' 'You don't know me? I sat on your lap when I was a kid.' And I'm peering up looking at him, do you know what I mean? 'You're not what's-'er-name's son, are you?' 'Yeah, course I am.' I say, 'Ah, mate, I'm sorry, I didn't know.' Because last time I see him he was down to here.

A mate of mine – I used to have two fields off of him for my horses – his father had the finest funeral I've seen. He wanted a good send-off, and he wanted lively music, you know. So what they done, his boys, they had a brass band, and they had two bagpipes playing, that song – what's-'er-name? And when I got down there, one of the stables was turned into a big bar, they was all dancing and singing. They was all drunk, dressed up in cowboy uniforms, there was blank cartridges going off – bang!

bang! bang! And the coffin was laying there! He was one of the best horsemen in the country, you know. And I see his boys – 'Hullo, Uncle Tom, come and have a drink!' So I said, 'What's it all about, what you doing, for God's sake?' He said, 'That's the way me father wanted it, mate, it's in his will!' And the brass band was going – da-da-de-de-da – and the guns were going off – bang! bang! – and everything. And they put him in the grave, and his boys had got two bottles of whisky, tipped it all in the grave, and his other boy was the other side with a bottle of spirits – all in the grave. He said, 'That's the way he wanted it, and he's going to have it like that, and that's it!' Ah, dear.

# Dr Jonathan Miller

I had a nanny who was death-intoxicated. My first feelings about death were always to do with the death of others, never my own death; it didn't occur to me as something which might happen to me. I was frightened of death because of the solemn mystery of it, the solemn mystery of corpses. I think my first feelings were connected with hearses – the name 'hearse' still has a terrible onomatopoeic sound, a sort of terrible susurration, a hiss of this approaching, silent, solemn thing. My nanny would say, 'That's an 'earse, there's an 'earse going by.' They were already motorized in my day, I never saw these plumes and horses; but I hated these dark, solemn oblongs that were to be seen inside these rather polished, skirted cars that used to appear. And the flowers on top, and the terrible purple of the drape over the coffin.

And I was always frightened of having to ... of the terrible possibility that one might see the body that was lying inside it. I dreamt about it, and thought that there was this sort of marmoreal immobility which overtook people, and that they were ... I remember dreaming some time of an aunt who I'd been told had died, and of somehow visualizing in some very vague way this slightly yellowed face, dressed in a black Persian-lamb coat, and this great crinkly Persian-lamb collar which was round her, and that this was what one would see if one was unfortunate enough to stumble across an open coffin. And the word 'coffin', the word 'hearse', could stain a day for me if I heard it mentioned.

The nanny ... Well, I can remember asking her a lot about death – 'What is it?' – and she terrified me once by telling me that it's 'the peace that passeth all understanding'. I mean – the idea that all understanding might be frustrated by it ... And so the idea of it being a completely impenetrable mystery was to do somehow with the idea that the corpse was something which could not, or *would* not, answer you. That you could address either this awful, sleeping face or, worse than that, those faces which I think I saw when she took me through Westminster Abbey; the terrible morbid vigilance of the effigies that lay up on one elbow. There was something terrifying about the fact that they were not just simply ordinary people lying down, that this was an impenetrable glance which passed beyond you to something, to some concern which lay in a space behind and beyond the spectator.

The funny thing is, I don't think that the idea of my own non-existence – either previous or subsequent to my actual existence – ever really occurred to me or disturbed me. It may have done, I may have suppressed it completely. But it was the thought that it overtook living people, and turned them into these sternly impenetrable and unanswering figures . . . Yes, it was the unansweringness of them, it was the mysterious solemnity.

It was particularly ideas of smells . . . I remember being terrified when I was a child, in our garden in St John's Wood, when my father had disposed of a bear's skull, and I came across it nestling in a clump of lily of the valley. And I kept on talking about this phrase which my father and mother told me about many years later, that I came in gibbering this phrase, 'the tooth of the bone, the tooth of the bone'. And it was always in my mind; this idea of the decaying and the dead was associated with this menacing fragrance. I didn't know about the body decaying, I knew they went into the earth. But far more frightening than the idea of putrefaction, far more alarming, was the poised, beautiful, sort of delicate fragrance of these lilies of the valley. And for me, for many years as a child, the whole idea of death was this menacing fragrance of these delicate flowers – they smelt of death. The bear's skull – I can hardly see the bear's skull; all I can remember is the smell of bone, the smell of the grave, the smell of laying out, of preparing the body. My nanny talked about being laid out, washing the body, the shroud. So that my fears of death were always associated with concrete fears of the corpse, the stillness, the unansweringness, and the menacing poise of it all, of which this fragrance somehow was the epitome.

There was never any question of being told about heaven or

anything like that. I suppose the only time when I ever saw it in terms of an eschatology, or of some sort of 'last thing', must have been when I was about eight or nine, and I would read Victorian editions of *The Idylls of the King*; and there was one day I remember having read something about the death of Arthur – once again it was this terrible thought of this barque, of a hand 'clothed in white samite, mystic, wonderful'.

I had, I suppose, a very Victorian view of death, because I had a Victorian nanny; it was to do with samite, shrouds, camphor, and jet and coffins and hearses. And catafalques, and cenotaphs. All of these strange things. My nanny would take me down to the memorial service in Whitehall; and again, there was this terrible thing she would say when I'd see these people gathered around a solemn, white monument. I asked her what it was and she said, 'They're commemorating the men that laid down their lives.' I had no idea of what being killed in war was ... But again, the image of these poppies, and these wreaths, and these people grieving ... For me, death in Flanders was a procession, very similar to the one by which people commemorated the death of those who had been killed – people *laying down* their lives was something equivalent to the gesture with which the relatives were laying down their wreaths. Somewhere in Flanders, in some sort of Last Post-sounding silence, people brought in this samite-shrouded thing of themselves, and laid it down. No, my parents never caught a whisper of this.

The first actual funeral I went to was in fact the funeral of my grandfather, when I was already fifteen. It had all gone then – I suppose that all my real fears of death, in this sort of infantile world of solemnities, and purples, and catafalques, and cenotaphs, and overturned guns, gave way to a biological view of death. Of it actually being, you know, a thing that overtook the body. I was already studying science by then, and I had a view of it that was much more concrete.

My taking up medicine wasn't anything to do with these early fears, it was because I was interested in biology. I went into it, you see, never really thinking that I was going to be a doctor – I thought I was going to be a biologist of some sort, and the best way to study biology and make a living was to be a doctor. I certainly wasn't interested in conquering the mystery of death, it was just that I was very fascinated by how the brain worked, and I was interested in how animals were classified.

But I remember my fear of death then was still ... It was a residual terror of the corpse – what it would look like, how I would react when I saw one. And I remember, I was in my last year as a schoolboy, before I went to Cambridge, and I took a job as a hospital porter. Actually, they assigned me to cleaning the floors in the nurses' home, but there was always the thought that I might be sent to the morbid anatomy room to do something, and I kept on pitting myself, saying, 'Today will be the day when I'll have to see a dead body.' I'd seen dead animals, but I'd not seen any dead bodies.

I never really thought ... I didn't think of my own death – fantasies of premature burial, or being this little corpse. I didn't think about illnesses. Though I was frightened in 1947 – that hot summer of '47 – it was a sort of plague year, and everyone talked about infantile paralysis. But I was frightened *concretely*. I had my tonsils out when I was about twelve or thirteen; at no point did I ever think that that was going to be death, I just thought this was one of the most wonderful experiments with consciousness. I just remember this keen, sort of throat-cutting smell of ether, it had the sort of cold glitter of knives about it, a kind of scalpel-like smell.

Certainly I wasn't frightened of it. The only real death then which came near to me was in 1943 – my mother developed double pneumonia, as they called it then; she became very ill indeed, and I think nearly did die. I was taken away to live elsewhere during her really serious illness. And I remember my nanny a year afterwards telling me, 'Your mother was at death's door'; and once again it became an image, not of her going away, but of this forlorn, samite-covered figure, standing at a doorway like that picture 'Love Locked Out'. Going into a beyond, in which further terrifying solemnities prevailed.

It's not that I was worried by annihilation, I never thought of it; perhaps in some sort of awful, selfish, simple way it seemed so inconceivable as not to be a matter of concern at all. Perhaps one forgets; I do remember my son, finding him sitting on the lavatory in floods of tears and saying at the age of five, 'I don't want to die, I've not had a long enough turn yet.' But what I remember is that it was something which might overtake people that I knew, that they might become unansweringly solemn; like, I suppose, the mystery of sleeping parents. It was also this idea that they were in fact gathered into and unto some sort of corporation or multitude, which was absolutely different from the multitudes of the living.

I remember once when my nanny hit me, and I was in the bath, and she saw the bruise that she'd raised on my arm and she said, 'Who did that?' I said to her rather timorously, 'You did.' And she leaned into the bath and sort of hissed at me and said, 'If you tell your parents I done that it'll be your last day on earth!' And once again it instantly coincided with this image, in what I'd been reading about Arthur's death, of his being lifted up into heaven surrounded by these quiring angels. It wasn't that I was dreading the place to which I might go, but it just simply aroused once again this notion that what death was was this solemn, incense-laden, lily-of-the-valley-smelling multitude . . . I didn't have any religious teaching, no, but I went in and out of churches and churchyards because my nanny was a church-goer. No, I never went to church services really, except for school services. But again, when I was at school, much of my images of death were Victorian images – light coming through memorial windows, stained glass, chapels commemorating those who had laid down their lives, those now in the peace that surpassed all understanding.

My inauguration into the actual dead, the first dead body I'd seen, was in the dissection room. I can remember this shivering congregation of novices, all scared about meeting the dead; we met in an echoing, stone-flagged basement antechamber to the dissecting room in Cambridge, and we were given a quick instruction in the conduct expected of us – you know, respect the dead, no larking around. And then these frosted-glass doors were thrown open, and then quite suddenly there was this sort of bright swimming-bath atmosphere, with voices echoing, and lots of tables, and a smell of formaldehyde, and of slightly rancid grease. And of these Pompeian figures lying on the tables, grey, their mouths often open in a lipless O of surprise, as if startled by some remarkable thing that they had witnessed at the point of death ... The jaw falls down, and then they had been fixed in formaldehyde in this posture, and I can just remember this strange, grey stubble of old men's beard. But they were un-recognizable as bodies, they were just simply effigies – not those solemn, frightening effigies, they were something else altogether. I was reminded very much of the photographs I'd seen of these Pompeian figures, turned into lava.

Immediately the whole horror of death, the previous image of it as this world of curtains, solemnities, and camphor, and grave-clothes, and ruffled samite had gone. And I can always remember talking to that little pock-marked, alpaca-coated attendant who was scrubbing up his hands in the row of sinks that lay at the end of the thing, and I said, 'What's it like working in here?' And he said, 'It's all right in the term when you gentlemen are here. It's the vacations I can't stand; when it's just me and them.'

But my next ordeal with the dead, the next actual ordeal, I suppose, was something which happened, as it always does, about three years after you start as a medical student. You've seen the altered, transformed effigies, but what I'd never seen was the recently dead. Oh yes, a total difference. You see, these figures that are lying in the dissection room are embalmed, and in fact they're just – they're flexible effigies, not dead bodies. They have a consistency of hard, vulcanized rubber. No, no feelings that they were human beings, nothing like that at all. Because they didn't slit in any way which was like cutting one's flesh, they didn't bleed; the heart was choked with a sort of red lead, like earth, like opening a flowerpot. But when I went into the post-mortem room, they were recently dead. And they had that faint candlewax, sort of tallow appearance, and they were flexible. And that was disturbing, because they had been human beings very recently. And there was that warm, butcher's smell, a mixture of a butcher's and a lavatory. It was a smell of newly opened gut, a smell of warm farts, piss. They were still very near to human beings, but unrecognizable in the sense that you couldn't see them as someone you might recognize in the street; they *were* recognizably people because they had this sort of ... They looked like someone that you might say to, 'God, you look ill.' That sort of awful yellow-greenness.

And then I saw patients die, and by that time it was already something totally different. Death was always something that happened to *them*, to this natural kind called patients. I suppose I was twenty-three, twenty-four now. Actually you very rarely saw death happen – they often died at night when you weren't there as a medical student, it was an event which you often missed. But it was a funny thing, it never occurred to me that it was something that would happen to me. I suppose intellectually I said, well, some time I'm going to be doing this, but I haven't got time to rehearse it now, or even think about it now. It was something that happened to this special class of people who were patients.

I don't think it was callousness, it was . . . Well, there's a very deep sort of ontological commitment which you would have as a doctor – you very gradually are somehow initiated into a belief that there are two natural kinds in the world. There are the patients; and then there are the upright, living kind, fully clothed, who are going about their business, who, it's true, intellectually you know are in fact the forthcoming candidates for this role, but you don't see the transition from one to the other.

I suppose around my forties I began to think, well, hang on – this is something which I'm going to be doing some time. I'd never had any life-threatening illnesses; I've had moments when I thought I might be going to die, say, in things like boating accidents, but it was the terror not of dying, it was the terror of drowning, the splashing and the horror. I suppose at moments I might have had pictures, rather romantic, Shelleyish pictures, of my white, weed-covered body, dragged and snagged in nets and things, but I don't think I ever saw more than that. Of course, in hospital there are all sorts of illnesses which, if you have some imagination, you have to think, one or other of these things is going to get me. But I didn't as it were, concern myself with that too much; and I suppose I do much more now, and I think, what is it going to be like when in fact I am dying, when I'm going through this process of recognizably approaching an end which is now given and assigned? And I'm perhaps suffering a lot, and then also saying farewell to it all . . . It's like crossing the

Channel – you get nearer to the shore, and you can actually, for the first time, not just make out this dim, insubstantial cliff, but you can see little houses, and cars moving across.

I get distressed by ... I get the thought that I now have so many concerns, so many associations, so many things which in fact I've experienced, which are going to proceed without me. It's the idea of, as it were, leaving a very complicated, busy scene; and it will be going on ... I sometimes think of this by analogy with my parents; I drive down Hampstead Road and think, good heavens, my mother's not here to see that I'm a driver now! I was always a person who never drove. My mother would never understand my huge children ... She's not here and can't be recalled to see these things. My father will never understand that I'm doing opera now, and doing all sorts of things. Yes, they died before I became a sort of fixture on the scene – that's how I think of myself.

I never grieved over either of my parents – they were rather cold and distant, or at least my mother was. I mean, I liked her very much as she got older because she amused me and I amused her, as we got adult we amused each other a lot. She died demented, so ... She had Alzheimer's disease and died quite young, she was only fifty-five. My father I never got on well with because he was so much older than I was, and a sort of heavy, lugubrious Jewish figure who wanted me to be Jewish and I just didn't want anything of it. But both of their deaths really had no effect on me at all. Retrospectively I sometimes cry about them. Because of there being failures to reconcile, things that could have been said – if only we'd had this talk, or something of that sort.

I did have this very strange moment, which again is partly to do with these nanny-images of death – it was a very strange thing. I really did not grieve over my father's death, I was relieved of a burden. He'd suffered from rheumatoid arthritis for a very long time; I didn't know what was going to happen to him or who was going to look after him. And then he died, in 1969, and I don't think I thought about him or dreamt about him at all. Until about ten years after that, perhaps less, Rachel and I were in Pompeii on holiday, in a cold, bright February. And we were walking around Pompeii, and we were both rather startled by the strange brilliant solitude of this place. There was bright sunshine, and these houses torn open to the sky, and this glaring scrutiny of this city of the dead, with no people around at all. And it had obviously struck my imagination in some way, that there was this place where there were no bodies – signs of habitation, but no bodies at all. A sense of people having been here – a *Marie Celeste* place.

And I went back to the hotel that night – this large Victorian hotel on the front – and dreamt for the first time, that night, of my father. He returned, as it were. It was a very strange dream, which somehow goes right back to my nanny's dreams of the First World War, and military Last Posts, and khaki, and cenotaphs. Because I was standing on the pavement outside Westminster Abbey, by Central Hall, Westminster, in a street café. And I saw my father's figure in military uniform that he'd worn in the Second World War – a Sam Browne belt and a very large peaked hat, which slightly shadowed his face. There was a sort of wistful look on his face; and I tried to cross the road to speak to him, and the crowds took him away, and I woke in tears. And I somehow thought that he had come back, with all those multitudes of other dead that had gone. It took Pompeii and all its inhabitants to bring him along.

With my mother – well, I'm president of the Alzheimer's Disease Society, and when I talk to public meetings about it I talk about it as an uncollected corpse, there is this terrible thing which is walking around, which the undertaker has cruelly forgotten to collect. Oh, I'm frightened of it. Yes, I am frightened. If I was told that I had a fatal neoplasm of some sort I think I would, well, steam up to a sort of fail-safe line; I would not go through the business of radiotherapy and things of that sort. Of course, as one gets older, these things start to ... Yes, there are specific dyings that I'm frightened of.

The fear of just not existing – no, I don't have that at all. I suppose every now and then, in a sort of sentimental, paranoid, Housmanesque way – 'Is my team ploughing?' – you know. The idea that the place will close over, and that other people whom I thought I was fond of and were fond of me will in fact get on with their lives. It's connected, I think, with something which was very early in childhood, at the age of about seven or eight – frosty, wonderful, welcoming Christmas parties, and of being collected slightly early, of there still being musical chairs, and of having to go before musical chairs, and jellies . . . It's being taken into the darkened hall, and the lights are on in the room, and half glimpsed there's a pretty girl crossing a lighted doorway, in an organdie dress, and laughing en route to some festivity that one now can't have.

Oh, I do feel – if one were thinking in purely objective terms about a rich, full life I have to say that it would be greedy to want to live on in the hope of getting – more jellies, more party games . . . But I would like to feel that in fact when the time comes there can be this Indian summer, you know, with a substantial and really fruitful life of achievement. Untormented by the quotidian disputes over reputation which are associated with being in the theatre – 'Trendy old Jonathan Miller once again has mucked up a great classic'! Say a healthy eighty. No! Eighty-five.

I think of my wife Rachel and my death in very complicated ways; I don't want to live long without her – I would be bereft without her, I think, now – but on the other hand the thought of her being bereft is also very distressing to me. One would like it to be fairly simultaneous, but of course it never is. I'd like not to be aware of the process of dying; it's related to the notion of a death sentence – of some preformative utterance which declares you to be now going through a period which is not just living till one dies, but actually dying. I would just hope to get whatever it is and fade very gently away, or else to be taken so that I was never aware of it. Or like this wonderful thing that happened to Penelope Betjeman. She was leading a trip in India. She got off her donkey, and sat on a rock, and said, 'Isn't that nice', and fell off it, and was unconscious and dead.

I don't want to see the grieving around my bed, either. I'd rather be at home, certainly; but on the other hand, what to me is distressing about deathbeds is the grieving of those who are left. That was why I think I worked that scene in *Traviata* so effectively. But Violetta herself – the funny thing is, the experience I brought to that was not experience I had had of seeing someone die, it was much more the domestic experience of simply seeing the frustrated panic of one of my own children, delirious from tonsillitis, who was unreachable, in a paroxysm of uncommunicating distress. Yes, I am frightened of that – of not being able to tell people that I'm in agony, of suffocation, of being at the bottom of a well from which one cannot ever attract attention. Terror, absolute terror. Occasionally one just wakes at night suddenly . . .

I do actually in some strange way – while I do not conceive of an afterlife – I do conceive a strange, attenuated, out-of-the-body experience in which I'm somehow tenuously present at my burial or cremation. Watching my own funeral. Or in fact not watching it, but being immobilized inside the coffin. Because I cannot actually conceive, can't make sense of the notion of total annihilation. Or I'm frightened of the fact that there might in fact be this residual consciousness which is not quite snuffed out. But I know it's impossible, it's meaningless. I think of consciousness as being strictly contingent upon a particular arrangement of cells in here, and when they are dishevelled beyond a certain point there isn't consciousness. I mean, considering how deep the unconsciousness is which goes with the minor dishevelment of sleep, it must be infinitely more profound and to the point of total annihilation.

I suppose I do have a picture – because of this idea of being taken home early from the party – that the dead are in fact cross, and like Hans Andersen's match-girl, that they're part of the multitude which includes the poor and the underprivileged and the starving. Noses pressed to the glass, and excluded from but spectators of the festivities.

In so far as I have any views of an afterlife, which are in fact involuntary, as I say, my most impressive metaphor, image, has been much more Greek than Christian – it's this awful land beyond the Styx, in which people are mourning their own deaths. It's not the altar-pieces of people being pushed into fiery furnaces on one side and raised to states of great bliss on the other; but just simply, as the Greeks saw it, this terrible cold steam-bath, some frightful, infinitely extended Baths of Caracalla, with shrouded figures sort of wandering in this steamy Fellini mist. I suppose I did that in *Orfeo*, when I actually did the scene of Orpheus visiting the underworld, and I just saw these shrouded figures, clothed completely in black, so their faces were hardly visible, just wandering. It does go back to Nanny's picture in a way, yes.

When I do have a vision of this vast steam-bath, I think it was influenced by a story I read in Jacques Le Goff's book *The Emergence of the Idea of Purgatory*. He has a wonderful vision, which is taken from a fifth-century pope, and it's absolutely terrifying. There was a cardinal who died, who had committed a minor sin of supporting an anti-pope or something like that; and the next day his closest friend in the Curia was taking his bath in the Roman baths, and in the steam a bath attendant came up to him, telling him he was in fact the cardinal who had died, and that purgatory was nothing other than being assigned to a different role in the here and now to the one he had occupied previously – that from being a cardinal he had simply become a bath attendant. I would be – well, I suppose some extremely unsuccessful rep actor!

I remember a very strange image I had of death. A friend of mine died some years ago, and the afternoon that he was dying I went to visit a friend of mine who had a cottage in Gloucestershire. And late in the day we made an outing to one of those little Cotswold villages where there was some painting on the wall of the parish church. Rachel and I and this man went in a car, down a sunlit lane, to one of those back villages which you can only reach by going down deeper and deeper lanes, and we turned out of the lane into this blistering sunlit village street, which was empty, a strange mid-afternoon solitude – it was almost like a sort of Tudor De Chirico. And we wanted to ask something about a house which was for sale; and there was this rather pinched, mean little house, with leaded windows, and dusty, and we knocked and couldn't get any answer, it seemed to be deserted. And suddenly a rather shambling figure in a dusty suit appeared from the back of this house, a working-class man, a caretaker, but he looked drunk and bewildered and had obviously been roused from sleep. He was the spitting image of my friend who was dying, exactly same as him; and what I felt was that my friend had died perhaps an hour before and that he was in fact transposed, not into the world of the dead, but simply shunted into an alternative body, and was distressingly bewildered by where he had found himself and wanted to ask us advice just as much as we wished to ask about the house. That he wanted to sort of reach forward and say in this heavy, countryman's voice, 'Can you tell me what I'm doing here?'

I do think, as you say, that it isn't just the moment of death, but that one is actually struggling all the time with deathly things, things which are very much analogues of death because they're transformations and losses of previous states. And a lot of the fear of death, when people are not really frightened of simply coming to an end, or of the pains of dying, a lot of it is to do with the fact that death might not be death at all but might just simply be being *undead*. It's in Dante, isn't it, this idea that hell might be actually being forced to simply re-enact the pleasures that you sought all through your life, constantly reliving the sinful pleasures.

I do have elaborate fantasies about continuing – sort of finding myself in a bedsitting-room in Derby and not sure who I am. I think this is after all what all these dreads and fantasies are about, the experiments we play, thought experiments, with the notion of personal identity. What is it to be oneself? Is it possible to be oneself and yet, in every respect, *someone else*? It's to do with my work in neurology, yes. Can one be sure of actually being oneself . . .? And therefore one does play these rather fearful thought experiments; that one will in fact continue after death, with all that is required to identify oneself as what one was previously, while in almost every other respect being other than that. Still feeling, but not being recognized as, Jonathan Miller. Above all, being so knocked off that I have an extremely dishevelled and befuddled view of Jonathan Miller, so that I don't even know where I am and what I am.

I think that's how the idea of hell on earth has been conceived – this early notion of purgatory not being another geographical place, in the gap between hell and earth, but some sort of alternative existence on earth like that. When hell really is hell it seems in some strange way endurable, as it was for some of the people who survived things in war which we can hardly bear to imagine. Whereas hell on earth is not in fact accompanied by torments, but by these disorders of ontology, of what *being* is.

I've always concentrated, when I was rehearsing deaths, on this muddle, the sort of unexpected, terrifying trivialities. Trying rather incompetently to do what you were doing when you were fully alive. People who've survived being shot just say, 'I found myself on the floor' or 'I was wondering why it was my shoe wouldn't stay straight.' I'm interested in very, very small, overlooked quotidian details. I always feel that what happens on the stage in moments of great drama are funny, unexpected trivialities. I didn't say anything with Gilda dying, in *Rigoletto*, I actually had her in a state of rather irritable discomfort − irritated by the fact that her father wanted to embrace her, and this was rather an uncomfortable position for her to be in. It's these sort of funny continuations of ordinary life, just with the selvage pulled off, frayed. I spend all my time trying to avoid the obvious theatrical moments, trying to get things right by the shock of unexpected triviality; like that thing that really made that wonderful essay of George Orwell's about the hanging in Burma − the funny little nimble-footed man on the way to the execution shed taking a detour around a puddle on the way.

Yes, I do think opera, poetry, whatever, are opposed to the idea of just meaninglessness. Because in fact what happens is that by improvising meaningfulness, by each contribution that's made towards this improvised meaningfulness, you make things more meaningful. It's a bootstrapping process; you bootstrap it up from nothingness, and create a contingent somethingness. And each time someone does something more in the way of improvising purpose it actually is a permanent contribution towards it.

Goodness − I do think goodness is worth while. Simply because inside this balloon of consciousness which we inhabit there isn't anything else anyway, and it would be intolerable to have to go through this without in fact committing yourself wholeheartedly to the idea of an absolute within that universe. The fact that it's not absolute within the larger universe is completely irrelevant. I'm never going to visit the larger universe − the only visitable universe is the one within which these improvisations hold sway, and therefore in that sense they are absolute and must be cleaved to, the morality is worth holding to. I don't feel daunted by the fact that it is ultimately meaningless, because I'm never going to visit the ultimate meaninglessness. I only inhabit the domain within which meaning has meaning, like I expect to be understood when I go out and ask for butter, and I expect the train to run, and if it fails to there is a reason. I mean, trains running on time, or the communicability of my need to get butter, don't count in the larger order of things; but the fact that it counts in my life, and that of those whose lives I share, is as far as I'm prepared to go with meaning – that's all that's necessary. I think in fact there's a hierarchy of meaningfulness, but the hierarchy doesn't, as it were, like a skyscraper, pierce through some ceiling into a domain of absolute meanings; it's capable of extending itself as high as meaningfulness can extend. And that's as high as I need it to go.

# JOHN SNELLING

It was in 1973 or 1974. I'd been working abroad and I came back to England feeling a bit under the weather and eventually went to a doctor; and he hustled me into hospital, and after a long period of tests it transpired that I had a form of cancer – leukaemia. I was thirty-one. Now that really brings you up against the fact of your own mortality, the fact that you're going to die.

Up until that time, like everyone else ... Well, I think one indulges oneself in a kind of illusion that in one's own particular case the gods are going to be lenient, that they're not going to give you the fateful summons – that everyone else can be carted off to the morgue, but that you as the favoured child, you know, will get off with eternal life. And this experience brought it home to me, rudely and summarily, that the gods didn't look upon me in any special way. It was quite interesting, because I remember on the first night that it had been confirmed that this was what I had, I went to bed with an absolutely ghastly feeling; it was a sense, a mingled sense of fear, and incredulity, and a tremendous sense of injustice – why me? And, you know, I really sort of harangued the gods, imaginatively I went up there and I really gave them a piece of my mind for this dirty trick.

But then I began to really feel this thing in my body, and as it progressed I became more and more sleepy and more and more tired ... And then the whole saga of that particular night was interesting, because although I went to bed with, as I say, these tremendous mingled feelings of anger and incredulity and fear – many things – I went through a kind of purgation in the night, through fear, in a way. I don't know what it was, but when I woke up in the morning I'd come to terms with it.

There's a line in Dr Johnson's writing somewhere when he says, 'Depend upon it, Sir, the thought that he is to be hanged concentrates the mind wonderfully'; and I think it did in an odd way cut through an awful lot of mental bric-à-brac and homed me in on the central issues, you know, the religious issues about what I was, what I was doing, what life was about. Yes, I was already a Buddhist, I'd started on that path; but this suddenly sort of rallied and galvanized all the religious efforts I'd been making and brought them to a new pitch. And in Buddhist terms I could make sense of it, and actually use the experience as an enriching one. I think I wrote a poem at the time, and my feeling was this: that the world is bountiful, it gives you a lot, but it takes it all back. But what it doesn't take back is the greatest gift of all – it's in all religions, there is in us some spiritual treasure, a pearl of great price, a hidden jewel.

I think that in normal waking life, when we think we've unlimited time ahead of us, we get so distracted by all the usual lures and seductions of life, the complications, that the spiritual jewel is obscured. But it's often a stark confrontation with death, or the possibility of it, that clears the situation. And one feels then, within us, the power of this tremendous thing; it isn't personal, it's not me, or my achievement, but it's ... it is something quite marvellous.

It's not, as I see it, it's not that Buddhism denies a self, some spiritual element in us beyond all the aggregates; what it staunchly refuses is that we put a name to it, or stick a face on it, or start to have ideas about it. Because it transcends anything that we can know or think. It is something that one can get a sense of, one can touch, feel close to, but never know in the sense that we can know each other, or know a fact, or know this flower. It's not graspable in terms of sense data, it is entirely other, it belongs to a whole different category of being.

The so-called *anatta*, the no-self or no-soul doctrine – it's not saying that there is no self, it's just saying that nothing you can point to is the self, you can't identify the self. And I think that the Buddha ... I think that this was a kind of medicine prescribed for the disease that we have when we conduct spiritual inquiry, of trying always to grasp this great mystery with the mind, to name it, to describe it, to start to think we know that it's a this or a that or it has these qualities. It transcends all those sorts of descriptions. It is an absolute; something, as I say, utterly other, and ungraspable and unnameable and unknowable, unknowable in the sense that we know anything else in terms of its sensual qualities or its abstract characteristics. We can't grasp it that way.

To let go of your ordinary superficial self, certainly you've got to have done your psychological work, you've got to have a workable ego to let go of, that doesn't fall down the moment it gets a little battering. Possibly many people haven't. But then what spiritual training does, basically, is it takes you beyond that ego to something greater, to this great mystery which is beyond the ego. The ego's there, but this thing is beyond it. The truth isn't complicated, it's quite simple, but it's incredibly hard to approach and sustain.

Of course if people were able to take the truth neat, then so many kinds of variant approaches to it, which make huge concessions to human needs, wouldn't have evolved. And I think a lot of these marvellous accomplished states of equanimity and renunciation are the ideal. I mean we can't, from where we are, expect to be able to practise perfect renunciation or perfect equanimity; these things are qualities, spiritual qualities, that take years or lifetimes or aeons to perfect. So it's impractical to suggest that we should be able to let go and be utterly unattached instantly – these things have to be worked at. And likewise, for a person who isn't unattached, who still has attachments, there's no concept in Buddhism that they should castigate themselves for this, it isn't wrong. It's absolutely natural that you have attachments, it's the most natural thing in the world; on the other hand attachment is also the cause of pain. In so far as it is the cause of suffering, you ideally begin, hopefully, to loosen your terrible grasp on the things that you hold on to for self-identity and security and comfort.

When I was told I was ill . . . There was a great deal of funk, it was pretty intense fear. I'm not saying I purged it through entirely, but . . . I was clearer in the morning, and I wasn't terrified, and I wasn't funk-ridden – in fact the other people around me seemed far more upset, come the morning. And it seemed to me that I was walking a road that beings had been walking for aeons, and that in a way almost some sort of vast, collective strength rallied to my assistance. It wasn't undiscovered country – human beings had been walking the road of death and meeting Mara, the grim lord of death, for aeons. That's a Buddhist deity – he's meant to have been the first man, hence the first man ever to die, and so in a sense he blazes the trail. It's not a trail that each man blazes for the first time. All sorts of beings have faced dissolution; this fact that beings have done this comes to our support, I suspect, in the moments when it really happens.

What happens to us, in traditional Buddhism, what happens when we die is that the various elements of which we're composed go their separate ways; but the delusion that we have a self and a person transmigrates on. If when a person dies they haven't transcended that, if they're still clutching an attachment to a sense of person, this will condition a new birth. It's a sort of disembodied grasping after incarnate existence. In Buddhist cosmology there's a doubt about it, to be born is an unhappy predicament to be in.

I find that there's a certain kind of mythic or poetic force to this view. It's as though deep in oneself there's a sense of having been dragged from one existence to another, repeating the same mistakes and encountering the same obstacles, and one's enormous efforts to overcome them, to discover really that what one's arrived at isn't worth that much anyway. There's disillusionment, there's pain, one goes on and on. This is the whole connotation, the quality of the Buddhist cosmology, and Buddhism itself – that we are dragging ourselves through untold forms of existence, most of them painful; tired, overburdened, wounded. And that what the Buddhist seeks is a blissful release from this suffering state, what they call *samsara* – the wheel of cyclic rebirth. The Buddha is the man who found the way out. Now, unlike Hinduism, you're not assured of release; you could go on, theoretically you could go circulating on and on in this great spinning ferris wheel for eternity. But you might encounter the teachings of the Buddha, and you might begin to practise them, and you might over many lives – or one life if you're incredibly lucky – perfect them. And you might discover the way out, which is the way to wisdom and bliss, and that is *nirvana*. And that is also the deathless, that is beyond the dualities of birth and death, where in *samsara* we are being born and we are dying; but in *nirvana* we are neither born nor do we die.

No, you wouldn't be *you* in that way. But I think the question hinges on who this 'me' is. If you identify it with your ego, there is a sense of loss. But if you discover your true self, the person who – we shouldn't even call it a person – that which is really you, that which looks out through your eyes, that which really feels, that which gets caught up with your thoughts, which thinks itself is you but is not, is something else; if you really find out what that is, then . . . Oh, the telephone! Sorry.

In terms of my imperfect understanding, there never really was a Rosemary Dinnage, this person; there was this great mystery, which is replete with awareness, which was both the stuff of your being and the spirit animating it. It created you out of itself, and it entered into you, as it enters into everyone, became confused with you. And through your spiritual practice you unravel who it really was, unscramble the whole pattern, the ideas that you put together to create a sense of yourself, the personal identity with a life history and tastes and memories and occupation and credit-card numbers, unscramble it from what was really there – you see what I mean? It's the difference between what was created by mind, through thoughts and memories, and what was really there. And it's that profound inquiry into who you really are . . . The mystery of yourself is the greatest mystery; I mean, scientists have unravelled just about everything, but the greatest mystery of all is, who is here? Who looks out through these eyes? And if you really look, as far as I can see, you can't find, can't come out with anything, and say, 'That is me.' It's a great darkness, but it's a darkness replete with light.

In my case I think actually the whole confrontation with death, the whole confrontation with cancer, leukaemia . . . I mean – I sound like an old Victorian schoolmaster – but I come from a generation that was spoiled rotten, we were soft and indulgent, and I really think it brought out the best in me. To live with this illness for fifteen years. It did stimulate me tremendously to practise, and I'm sure that's very, very important – one can put off practising. I think that the benefits of having practised will become apparent at death, the more you've meditated and been able to clarify yourself, so that you no longer identify with every little phantasm and chimera that rises up in your mind. I'm sure that when we die, we don't . . . It isn't a nothingness . . . I'm sure consciousness goes on from moment to moment, or there is a sequential progress through apparent time, as there is on this plane of existence.

After death – well, yes, potentially the craving for existence could induce one to find a new body in which to be born. According to the Tibetan tradition, we go into an intermediate state, the *bardo* state; at the moment of death they say we're confronted with enlightenment, the primordial experience it manifests as a clear light. And if you can see it for what it is, if you're that aware, and clear, then you're released; but if you're not, then you progress on and meet all kinds of apparitions, ghosts and figments of your own imagination, goodness knows what archetypal forms – Hammer film type milieu. You can be terrified and driven out of your mind by these, but you also get other chances; other lights appear, which represent high, spiritual states, and again, you know, if you go to them you are assured of some kind of realization. But if you don't, you keep going on and on until eventually you start to want to find a new body into which to be reborn.

Well, taking it literally – I don't know. I don't know. The near-death experiences that people have reported after resuscitation – yes, they're different, but I think it all hangs together, it makes sense. I mean, I only speculate, but it kind of feels right in the bones sometimes – it strikes me that quite possibly what you actually see when you die is very much conditioned by what you're expecting. Particularly if you're Christian, and you've been steeped in the Christian pantheon – there's no doubt you'd probably see angels. I suspect if you're a Tibetan you see Bodhisattvas and Buddhas and if you're a Chinese you maybe see Taoist deities. Agnostics – well, they probably see some kind of rationalist thinker type, like Bertrand Russell!

I came across Buddhism when I was travelling in the East in 1971, 1972. My father, I think, was an agnostic, with not much of a feeling or liking for religion, and my mother was a kind of nonconformist Christian who had occasional guilt-ridden bouts of religious fervour, followed by periods when she was reasonably healthily weaned off it. I never found much in Christianity. But trekking through the Himalayas, you came across Buddhist monasteries, and I was just very attracted – there was a quality I liked. I've always felt at home in Buddhism. Some might say that a lot of us who are attracted to Buddhism were Buddhists in former lives, and we just happen to be reborn in the West. It's a question of: am I a Westerner interested in Buddhism, or a Buddhist who's been reborn as a Westerner?

So my illness in a way sort of galvanized me, it made me practise my Buddhism the harder, because I thought time was running out; I thought it was very important to be well prepared for death when it came. On the other hand I think it's held me back, held me back from embracing life fully. I think I felt that life was too . . . I began to get a terribly heightened sense of the precariousness of it, that one couldn't rely on it; so, as I say, I drew back from being too involved. You never know, if you take on any new job or situation, whether your health will hold up – you know, if you take on anything big, whether you'll live to see it out. It creates a tremendous sense of precariousness, a lot of anxiety. And there's also the whole business of combating and fighting the disease, you have to struggle with the disease. Operations, chemotherapy, radiotherapy – I've had the lot. I've just had my spleen out now; it's a feature of leukaemia that the spleen just swells up to gigantic proportions.

There's obviously an optimum amount of time where you confront the fact that you're going to die, you do something about it. You can, like I did, you can confront your death, you can have a period of absorbing that, and integrating with the knowledge. But then you live on and on, so you realize, well, you know, I can't drop everything – I've got to plan, I've got to think about how I'm going to earn my living, where I'm going to live, whether I should marry or not, this, that and the other. One has all the problems of life as well, and in a way it's hard to keep both balls in the air – the fact that you're going to die and you've got to live. And in some ways I'd say this: the problems of life are more difficult than the problems of death; actually preparing yourself to die, and doing it, isn't so difficult as working out your problems in life, in my opinion. Trying to fulfil one's potential in life, trying to meet one's challenges, do the work one has to do here, I suspect is more difficult than hopping the twig – which is, in a way, all about letting go and just jumping off.

The whole question of life and death ... You know, it's incredible how trivial our society is. Television and all the rest – it trivializes everything, it turns everything into a cheap laugh, it glorifies the vain and the vacuous. But the real, awesome challenge of our predicament as human beings, sandwiched between heaven and hell, life and death, is incredibly awesome and challenging – it has real grandeur. We live in a saturation entertainment culture and we don't look at the real questions, the perennial questions that bear upon human life and that really are the interesting ones. And life becomes far more interesting, and an adventure, if we face these things than if we sweep them under the carpet and they just become monstrous fears. The fact is that human existence, the lot of being a human being, is quite an awesome thing. I don't now find death as frightening as the challenges that beset me in life – can you understand that?

And you have to experience both sides of human beings. You have to be careful who you tell that you're ill, for instance – I've lost a job once because they found out. It's funny, you experience people's wonderfully supportive and kind sides, but you also see their ruthless and frightened and hitting-out side. The irony of it is that often someone can be terribly kind to you and terribly unkind – the truth of people isn't simple. Now that's the funniest thing I've ever encountered – somebody who was incredibly kind to me was also incredibly unkind. I mean, we think that the human race polarizes into angels and devils, but you can, when you're so terribly ill, discover both sides of people. I don't know myself, if I were in the position of being supportive, whether I would funk out or always soldier on – I don't know. I do think that one should, and I do think that whenever one doesn't rise to a challenge like that, one fails, in an odd way, quite deeply.

But I've noticed in cancer groups that people have as much a problem with their families and immediate friends as they have from the disease. And I think that in an awful lot of cases people die because they feel it's more convenient for other people if they're not around. I *do* think the mind affects the body – I've heard of people who have been perfectly well and decided that they were going to die, not going to go on under those circumstances, and they've died the next day. I think if you put the signal through to your body that you don't want to live, you can go in a very short space of time. The other thing I think is that you can go on indefinitely sometimes, if you're determined to. I have a strong suspicion that the human body isn't like a car, where if one part goes, the car breaks down.

I think I do have a strong will to live, yes. One resolution I make is that I'm not going to die before I've accomplished what I should accomplish, I'm not going to die before my time. And I repeat that to myself. It's a funny thing, we seem to believe that health and sickness, and strength and weakness, are sort of complementary to each other – that if we're eighty per cent strong, then we're twenty per cent weak. It's not like that; I think we can be kind of eighty per cent weak and eighty per cent strong, have an eighty per cent disease but an eighty per cent will to live that more or less balances out. It's not a matter of sitting down and rationally making up your mind. It's something else in us, there *is* something else in us. It is some force that wants to accomplish something, that comes through us, and that governs our life to a very large extent.

But I don't think you have to accept a kind of pallid, guilt-ridden Buddhism, I don't think that's native to it; it's a kind of Western version, that self-hating and self-abnegation, the guilt because you've got an ego. Perhaps in the East they don't have the same hang-ups that we have. I remember in India spending quite a lot of time beset by beggars, and I remember also seeing lepers; and I noticed these people had a glint in their eye, they had humour. They were amused that you were shocked at their hideous sores; they were by no means crushed. An awful lot of people in England, the unemployed, for instance – George Orwell's kind of men, bent, shuffling in the dole queue – they carry a far worse burden of stigma than the Indian beggar and leper.

We're lacking a spiritual dimension to life now. I was thinking today that unless one really has a spiritual quality one is in a sense a hollow man. Sooner or later hollow men cave in, don't they? Oh, some of the most grotesque, vain, inflated people go to churches and Buddhist temples nevertheless – yes, I'll certainly buy that one. Why? Why are we like that? Why anything? I can't answer that question. It's just the fact, we are what we are. Why do birds exist? There isn't a reason. Buddhism just says, 'What is this world, and how do we get through it?' It points to the way things are.

In the basic Theravada view, death isn't really something that happens at the end of our lives, death is something that happens from moment to moment. Every moment is a birth and a death in itself. And I suppose the central thing in encountering them is how well one is able to let go of the past and embrace the unknown, which is the new. The actual dying process, when other people will start making decisions for you, what is going to happen to you, where you will be put – that is a worrying stage. If you could be sure you would be among sympathetic people, who would honour wishes, and not start pumping you full of this and that . . . But hopefully you will have ceased to identify totally with yourself; if you've got a slightly wider perspective and you're able to look at yourself from without, then maybe it's easier to die, easier to let go. And there's that great line from Oscar Wilde, isn't there, as he was dying in this cheap, tawdry hotel bedroom in Paris, and he looked up at the wallpaper and said, 'Either that paper goes or I do'! I think that's marvellous, that capacity that human beings have to step outside themselves and see how ludicrous it all is. It dovetails with the Hindu notion that life and death, the world, is all the sport of the gods. Sport and play.

# Tessa Warburg

Fifty-seven is so much younger than we expected — we had expected to have another fifteen to twenty years together. We both knew he was going to die, and we both wanted to do what we could to be together during that time. Because we were very close, and so I knew it was going to be a most horrible blow to me. But nursing my husband at home for six months, I think, gave me the chance to do my very best to the very last. It was going to happen to one or other of us. We had often discussed it; and, I suppose, if I'm to be honest, we both knew that he would die first and that he would die relatively young. I don't know, we must have sensed it. He always was careful to make provision for me, he encouraged me to have a career so that I'd have something to do afterwards; and this was long before he got ill. He was a most remarkable, generous man. There's nobody else who can replace him.

I'm a Catholic, a convert actually, though my mother was a Lutheran. To be a Lutheran in Vienna is very odd, you see — it was either Catholic or Jewish there. She was American, and my stepfather was very anti-Hitler, he was editor of an anti-Hitler newspaper — that's why we came over here in 1938. I was nine; and I was fourteen when I converted to Catholicism. It wasn't an unhappy childhood at all, but I think when my mother divorced my father I just learned to be independent, just decided, you know, that all this business of depending on parents doesn't work; and in fact I turned to God instead. That's why I got so angry with God when Jeremy had to die!

The first thing I can remember about death was looking at pictures of soldiers in the war between China and Japan — I remember thinking about it. Then of course I was very aware of death during the war, because we lived twenty miles south of London, and we had the bombers going overhead, and then the doodle-bugs. My sister and I went to school about seven miles away on bicycles, and these doodle-bugs were sort of overhead and when the motor stopped we dashed into a ditch. We used to quarrel, as sisters do, but when the doodle-bugs came overhead I stopped and waited for her, because I knew it was dangerous and we had to be together. And then in Vienna, when the SS were actually in the streets, in the tanks . . . Oh yes, I was very aware of death. I remember being primarily scared of being maimed, because in England we were near East Grinstead, where there were all these RAF people who'd been burned and had plastic surgery.

My own father was eighty-six when he died – it was cancer of the oesophagus – and they did one of those huge operations and then pretended he would get well. I think the doctors do it because they're afraid, they're afraid of death themselves. It takes a lot of courage to stand out against them – they're kind of promising you something which actually they cannot give. But they can't seem to admit that they can't give it to you. I think my father was angry when he died. My half-brother was in charge, and he insisted on keeping him alive to the very last – they kept drips and things going, they took X-rays to the last moment, the whole business of modern medicine. It's completely and utterly mad. I think he was angry with us all for letting him live on.

My husband was so much younger. He did say he didn't mind dying, but when it came to the point he did want to live. It was a long-drawn-out suffering from cancer, you know, it took a year for him to die. He was at home, and the Health Service was absolutely fantastic about supporting us. I don't think people realize that they can do the nursing at home; they think the experts have to take over, and it's complete rubbish, there are no experts. We just had the district nurse. There isn't much to do, you see, with somebody who is very ill and paralysed. Morphine comes in slow-release tablets now, so you can control pain without injections. Many of the things are not that difficult to do. The most difficult thing was the moving of a very tall man, but we learned how to get over things like that. I think many relatives don't realize how little you need to do; and I think if they're encouraged to contribute to the nursing, it's an enormous help to the survivor to have done that.

At the beginning nobody would tell us the truth. I do want to get that across. We went to see a consultant, who was unbelievably aggressive to start with. Now I would know how to judge him – then I just couldn't understand why he was so aggressive, but it was because he knew he couldn't help. Apparently he could tell right away, but what he said was, 'Oh well, we'll have to have X-rays, we'll have to have scans, we'll have to have this and have to have the other.' And that went on and on and they never really told us the truth. My husband had kidney cancer, with bone metastases. We were told that the smallest amount of time he had was two years, and the largest ten years, but it wasn't true. We were very upset, because we asked directly, we said, 'Please tell us the truth, we want to know, we are not afraid.'

And they told us the radiotherapy could cure the bone cancer; now actually the radiotherapy was very damaging, and we should have been given the option of choosing. What it did was it made compression fractures in the spine which were unbelievably painful – well, we didn't know any of that. There was this on-off business – people told us he was dying, the next minute he wasn't dying, it was just horrific. This comes out in the book;* we were both very keen that other people should be spared this . . . Well, it just made it so much worse. The book is a diary of what he felt, what it feels like to know you're dying.

One of the radiotherapy consultants finally told me. And Jeremy said to me, 'What did she say?' And I said, 'Do you want me to tell you the truth?' And he said, 'Yes', and I told him.

He expected it; he said, 'I've known for some time that I'm dying, because of the sort of pain it is and the way it feels – it's as though it's sort of clawing me to death.' I do think stress can come into this disease, yes. He'd been very successful as an academic, but he gave it up because he wasn't really interested in it, he wanted to write fiction; but it was unsuccessful. I do think that had something to do with it, I'm quite sure. He could never get over the fact that it really didn't work.

He kept his mind up to the last, to the very last. In fact his last words were he wanted me to write up his diary. Many people

* *A Voice at Twilight*, London: Peter Owen, 1988.

were impressed that he was actually doing something through this impossible illness. He felt strongly that things could have been so much easier for him, and he wanted to do something for others in his position. He felt a great bond with other terminally ill patients, whether cancer or whatever disease. And he kept his mind in spite of the enormous dosages of morphine. He put into the diary his actual thoughts as he lay dying, what he actually felt. He wanted to record his thoughts, because he felt people didn't understand the dying. And that I think is true, people do not understand. So many people are afraid.

I'd like to think the diary might have practical effects. He did go into hospital for short breaks during the time, you see, but in some ways that was awful. For instance, in a hospital you're not allowed to keep drugs by you, they have to be dispensed by two nurses, and if there's a time-lag of an hour it can cause quite serious problems. At home I had the help of the domiciliary nurse from the hospice who taught me. But then some GPs refuse their patients access to the hospice nurses – the hospice is only allowed to help with the agreement of the GP, and if a GP turns it down, that's it. They have prejudices, I suppose; they think the hospice nurse is taking over their authority. Our GP was a very, very enlightened woman, and she said, 'Let the nurse tell us what to do and we'll do it.' Very often I could work out something that nobody else was interested enough to work out – for example, that I could sometimes add what I used to call a slug of liquid morphine just when it was needed.

It's very honest, the diary, so that it can be quite shocking. But I think if a person who was very ill read it, then they would feel less guilty about some of their thoughts. Because sometimes he did feel angry – he often said, 'Well, why do *I* have to die?' Someone might say, 'Why *not* him?' – and I'd think, well, you try it! I've never felt anger with him for leaving me; but I think the anger did come through before he died. I mean, we did get angry with each other in a way that we hadn't before. We were both surprised and I think a bit shocked. What happened was that all of a sudden he would get sulky about something; and I would feel, my God, I'm doing all this and all he can do is be sulky! And suddenly, you know, one would explode – and we thought that illness was supposed to bring you closer together, but we suddenly found we had these angry scenes. I had to work quite hard at reconciliation, because he wasn't in a very good position to defend himself. And obviously I felt guilty about being angry with a man as ill as that. But on the other hand we did find it in some way releasing – we always felt we could say what we wanted. There was a period I think about three months after he was paralysed when we had this anger, I can't remember precisely. And then after that it didn't occur again. It had gone. There was nothing to be angry about.

And then the children – we were both very fond of our children, but there came a time when we no longer wanted them to visit so often – it was too much for both of us, particularly him. He just wanted to be with me, and I wanted to be with him, and really we didn't want to be interrupted. You see, they would come and they would say, 'Well, shall we have a tape on, or watch some television, or play a game?' – all that is beside the point. The visits became hard, in the sense that he couldn't concentrate on them, he was no longer in the world sufficiently to be able to cope with them. They were young, and he just wanted his wife there, really – basically that's what he needed. And all we did was just sit there, perhaps in silence, all we could really do was hold hands. He was what he called 'out of this world' already – I mean, the news, for example, he didn't really care.

He was very happy that he had been a good father; he'd taken a great deal of trouble, spent time with his children, something that hadn't happened in his childhood. And he was very, very pleased at that. He felt that and his marriage were his big achievements really. He didn't really care about the academic stuff – strange, because he did so well in it, but he just didn't care particularly about that.

I didn't want a living-in nurse, I would have had to cook for her and think about her. I felt it would be an intrusion and a nuisance and would exhaust me. What I had was a baby alarm call; I went up to bed, and I could hear any noise he made, and then I could rush down. I used to do some of my own work as well – looking after him, I needed something . . . I set it up quite specifically. I knew Jeremy was going to die; I knew I would be devastated; and then I thought, I'll get this going, and then I'll have something constructive that I can do. Though I was so close to him, I had to have some escape. I'd go and visit him, then he'd sleep, we'd have a meal or coffee or something like that, and go out again. It was very nice that one could sort of keep calling in on him.

I thought he would want to die quickly, but he didn't. He was so keen to live, he used to say, 'Another day, another day of life'; and I used to think, if you're that keen I'm going to do everything I can to keep you here. And so I wouldn't wish him a single day less. I am glad that I held on – I think I was afraid of losing, of getting over-fatigued. And so I suppose in that sense I was glad he died when he did, because had he lived another three months I might have begun to run out of puff and not been able to do it – I wouldn't have liked that.

I think I was always religious and believed in the life hereafter, so perhaps it takes some of the sting out of death. But my parish priest didn't really *do* anything – he did eventually come to visit, but he refused to discuss anything religious, so it wasn't a success. My husband was very disappointed. He wasn't a Catholic, but he believed in a God. I think the priest thought he was putting my husband at his ease by talking about the weather and things like that, when my husband wanted him to talk about God. And after Jeremy's death . . . The priest said to me, 'Oh, I should have come round', several times – which is true. I think I would have liked him to have offered to come round and talk, yes. He seemed to be so busy making money for the church that he forgot all that. They seem to talk about so many other things – anything rather than the thing which is still with us and is not going to go away.

My husband was quite convinced that he would survive in some form; he was also quite convinced that he would be there to help his family, that somehow or other he would be able to get into their thoughts, and help them in some way. And I've felt quite strongly at times that he has helped me, yes. It was so quick in the end. My daughter was sleeping in the room with him – we were all in the house, we were taking it in turns. And I'd been to visit him, and he said, 'Go back to bed, you'll get exhausted' – it was about three in the morning. My daughter was there, and I said, 'Well, just call me if anything changes.' And then she called us, and we all got there, and then almost as we were there, the head was straight and then it lolled; but that was it. That was it – it was so quick in the end that we couldn't really believe that he was dead, finally dead. So it was almost as though that moment wasn't particularly significant.

We had worked together, discussed each other's work, we were very involved; we knew that one of us would have a horrible time after the other one died. But we still thought it was worth it. And as he said, it's no good complaining, we've had thirty-two years of a happy marriage, you know, how can you complain about that finishing? I had preparation; and in fact I always felt he helped me through the grief. Because it wasn't, you know: now he's ill and then he died. It was a gradual withdrawal from life. Gradually he would get less and less interested in the world. And obviously that conveyed itself to me. I would let go gradually, I suppose. People say to me, 'Wasn't it awful nursing him?' and I always say I'm glad I was able to do it. It's awful at the time, I'm not denying it. But somehow or other you can get something wonderful out of it. You still have that awful grief and that sense of loss, and you'll never get over that entirely, because the person will never be there physically. But if I've got a message, it's try to do the nursing at home, because both you and the patient can be immeasurably enriched by this experience, and nobody can take that away from you.

But there was an extraordinary thing that happened to me after his death – I felt I wasn't worth anything, sort of what I'd call a Cinderella syndrome. *Aschenputtel* – ashes, yes. I hadn't expected that I myself should feel that I wasn't worth as much as I had been as a married woman, I was very surprised at that. I was never a dependent wife, it just isn't me. But I felt that the rest of society . . . Well, I know why I felt it, because it was obvious in bank managers and people like that. I mean, they would take the attitude of, you poor little thing, you can't possibly cope – which I didn't much take to.

Each time I saw this reaction I used to say, 'Of course, my son will help me'! And I thought to myself, it's the first time in my life I've understood what the feminists are talking about. It was because I was a woman. For example, probate, which I did myself . . . My husband had his bank and I had mine, so I went to his bank to collect the house deeds and various other bits and pieces he had there; and the bank manager said to me, 'Well, do you need any help with this, that, and the other . . .?' and I said, 'No, I'm going to do probate.' And he said, '*You*'re going to do it' – you know!

Yes, it is often done by solicitors, but solicitors charge a lot of money for it, and it's actually very easy. I mean, for somebody who's used to dealing with forms and things like that, it's absolutely nothing. I had a friend who was widowed and she was actually very poor, and she didn't want to turn it over to a solicitor because even for the very small estate it would have been two hundred pounds. She was very resentful – they would *not* let her do it. She was someone who had been very dependent on her husband, so she was not in as strong a position as I had been. She in the end allowed them to push her around, but she was very upset about it. Again, I would like to convey to other people what they can do to protect themselves.

Somehow or other, the word 'widow' . . . It's almost as though people would just sooner you threw yourself on the funeral pyre. Just as the nurses thought I should stop doing any work while Jeremy was ill, because I was a woman and that's all that really mattered. I mean, my gardener, for example, without even notic-ing what he was saying, he came along and said he'd always help out, he's a nice chap; and then he said, 'Of course,' he said, 'I've got my widows' – forgetting entirely that I was a widow. He thinks of them in a deprecating sort of way. So when you're left on your own you have this feeling, you know: how am I going to resist society in this? – I don't want that, I don't like that . . . Fortunately for me I have work to do and then I can get, I suppose, my own persona back.

My children have been particularly nice, they invite me to things – it must be awful to be bereaved and completely alone. People say there's embarrassment when you talk about the dead person. I like to talk about him with people who have known him – why not? And I've found people don't seem to mind; that's been very fortunate. There's nothing worse than this awful business that you have to hide it, as though it isn't quite nice. Well, it *isn't* quite nice! Life isn't, is it?

Yes, my religion is a help; but I find I'm religious just by nature, and I need my religion just as much when things go well as when they go badly. I can't say that I pray in the sense of saying the Our Father or the Hail Mary particularly, except in mass; but I have a conversation with God, if that makes sense – that's to say, I feel things coming back. For example, there was that time when I was very angry, I was very angry with God for allowing this to happen to what I considered a very good man. I got really very angry, and this went on for quite a long time. But gradually, because I still went to mass . . . I find it enormously helpful when a whole group of people are worshipping God – sometimes you can sort of feel, you know, 'when one or two are gathered together in my name' – it makes an enormous difference, it all seems to be lifted up. And then a sort of peace would come.

I don't think God makes any illness happen – *we* make them happen. I think we do in some way choose, I think we influence far more than we actually realize. I think that we talk ourselves into all kinds of things, not as individuals necessarily, but as a group of people – I mean, for example, this extraordinary strength of the society around me, making me feel worthless as a widow. I think that we, together, actually cause the bad as well as the good, and the thing is that we can do the good and that we can resist the other. I think even that we invent death, so to speak – I think, you see, that Jesus was the son of God but that we could all be like Jesus, if only we could believe properly. Yes, I do – I think we could walk on water, I think it's only because we choose not to that we don't. Because if you think about it, there's so much that if you believe you can do it, suddenly you can.

The great help for me was doing Jeremy's diary. Because suddenly everything stops and you're left high and dry, without anything to do, having done it every minute of the day. Fortunately there was that I could do for him. It was very hard to do, because you had to relive it all the time, so I used to sit there with tears pouring down my face. But because I did the diary for him, and said, 'Now help me with this, I'm not going to be able to do this on my own', I had the feeling that we were collaborating as we did when he was alive. We went through it all again together. But I found that once I'd proofread it, it seemed final then. And there was a sort of – 'Now what can I do for him?' And I think I do cling to trying to do something for him, because that's what I liked to do. Probably I should now shut the door and leave it – I hope I can do that, but I do find I am resisting it. My daughter thinks that it's a mistake, that I ought to really do things for myself, and I find I do resist that. But it's only sixteen months since he died.

People say, 'Well, you could meet somebody else'; but it could never be a replacement. For a start, you cannot have anyone else to share your children. And thirty-odd years of a relationship, you can never replace that. I feel as if he would tolerate my remarrying, if I wanted to do it, but I don't think he would feel particularly happy about it, no; in a sense I think he'd feel betrayed. And in a sense also I think I would be betraying him, I think I'll always feel that. He *said*, 'Don't feel you can't marry again'; but I felt he was being kind. I suppose deep down I feel that I'm married to him and that's that.

I feel, I suppose . . . that he's just around somewhere. I think he has had his purgatory already, I don't think there's any need for that. At some times I can pick up parts of his soul, spirit, or whatever you like to call it, certainly sometimes I feel quite strongly . . . It could just be imagination. I mean, there are times – very often – when I think something to myself and I'll hear his answer. But perhaps that happens to a lot of people. Sometimes I'll ask him questions, and then – well, it's hard to believe it's an imagined answer, because he'll say something like, 'Of course I know that, don't be so stupid', you see. I always get an answer, and not necessarily the one I'm expecting. And some-times just, 'Well, I don't know why you're fussing about that' – that sort of thing. And just occasionally a sort of feeling of arms round one's shoulders, you know. I *feel* it to be him. I feel that he is there; that's quite strong. That he's there, still *interested*.

No, I never feel haunted – I thought about that, but I never felt it at all. I thought, I'm in this huge house by myself, is it going to creak and am I going to think he's walking down the stairs? But I never did. He always said, you shouldn't be in that house on your own, it's so remote; but there I am, living there . . .

But there was one day . . . It sounds insane, but we had this enormous oak in the garden, and because my husband was such a big man, I suppose, I equated him with this oak; and this was suddenly torn down in a gale, not the recent big gale but another one. I knew there was something wrong with the tree, so I knew it could happen, but it was a terrible shock – almost as though he had died again, or he was *really* dead. That sort of thing. So one does imagine things.

# Rabbi Albert Friedlander

Living through conditions where everyone, all the outside world, said to me as a child, 'You're inferior because you're Jewish', probably the way I compensated was to say that either they are right and I'm inferior, or they are wrong, in which case being Jewish might be superior – I overcame my inferiority complex in that way. Then just thinking through: well, if it's good and right to be a Jew, what is the best kind of Jew? The ideal then would be to be a rabbi, of course.

We survived through the *Kristallnacht* – the November '38 pogrom in Berlin – but in 1939, early in January, I was able to flee with my family. I was eleven. We escaped to Cuba, stayed for a while, and then came to the United States, where I grew up. I was chaplain of Columbia University in New York, but I'd married a London girl and in the summer of '66 we came here, and we've been here ever since.

So I think that from the time I was ten or eleven years old I was pretty much convinced that I would at least become a Jewish scholar. Whether I would serve a community was something else again; but being a rabbi means being a teacher, and many rabbis can become, let's say, university professors or hospital chaplains or writers, and work in various areas, although the bulk of them will take on congregational commitments. I'm still the dean of our seminary here, and as the rabbi of the Westminster Synagogue I give sermons twice a week and hold regular services.

Oh, certainly I had persecution at school in Berlin – being beaten up continually, until I had to be taken out of the general school system and put into a Jewish school, being in an attack on a Jewish rowing club when it was stormed by Nazis, arrests by the police and interrogrations when I was ten years old, going into hiding during *Kristallnacht*. Experiencing, I think, quite a bit of persecution. Later I realized that many of my friends who did not escape died in the concentration camps; I don't think I realized that till the mid-forties, but certainly one could sense danger; one knew that there were camps, even though they were called re-education centres. We were aware that they were at least places of torture. But in the immediate family circle there was no direct encounter with death as such.

That time I mentioned when we were at this Jewish rowing club outside of Berlin, my father and brother and I were hiding in one room, and the Nazis broke down the doors with an axe. And seeing that axe come through the doors of the room, and becoming bigger and bigger – I certainly thought about death then. When finally we were permitted to leave without being harmed, my mother and sister in the next room had already seated themselves on the edge of an open window, because they thought that if it would be a case of being raped, being attacked physically, they would throw themselves out. One could not help but think about that, even long after the event; so there was the death that comes out of violence, call it almost a fear more of fellow human beings than of death itself.

At home we attended synagogue, but we did not have a kosher home as such. My mother was a very devout and believing Jewish woman, but she was not Orthodox – one didn't have to be Orthodox to be devout. Certainly there was a very deep, quiet religious faith which was part of my mother's life, and it communicated itself to me. And the fact that we did attend synagogue services, and I did go to a Jewish school, all helped to make me feel that I was part of a religious tradition. And certainly I prayed, and felt that I was not doing this because I was conforming to the wishes of parents, but because I wanted to pray. I think the basic teachings, even then, of Judaism that I was taught were that there was life after death; in Judaism in any event there is no very clear distinct picture about heaven or hell, but a very firm belief that death is not the end, but that there is a different, new, separate kind of life that takes place then. I would already be aware, let's say, of my mother lighting memorial candles on the anniversary of my grandmother's death – so there was the knowledge that people remained aware of those who had died, that we had ceremonies that continued to keep them alive for us in some fashion.

I think once I had decided to become a rabbi, it became part of my task to deal with death in terms of helping others and incorporating it into my regular activities. I suppose I was a young rabbi of about twenty-four when I had a call from a member of the congregation that her husband had died. He – the corpse – was still seated at the table in the dining-room. I think that was the first time I saw a corpse, and I had to sit by the body through the night, because it is part of the tradition, our tradition, that a body would not be left alone at any point after death until the Burial Society would come and take care of it. Often a group of men would come in to spend the night, saying psalms, keeping the body company, from a sense still of the dignity of an individual who at this point could not be simply viewed as empty clay, refuse, to be left alone.

Today most people die in hospitals, and there is little of the more or less traditional Victorian death scene at the end of a novel. But nevertheless I think I learned from those first encounters, and also sitting down with individuals, I learned that one had to accept death as part of life, that it was not that here was a complete caesura, everything coming to a total stop, but that one still cared for the person who had died, one cared for the family who surrounded that person. And that also, no matter how many sophisticated concepts one has about death – what it may be, what it may not be, whether it is the end or not – that I think probably for clergy in general at the moment of death, entering the house of bereavement, one does not spout theology, one simply deals with the reality of hugging the widower, of saying a word of comfort, of sitting down with the children, of trying to be practical and help make arrangements about the funeral. There, then, one does not think so much about the dead as about the living; but I think that is part of Jewish life.

If you say, 'Well, what are the basic Jewish teachings about death?' certainly we would say that from ancient times we have believed that there was an immortal soul, that there is a spark from the divine, from God, which rests in every human being. But there was never in *any* civilization or religion just one clear concept of death, but many parallel concepts. In biblical times there was a kind of folk eschatology, people who believed in an after-existence in Sheol. There's the story of Samuel being summoned up by Saul, the king. Samuel had, in terms of Jewish tradition, rooted out all soothsayers and necromancers from the community; but suddenly when Samuel was dead and Saul was about to go to war, he wanted to talk to Samuel. And they found him the old woman of Endor – not really a witch, although she's always called that – a wise woman who looks at Saul and says, you know, 'You're going to kill me, I'm not supposed to do this.' He says, 'No; summon up Samuel for me.' So there is, then, this shade of Samuel who tells Saul, 'Why bother talking to me now? Tomorrow we'll be together, tomorrow you'll die.'

You see, there are folk beliefs – on the whole the concept of immortality develops slowly. In about, let's say, the time of Jesus, which would be more of a reference point for you, there were two religious parties in Judaism, the Sadducees and the Pharisees. The Pharisees were the more liberal 'people's party', who said that beliefs grow and develop and who believed firmly in the immortality of the soul, whereas the Sadducees, who were the priests, refused to accept the concept of immortality, saying it was not present clearly in the five books of Moses, not present in the Bible, and that they refused to accept any new notions. But the Pharisees, who became the rabbinical party that survived after the destruction of the temple, were then the great teachers of Judaism, who said, 'We believe in immortality, we believe in a final judgement, and at the end of days a physical resurrection of the body at the time of the coming of the Messiah, the establishment of the Messianic kingdom.'

Those beliefs are part of the Jewish tradition; but we would have to be very careful and say that there are many parallel concepts. They are all stories, they're developments; certainly there was for a long time, and there still is among many Jews, the notion that there will be a resurrection of body and soul together; and at that point, at the coming of the Messiah, there will also be a time of final judgement, and it will take place in Palestine, in the land of Israel.

You see, Judaism does not have a really clear notion of heaven and most of Judaism clearly denies a notion of hell – it simply seems to us impossible to conceive that the finite amount of sins that a person may commit would be followed by an infinity of punishment. I mean, you can always find some Jew who believes it, but the vast majority simply would not accept the notion of hell. And the rabbis actually had a fairly unclear notion of paradise; heaven could be called the *Yeshiva shel ma'alah*, the academy on high, where one could study twenty-four hours a day – that was not everybody's notion of heaven!

What we centre on is the very firm conviction that the soul as such is immortal, that when somatic death occurs the soul does live on. This then can give rise to many varieties of belief – Jewish spiritualists who will call forward wandering souls, metempsychosis believers . . . You have in Jewish literature, for instance – there's a play called *The Dybbuk*, that's the soul of someone who has died which enters another person. When you enter a Jewish house of mourning – although most Jews don't even associate it with this – the windows and mirrors and all reflecting surfaces would be covered up, and the old notion of course was that if you looked into a mirror after a death, the soul of the departed might enter you and take you over. But this is folk belief rather than teaching.

Basically we say that we live in one world at a time; we shouldn't spend too much time thinking about heaven, or even link ethical action with rewards in heaven – being nice to someone because you're getting credit points for heaven, because you're getting a reward. So Judaism says the good you do is rewarded by the good itself, the evil that you do is punished by the evil in this world – even though it's sometimes very hard to accept this when one sees evil flourish, and even though in some Jewish writings there is an attempt to reconcile those who think in that fashion by assuring them that the evil will be punished and the good will be rewarded in the next world.

There is a particular ethical dynamism in the Jewish teachings that says that if one doesn't have the option of being rewarded in the next world, the only way not to suffer so much is to create a better world now. It's been said by teachers that this ethical dynamism is a difference between East and West; that Buddhism and other religions from the East say that you have many sufferings, many hungers that cannot be fulfilled for you, and what you have to do is just adjust yourself to that reality. That if you do not get enough food you must learn to live with hunger, that you yourself must change and be part of the overall stream of development. In Judaism it's been much more that if one hungers in the world, one should change the world to create enough food for all; that if it is an unjust society, one does not conform to that society but one must try to change it.

Judaism says we are part of *this* world and it's the only world we have; it says that we'll die with confidence that our soul will go on to a new life, a different life, but meanwhile we don't think about it here in this world at this time. We're very much this-worldly – let us try to create a better world. And in many ways, for example, Judaism would say that one doesn't sit and wait for a Messiah to come to bring in the better world, but that in a sense the contribution of every human being is necessary towards creating a Messianic world; that therefore rather than waiting for death and release and going up to a more beautiful, carefree world, one has to live in this one. And we'd say that suffering is an aspect of society that we have to accept, but it doesn't mean that we have to surrender to it – we are impelled to try to change it.

I think that's why you find so many Jews involved in causes of social justice, charitable work – one doesn't simply say it's fate, or it's decreed, one has to express one's concern *now* for others. One doesn't leave them to the mercy of fate or of an inscrutable plan, but says, without challenging God, that we accept that we are God's partners in the creating of a better world. We don't have a monastic tradition, no – there are some tiny sects, there are some individuals ... But to us it is almost criminal to say that you can shut yourself off from the suffering of your neighbour – you cannot just sit and try to purify your own soul. You might view it as a short-term system of discipline – I could visualize a Jew saying, 'I'll spend six months in a Zen monastery in order to develop my way of thinking and get a new view', but not leaving the world. It would be to learn from the Zen Buddhists, or anyone else, how to be a clearer thinker and then to apply that newly found talent for the benefit of our society.

If someone comes to one and says, 'I have three months, six

months, maybe a year left – what should I do?' – again, for Judaism, it's a more practical matter. It's not to say, 'God will take you in his arms and bring you to paradise.' This month one of my very dear friends, a rabbi in his fifties, sadly died of cancer, and he knew about it for about six months. I and other rabbis would come and sit with him, and I think it was really more that he could let out some of the bitterness – he knew all the answers we might give him. I think we can always say, 'Trust in God' and 'Remember we believe that your soul will continue once your pain and suffering in this world has ended.' But I would think that that, in a way, is not often used in our tradition; what we say at this point much more is, 'If there is a limited amount of time left to you, how will we put your earthly affairs in order?' At that point one comes more as a friend and not as a teacher of theology.

Towards the end one comes with prayers that are a spiritual house-cleaning, as it were. When I come to a dying man, it can happen that he'll become very frightened and say, 'I'm not that ill – what are you doing here?' So there are even standard prayers, where the prayer-book says, 'At this point the rabbi says to the person to remember that many people have recited this prayer and recovered, that it does not mean that this will be the very end, even though the likelihood is that the end is approaching.' That is very much part of the prayers at the very end. But I would say that in the six months or so before death one does not sit and utter very noble thoughts and speak about heaven – at this point the rabbi is more a teacher and friend.

Of course it can happen that a person asks me, 'Rabbi, what are your beliefs, what do you feel, what can you say?' – then I would speak of my firm belief in the continuation of the soul. And with some very rational people who would argue and say they don't believe it, I think at times I've talked of the second law of thermodynamics – that, all right, you can take a piece of paper and burn it, and it's transformed, but it hasn't left the universe, and how much more does this apply to the soul, which directs and commands the spiritual? That spirit is stronger than matter, so why should spirit be excluded from the law of conservation?

I think many Jews do believe that they will meet those who've died; and again it's not a matter where we would argue for or against. If someone comes to me and says, 'Will I not meet my husband who died ten years ago?' I can say, 'This is part of your faith, and I feel that you are right to believe this – what can we know?' I would not argue about it – at a point like this it would be heartless and cruel for me to argue about it. I think in an adult discussion group, a study group on the nature of death, I would say we do not really have this clear an idea. You see, Judaism is not really a theoretical, theological religion. Even though rabbis will spend a lifetime studying, even then, if they disagree on something, they might say, 'Well, we'll table this problem until the coming of the Messiah – right, tabled indefinitely!' When it comes to ordinary Jewish life, Jews very rarely ask each other, 'What do you *believe*?' Even when you come to the distinction between Orthodox and Reform Jews, there would be far more argument about daily practices, very little in terms of dogma. We very, very rarely argue about a set of theological beliefs; there is no Westminster Creed or Oxford Confession or Nicene Creed to be memorized and recited.

I think partly this has been due to the fact that we have lived as a community, sometimes a ghettoized, a forcibly restrained community since the late eighteenth century and early nineteenth century, characterized as Jews living together by the outside world, and it wasn't really until the nineteenth century that there was a break-up into Orthodox, Conservative, Reform, Liberal – things of that sort. Until then, in the ghetto, even the *apicoros* – this is a term coming from Epicurean, which means a doubter, a sceptic – was part of the Jewish community, and no one thought he was not a Jew. So it was not a question of testing a Jew by demanding the belief points one, two, three, four, five, but 'Are you identified with the Jewish community? Do you practise?' Somewhere rabbis have written that there are no Jewish dogmas; there is the assertion of the oneness, the unity of God.

I'll tell you what happens when a person is about to die. First – in a traditional community certainly – the community may get together a quorum of ten adult males to sit in the synagogue to recite psalms, in the hope that psalms may somehow have curative powers and that through a miracle the person might be saved;

even when they're clear in their minds that the psalms will not as such have an effect on recovery, they are a way in which the community says, 'We want to do our utmost for this member of the congregation, we want to pray, we want to hope, we want to share this prayer and hope with the family.' Towards the end then the rabbi or friend comes and recites some closing prayers, including the affirmation of faith, the *Shema*, which is 'Hear, oh, Israel, the Lord our God, God is one.'

When death has taken place – well, in an Orthodox community burial must take place within twenty-four hours, but in the non-Orthodox Jewish community it very often is delayed several days, because Jews are scattered over the whole world, and family may arrive from America or from Israel, and allowances are made for this. Cremation is practised in the Reform and Liberal community; the reluctance against cremation arises out of teachings related to the physical resurrection of the body, and in some ways also I think is due to the fact that Jews want a place to come and recite prayers. What is becoming more the practice in the non-Orthodox community is that the urn is interred into a small plot, with a gravestone, so that the family can still gather there annually.

When the person has just died, the body is prepared, either by the Burial Society or in the modern funeral parlour, washed, and a plain white linen garment put on – the interesting thing is that on the holiest day, Yom Kippur, the Day of Atonement, these white gowns may be worn already in the synagogue. For men, generally their prayer shawl is taken and draped around the body. Prayers are said, the body watched over. And at the time of the funeral there is still the ancient ceremony of cutting – that is, the rabbi will cut either part of a man's suit or part of his tie, or more modern people may have put a piece of black crape on their dress or suit and that will be cut – this rending is a sign of grief. A service will be conducted, mainly in Hebrew, with a eulogy; the body is accompanied to the grave and more prayers are said, then a shovel of dirt is thrown upon the coffin by all the mourners, who in this way participate in the actual burial of the body. Some more prayers, then one washes one's hands – in some ways the old concept of the uncleanliness of a corpse survives, and in order to purify oneself one washes one's hands before one leaves the cemetery. Actually Cohenim – the priestly descendants, those who have the name of Cohen – in an Orthodox community would not enter the cemetery, because they are not supposed to come near a body.

A memorial candle is lit, a twenty-four hour candle; then that evening – *Shiva* means seven – for the next seven days at evening the friends and family would come together and recite the evening prayers. There may be a sermon the first day or so, a eulogy as well, or it may simply be the saying of prayers; but friends come together – except on Friday night the *Shiva* is interrupted so that members can go to the synagogue, and then Saturday night the counting of the seven days would resume. It is a psychologically totally sound practice; from the most intense grief – the tearing of garments at the burial – you have seven days of mourning where most of the mourners would stay in the house. The *Shiva* is part of the *Sheloshim*, the thirty-day period; for thirty days after the funeral there would be a formal abstaining from entertainments, pleasures, one wouldn't go to parties and restaurants and so on. Then for the eleven months after the death the male chief mourner is expected to go to the synagogue every day and to participate in the service in order to recite *Kaddish*, a mourning prayer, showing that throughout every day he does recall the person who was loved and is now mourned.

Oddly enough, it's not rare for this to be done. Actually they're supposed to go three times a day; now quite often they only go once, but even those who do it three times a day, they might stop by the synagogue at seven or eight o'clock in the morning, go on to work, go to the late-afternoon service, which is then linked to the evening service. No, the widow doesn't go – this is still the Orthodox pattern – I think a male member of the family would go to the regular daily services. So this takes place for eleven months, after which the gravestone is dedicated, which is a big service for family and friends. Then that ends the mourning pattern; it goes from the most intense grief to the formal observance, and this pattern of returning to normalcy can bring one through the grief and back into the community.

Then on the actual anniversary of death, each year, one lights a twenty-four-hour candle and says prayers – it's called a *Yahrzeit* candle, it's a memorial. It is lit and prayers are said, and so each year at least after the year of mourning there is still a reminder, as long as the father or son or other relative survives. And then, too, there are about four times a year when in the synagogue, the liturgy, one has a memorial service and people come to that and say the memorial prayers. The Day of Atonement, the most solemn day – this is a memorial service for everyone, for the martyrs who've died in the past, for those who have no one to mourn for them; for our own loved ones we have this special *Yizkor*, the memorial service, in which we recall their life and remind ourselves to be true to their memory.

I do believe it to be a support to the family, and to friends, because friends may not know what to do – 'We couldn't go to the funeral, but this week we'll stop by the house during the *Mimyam*, the evening services.' It gives them something that they can do, and in a society like Great Britain's where stiff upper lip and repression are present, here at least is an opportunity to weep. The family generally sit on low stools, and they openly and physically express their grief, and in this way it is not bottled up. The disadvantage may be that often, after the week of being so totally surrounded by friends, suddenly it's over, and they may be lonelier two months afterwards than at the time.

So much of religion revolves around these rites of passage, and death is one time when the whole community, even if they are very far from the synagogue, come to us. Sometimes they don't know what to ask for, what they want – sometimes it would be simply sitting and saying prayers with them, or talking to them. It varies quite a bit here from my American practice, where people were much more open and in a way expected much more from their rabbi. I think it's part of this coldness, of British reserve; someone might telephone and say, 'Rabbi, my husband, my wife, has died', and when I say, 'I'll come right over', there would be hesitation and embarrassment. Two nights ago the wife of someone who was dying of cancer in hospital phoned me to ask about arrangements for the funeral, and when I indicated, 'Well I'm coming over to the hospital to say final prayers by the bedside', she was amazed, she hadn't even thought that this was necessary. I don't know – I think there is a reserve that comes more from the outside than the Jewish side.

I don't have a fear of death myself, not at the moment. Rarely. Some years ago, in the States, I was swimming off Long Island and was pulled out to sea by the undertow. My wife was highly pregnant and a heart patient; she was on the beach and didn't realize what was happening, so I couldn't call for help. But although I was very much aware that this was a situation that could end in death, I think I just concentrated on swimming more than anything else. Maybe afterwards, as a residual fear, I found that I didn't enjoy ocean swimming that much any more. Perhaps I will have more fears as I grow older.

When I had to sit by the body throughout the night, as a young rabbi, I think there was no fear as such, there was a certain calmness. There was more a concern for the young widow, for the babies. I would think about the man, whom I'd respected and liked, I would sit there and read my book of psalms, but really I felt no fear. This year, not so long ago, I had to sit in the mortuary room of a large hospital, and it's really cold in there. This was unusual; the family were fairly traditional, it was a young woman who had died, and the husband said, 'I cannot bear to think of her being left all alone – Rabbi, will you go and spend the night there?' Well, no, it wasn't a particularly good experience! But it was a duty, it was a matter of pastoral caring for them.

There is one rabbinical teaching that says, 'Repent one day before your death.' Of course the answer to the puzzle is that however near the day of death you don't therefore repent every day – I think it almost means keeping your books up to date, living to the full, trying to undo the harm that you've done as quickly as possible. We have our ten days of penitence where we have to visit people that we might have wronged only faintly and ask them for forgiveness. But, you know, it's not as though we were Etruscans and worried so deeply about death that we're terribly afraid of it – we accept it as part of life.

No, I don't think the Old Testament God, as you would call him, is a punishing God, he is a God of love. If you look even at Christian teachings, Jesus was asked, 'What are the basic teachings of religion?' and he says 'First love the Lord your God with all your heart, will all your soul, with all your might'; and that is taken from the Book of Deuteronomy, it is a teaching of the Torah, of Jewish law, that Jesus knew to be so much part of Judaism. The Book of Job – the whole concept of that is that the righteous person does not have to fear God. Job suffers, and he challenges God, he says, 'Why?' And in the end the point is that God replies to Job – not to Job's friends, who come and say, 'Suffering is good for you, suffering is a consequence of sin, you must be punished' – all this God discards, and says, 'Job spoke more truly than any of you, it's simply that my plan is too vast for humans to understand.' At that point it is Job who is exalted.

Of course, the whole question as to why the innocent suffer continues. But it wasn't God who carried out the holocaust, it was humans; and if we live in a world of free will, there must be evil as well as good. If we were just automated puppets who could not do wrong, then we wouldn't be human beings – there can be no good unless there is the free option to do evil.

And what do you really mean by forgiving? Ten days of atonement deal with the fact that we must try to forgive each other. But when a Nazi comes to me and says, 'I've killed – can you forgive me?', I can just say, 'Look, you have to take it to your victims, not me; but your victims are dead. I can't speak for the Jews you've killed, or the gypsies, or the homosexuals, I cannot say on their behalf, "I forgive you." I'm not like a priest, who speaks on behalf of God. You're a Christian; you must pray, you can confront God, God's mercy is infinite. But *I* cannot speak for God.'

I've just returned from speaking at the *Kirchentag* in Germany, where 180,000 come to a meeting, and the fact that I meet with Germans, that I talk with them, that I work with them and their problems, shows that I'm not having a blanket policy of 'Hate all Germans'. But at the same time to talk about being forgiving is, I think, a very Christian concept. Christians, I think, imagine that we Jews hate those who have wronged us, and that it would be better for the sinners and also for the victims if we said, 'We drop our hate, we forgive you.' But this is a category of thinking where ... we won't act, we won't stereotype, we won't accuse *en masse*; but if I meet a Klaus Barbie, I cannot say, 'Klaus, I forgive you, as far as I'm concerned everything is wiped out.' To us that is a way of thinking that simply doesn't enter into our categories of thought.

Who am I to speak for God? And whom am I to judge others? Because we don't set ourselves in God's place and forgive or do not forgive, we also cannot judge other human beings. If they have committed sins they must be tried, let's say, by a jury of their peers, they must be judged by God, but it is not my function to say 'good', 'bad'. I can fight against the consequence of sin, I can fight against Nazis or murderers or rapists and try to create a better society, but I'm not the judge and jury. I can only give them to the earthly and to the heavenly courts, to be tried by them.

# Ben Helfgott

When the war broke out I was nearly ten years old, and so my preoccupations were those of a normal child – ours was a very happy home. Although I was a child I was very much aware of what was going on around me, the evil influence of what was going on in Germany – the Jews being driven out, and many of those who were originally from Poland being sent back there. There were some people from my home town who originally left and settled in Germany – now they returned. And then towards 1939, the outbreak of the war, we were more and more aware that war was coming. Everybody was very concerned about the future, and although I was a child I also felt it – I had a very early political awareness. People were often congregating around the wireless sets, always listening to what the latest news was.

I was born in a place called Piotrków, forty-two kilometres away from Łódź, with a population of fifty thousand people. Anti-Semitism in Poland had got worse; after the death of Marshal Piłsudski in 1935 conditions in Poland deteriorated as far as the Jews were concerned, because the right-wing party took over and they had strong anti-Semitic tendencies. And as time went on, in a strange sort of way and in spite of the Nazi menace, the Poles in those days were thinking of gaining colonies. It was a semi-fascist government with an expansionist outlook, very anti-communist.

Piotrków was a progressive town, in fact it was a socialist town. There were still many Jews who were very Orthodox and wore the kaftans and peaked hats, but that was declining very fast. I spoke Polish at home, though my parents between them still spoke Yiddish to each other, my grandparents spoke Yiddish. There were songs we were singing at school that now seem so ridiculous when I think about it, at a time when the danger was so imminent – 'We are seeking colonies abroad'! The Poles were menaced by the Germans; Slavs were considered *Untermenschen*. But the Jews were to be completely eradicated. Obliterated from the face of the earth.

I remember the invasion vividly, very vividly, it's just like it happened today. It was Friday the 1st of September 1939, and we were on holiday at the time and we were making our way home because, although we were not Orthodox, my parents kept the Sabbath. My mother wanted to be back early in the morning so that she could prepare for the Sabbath – we'd been in my mother's home town, where my grandfather was living, and my aunt and uncle. We left at about seven o'clock in the morning and we were scheduled to arrive at nine-thirty; but once the bus had started, every so often it stopped and we had to run into the woods or to the ditches because the planes were overhead, the bombing was taking place . . . And this journey was supposed to take two hours, but we didn't arrive till six o'clock in the evening. Everywhere we stopped we heard sirens. We heard bombs falling; and that was the first day.

The following day my town was bombed. We spent our day in the basement, and after the bombing there was panic and people were leaving town, running towards the east; because there were already rumours that the army was getting near, they were moving very fast. The Polish army was in disarray, completely disoriented. Like most people, my parents decided to leave home. We were caught up, on the night of the 2nd of September, we were caught up with thousands of people on the road. After travelling all night we reached a place fifteen kilometres away called Sulejow where the atmosphere was tranquil and peaceful. We stopped there, and for a little while it seemed as though war would never touch that place – everybody walking around, saying, 'Well, maybe it's not as bad as we think.' The weather was absolutely beautiful, it was like a summer's day. I remember playing outside with other children and my two sisters.

Suddenly in the afternoon, without any warning, German planes swooped down very low and started dropping incendiary bombs. Sulejow was a small town, almost like a village, a population of about five thousand; most of the houses were wooden houses with thatched roofs. Within seconds the whole place was in a conflagration, everything was burning. What happened was that just about a minute before, my mother must have heard the planes and she came running up and she grabbed me and she pulled me into the house where we were staying – this was one of the very few brick houses. A few seconds later all hell was set loose. We were all frightened, because people were shouting and screaming and praying, others were coming in from the street, so that at that moment we were probably about thirty or forty people there. All around everything was burning – we saw people running in flames. We heard the noises of cattle and horses and cats and dogs, all burnt, screaming – it was hell, you know, Dante's *Inferno* must have looked like this.

It was the first time I saw people burning, and I saw everything burning, people screaming and crying. Then for a few minutes the bombing stopped, and the door opened and we all started running towards the woods, because the smoke and flame was all around. And as we were running the planes swooped down low and they were just shooting at people, strafing, and people were falling, all around us people were falling. When we got into the woods, there again another hell was before us – people were running in all directions and families were separated, they were all shouting the names of their loved ones and their echo in the woods was reverberating. It was bedlam. But we were together somehow, it was my mother's presence of mind really; she kept us all together and we were running together. We got into the wood and ran as far as we could and sat down, but as we were there people were passing by – 'Have you seen so-and-so, have you seen my brother, have you seen my sister?' And they were running around completely insane.

The next few days we were travelling, we either walked or travelled by a horse and cart which my father hired – because there were no cars, in my home town there were only two cars altogether. The invasion had started on Friday and the bombing of Sulejow was on Sunday; on Tuesday, when we emerged from the woods, to our horror we saw German troops. There was no point in going any further. So we decided to return to my home town. On our way back we passed Sulejow. The stench that was there from burnt and decaying bodies, human and animal flesh, was indescribable – it will always remain in my nostrils. There had been five thousand people living there, and there must have been an influx of a few thousand more; but the tally of deaths was about four thousand. They kept clearing bodies, right from the very beginning, but there were still hundreds of charred bodies, unrecognizable, most of them just the bodies without legs, without heads, all lying around everywhere. And the smell, the stench. This stench has never left me. God forbid I should have to smell this again, but I would always know what human burning is. It's stayed with me ... Many years later, I was in Poland and I was in a coach with a group of people that I was travelling with to commemorate the twentieth anniversary of the uprising of the Warsaw ghetto. We were sitting there talking and suddenly I realized that we were going to go via Sulejow. I was telling my friend who was sitting next to me what had happened, and suddenly as we were getting near I smelt the stench of human bodies. I know it was only in my mind, but it was so uncanny.

At the time I was in a stupor. I was always from my early childhood an avid reader and by the time I was ten years old I'd read thousands of books; and I would let my imagination go wild, you know, when I read cowboy books or any other kind of adventure books. And suddenly, here I was ... And it was so completely different from my imagination. It was one thing when you read and hear stories, and another when suddenly you're confronted with the reality. And this was only just the beginning.

When we got back to my home town we heard a tale of woe that was almost as frightening as what we experienced during the bombing. We were told that as soon as the Germans entered my town they took out Jews indiscriminately and shot them in the streets, and they cut their beards off and they made them crawl ... That was just on the first day, and this bestiality in one form or another always threatened us. They were searching Jewish homes, they were taking goods away from shops and valuables from homes. They said that they wanted 100,000 zlotys within twenty-four hours and if they won't get it they'll take out the first hundred people and shoot them. There was a big panic, you know, trying to get this money together – how do you raise money when suddenly the whole normal banking system has come to an end? It was all confiscated; anyone who had a business, the business was just stopped there. Some people had money, some people had valuables or clothing which they could sell, and they could buy food from the local farms. But some people of course hadn't, and they were dying of starvation. So it was a question of survival of the fittest really.

By October there was an order that all Jews had to move into the ghetto. Piotrków was the first ghetto that the Nazis established in Poland. We were ordered to move in by the 1st of November. Before the war, in the area which was now assigned to be the ghetto, there were about two to three thousand people living. Now fifteen thousand people were ordered to move in there. Some were brought in from far away; for instance, there came a whole community, an ancient community, from Gniezno near the German border, very cultured and a cut above any of our communities. I think there were about fifteen hundred of them. And they were the first people who started dying off. Because they arrived destitute, all their belongings had been confiscated . . . Of course we helped them with accommodation, but the accommodation was – well, today I don't think anyone could even begin to think about this. What used to be a sports club, a very sort of derelict place, about seven or eight hundred people were pushed in there, one on top of another, on bunks. And the rest were housed in the synagogue. It was a beautiful place – the stained-glass windows, the murals, were the pride of the community. Now suddenly this was turned into a place where over five hundred people were living. You can imagine. And because the sanitation was poor – in fact there was hardly any sanitation – and because they didn't have sufficient nourishment or change of clothing, within a very short time there developed an epidemic. And from there, the typhoid epidemic spread throughout the whole ghetto. That took a toll of thousands of people.

The interesting thing about human nature is how quickly one gets used to disaster, how quickly one gets used to the good things and the bad things. And it was a question of simply adjusting oneself to it, very quickly – if not, one would have to go under. My father was a very enterprising man, he was a man of great courage; he was supposed to stay in the ghetto, but he spent most of his time outside. He organized the smuggling of food into the ghetto, and of course he was risking his life, because if he were caught he would have been shot. In fact, what he did was so remarkable that when I think about it today I just can't believe it – not just that he had the courage to do it but the imagination, the enterprise. But people were dying, including people known to my family; you could hear, so-and-so died, so-and-so died. The typhoid, especially the typhoid. Typhoid does not know the difference between poor and rich. And elderly people, who would have had a chance to live a while longer under normal circumstances, they died earlier.

We lived in the ghetto for about three years. It was a long three years. There was no more schooling for Jewish children, schools were shut as soon as the Germans entered the town. Private lessons were given for the few people who could afford it; but it took some time before this happened, because the first few months, the first year, we were living in a kind of limbo – nobody knew exactly what was going on. Radios were forbidden, anybody caught with a radio would be shot; but there must have been radios in secret because we usually heard the latest news. I spent a lot of time outside the ghetto at the beginning, I even used to go to the cinema. Of course my life was at stake. But somehow I did not think . . . When I told my mother about it she gave me a hiding and she made me swear that I'll never go out again. But even though I did understand what was involved, I did not want to believe it – I always thought that this won't happen to me. Really, when I was outside the ghetto I was not so much afraid of the Germans as I was afraid of the Poles. Because there was no way the Germans would know I wasn't a Polish boy – I didn't conform to the German stereotype of a Jew, I had blond hair, I had a short nose – but I was always afraid that some Pole would denounce me. That was my greatest fear.

You see, the Poles were looked down upon by the Germans, and in turn the Poles were quite happy about the way the Germans were dealing with the Jews. They felt, well, they're not so badly off themselves because the Jews are worse off. And it was a kind of *Schadenfreude*, you know; when the Germans first came in, some of our Polish neighbours said, 'Well, now you will see what the Germans are going to do to you, they will teach you a lesson.' I'm not saying that all Poles behaved like this, nor a majority – but a large number did. It was enough to make us feel that we were completely abandoned and that we had no friends; we lived in a hostile world. Even if we were prepared to risk our lives to get outside, we were not safe because few people were ready to help us. I understand that the Poles couldn't help the Jews because they were afraid if they did their own lives were in jeopardy, and I don't know what I would have done in the same circumstances. But that is not the argument; the argument is that the Poles were not passive, they were actively helping the Germans to destroy us. More often than not, a Pole would go up to a Jew or Jewess and say, 'I know that you're Jewish. Unless you give me some money I'll denounce you to the Gestapo.'

Now that is the tragedy. And that's something that unfortunately today many Poles don't want to accept. They say that this is Jewish propaganda. But I can assure you, whoever you would talk to who lived through those tragic days will tell you the same. I'm not anti-Polish; on the contrary, I was as a child as patriotic a Pole as any other child was. That's why I remember those songs, I was singing with great fervour that Poland should be a great empire. And even today I feel very much with the Poles who have got to put up with a system that they never wanted. I simply try to put the historical truth in proper perspective.

By the beginning of January 1942, at the Wannsee Conference, the Final Solution was decided, and the order was to liquidate all the Jews. The Germans did it all very scientifically. Each town was scheduled for liquidation for a particular date; they knew exactly how many people they can gas per day in Treblinka, and in Piotrków at that time there were 24,000 Jews. They decided to leave 10 per cent; and 22,000 Jews were rounded up between the 14th and 21st of October. They were taken in railway trucks and sent to the gas chambers of Treblinka. Within seven days these 22,000 Jews were exterminated.

Meanwhile, during 1942, there were all kinds of rumours in Piotrków; that they were being taken to the steppes of Russia for resettlement, but there were also many who said that they were taking them to the gas chambers. But it was very difficult for anyone to believe that. At that stage I was working in a glass factory, and it was very near the railway line, and as the trains were passing by carrying the human cargo, the Poles were joking, they were saying, 'Oh, more of you are being sent to be made soap of.' We didn't believe it. We laughed as well – what else could we do? But the rumours were there; and nobody came back . . .

But I had around me – strange as it may sound – a belief of invincibility. That nothing can happen to me. There were many times when I was frightened, absolutely terrified; but I had a great belief in my father. He would not allow any situation to get the better of him – so many people collapsed, just didn't know what to do, but my father, somehow, whatever the situation, he always seemed to have presence of mind and courage and resourcefulness. If I wouldn't have had that confidence and my father's support I'm absolutely certain I wouldn't be here today.

I was growing up very quickly; on the one hand I was still a little boy, on the other hand I was very much a grown-up. I lived amongst grown-ups; you see, in the ghetto there was a curfew at eight o'clock, so that's when I would indulge in my world of make-believe, delve into books, or else the neighbours in the building would come and sit and talk and discuss things, play cards and so on – there's hardly a card-game I don't know! I used to follow my father – I was the only son, and just my two sisters. I used to sit and listen to them talking politics, and I knew what they were talking about, because I would be on the move outside the ghetto most of the time, and I would often stand by the newspaper kiosks and read the headlines and read as much as I could from the papers. So I was familiar with the names of Chamberlain and Churchill and Halifax and all the political leaders of the time. People were still optimistic, they said, 'America will soon join and the war will soon be over, they can't go on like this and they will never win', and so on.

By October in 1942 I was the only member of our family who was working; in the main, children didn't work, because they were marked down for liquidation. But in my home town there was a glass factory and they allowed a certain number of boys to be employed there. My two sisters had been placed outside with two different Polish families, they were out of the ghetto by about August, September. My mother was the only one still at home, and I was working, and my father spent a lot of time out of the ghetto because he had a permit to go to the villages to collect rabbit-skins to be used for fur linings for German troops serving on the Russian front – at that stage they were suffering a great deal from frost. But in fact he didn't collect the skins – he was smuggling in food, and he used the permit as a perfect alibi.

At the time that the deportation took place it so happened that I was working on a night shift. I had left the ghetto at eight o'clock in the evening, and my mother was at home with her youngest sister, my aunt – my father happened at that time to be outside the ghetto. In the morning when we finished work we came outside the gates, they counted us up, and we were ready to march back to the ghetto. Suddenly there was an order to halt us. Because we were told that the deportation was taking place now. So it started off in the early morning of the 14th of October. The ghetto was surrounded; like everything else, it was all organized, every day street by street. But those who were working in the glass factory were kept there – they gave us a place in the stables, where we were sleeping on concrete and straw.

When the Jews in the house where we lived were ordered to the selection point, there were one or two there from the factory who were set free. When they arrived at the factory on the second day I asked them, 'Have you seen my father, have you seen my mother?' They said, 'No.' I said, 'Sure?' They said, 'No, definitely they weren't there at the deportation.' So I immediately was calmed down, because I had such confidence in my father that I believed he had done something – even though he wasn't there at home that evening, he must have done something. And two days later, when we were still in the glass factory, one of the Poles in the factory came to me and said, 'I have a message for you: everything is all right, don't worry.' He said, 'Somebody told me to tell you.'

After the deportation was over, we were ordered to go back to what was now the small ghetto, because the big ghetto was liquidated – just the adjoining houses of two streets. The remaining 2,400 people were going to live in an area where before the war about 200 people lived. So when I came back . . . It was like, you know, being in the middle of the sea tossed around with thousands of people and then you suddenly wake up and nobody's around you. The houses were cleared out and all the valuables and everything else were sent to Germany. People had been ordered to go out just without anything. Everybody was gone. In the main those who were left behind were able-bodied – very few women and children were left.

After a few days my father's brother came in with his wife and child, my mother's two brothers and their wives and one of my cousins – they were in hiding outside the town during the deportations. So practically the majority of my family were at this stage alive – it was really almost miraculous. I had an idea where my mother and sisters were hiding and I knew whom to contact to confirm their whereabouts. About two weeks later I decided that I'd better find out what the situation was, and when I went out to work one day I managed to detach myself from the workforce and I went outside the town to a Pole who was working for my father, helping him to smuggle food into the ghetto. When he saw me he went berserk, he said, 'What the hell are you doing here?' I said, 'I came to see my father and my mother – do you know where they are?' He said, 'Yes, I know where they are, but I can't take you there now.' He said, 'So many people were killed the last few days, and if they catch you here they'll kill me and everybody else – get out of here!' He started shouting at me. 'Come back later, later at night when it's dark.'

So I went out, very dejected, and suddenly I heard, 'Jew, Jew'. I got frightened and I really started running, and I could hear behind me boys shouting, 'Jew, Jew'. I was not far away from the park; I knew that park well, because before the war we used to play hide-and-seek and used to know all kinds of hiding-places there, so I went to one of them that I still remembered – it was really a hole more than anything else – and I covered myself up. I was quite a small boy. I could hear the boys looking for me everywhere, and after a time they gave up the chase, and so I stayed on till it got dark. And then I went back to this Pole and he took me to my parents.

I learned then that my father, when he was outside the ghetto, had heard that the deportation was going to take place in the morning. So he made his way back to the ghetto under the darkness of night and took my mother and my aunt to a hiding-place. He was really a very brave man to take this risk. And lucky, yes. Unfortunately at the end luck was not with him.

And so I was reunited with them. It was, it was ... Well, if anybody could have seen that scene at the time ... It was the first time in my life I was without my parents and for the first time I realized what it meant being without parents. You see, one always takes one's parents for granted. It was such a terrible time, people were so completely overtaken by events, their senses were blunted. So there was I all by myself, and I knew that somehow my little sisters were alive, my parents were alive. That kept my morale up. At the same time, it was a very strange feeling, suddenly being without parents. Yet I still did not believe anything could happen to *me*.

My father decided to come back with me to the ghetto – I told him that people were coming back, things were returning to a kind of normality. So we made our way to the glass factory and waited till my shift came out; but then we had a problem, you see, because they used to count us every time. But we managed to slip in with this group to the ghetto late at night, only to be told that a number of people were killed in the afternoon and all hell was set loose once again. Two Jewish policemen were caught trying to save their parents and they were shot and just left there in the street. No one was allowed to touch them, you just had to go through and pass by. To teach everybody a lesson. Because they tried to teach us lessons all the time.

My uncle, when we arrived, went mad; he said, 'Why didn't you tell me you were going to bring your father in? – this is the worst possible time.' Because only those who were working or were part of the administration, they were the only ones who were entitled to be there. The illegals usually were rounded up and sent away to the gas chambers; but now what they were doing was shooting them. The following morning my father together with my uncles went out to their workplace, where there were about sixty people working. My uncle was in charge of the group and he managed to put my father's name down on the list of those who were working there from the time of the deportation – this meant that my father was immediately legalized. It was again taking big risks; but my uncle did it with the co-operation of the Pole who was in charge, and this Pole was also a very close friend of my father's, so he was prepared to do this for him.

Then, soon afterwards, my mother sent a note to my father telling him what has happened to her. The wife of the Pole where they were in hiding had a lover who was working for the Gestapo, and she told her lover about the fact that she's got these two Jewesses hiding, and she arranged for him to come there one evening and to take everything away from them, even their wedding-rings. He said to my mother and my aunt, 'If you don't leave I'll take you to the Gestapo.' So my father immediately arranged for them to come back to the ghetto. And at the same time – everything happened very quickly – we had the same situation happen with my eight-year-old little sister. The villagers were pressing hard on the Pole who sheltered her. He just loved my sister, that Pole; when he used to come to our place he said, 'I'm going to look after her, she's such a beautiful child.' She was Aryan-looking, had blonde hair, her Polish was absolutely impecc-able; and no one, not even a Pole, could ever know that she was Jewish. This Pole used to take her to church, and when she came back she was saying her prayers before she went to bed, you know, she was really behaving like a Christian child. When he brought her back he was crying.

Then something happened with my other sister; she was to-gether with a cousin, who was about eleven. This cousin disap-peared in a mysterious way: the Pole that was hiding her said that she went out, there were contradictory statements, and nobody knew exactly what had happened to her. So when we heard that this cousin had disappeared, my parents decided to bring my sister back. Up to the present day the mystery hasn't been resolved. My aunt survived, she is still alive, but she's never been the same woman. Whenever she starts talking about her child she's in tears; her whole life has been clouded by it. After the war she was still in her early thirties when she was liberated, but she wouldn't have any children, she lives constantly in the shadow of her child. The wound is that much deeper because she really doesn't know how the child disappeared – she sometimes imagines that maybe she's alive somewhere, maybe somebody took her . . .

Now we were all five back in the small ghetto. The Germans knew that there were quite a number of people who have come back. Just then they decided that everybody who is now living in the ghetto would be legalized and will be receiving rations. But after about two weeks or so they gave an order to round up all the people who have returned from their hiding-places since the deportation. They were rounded up – there were about 520 of them – and taken to the synagogue. Once there you were as good as dead, because it was a clearing place – people were either taken from there to the deportations, or to the cemetery to be killed. They took my mother and my younger sister, my middle sister was left. It was early morning when they knocked and they picked them up. I was just thirteen then.

My father managed to obtain a permit to release my mother, but he couldn't do anything for my younger sister – there was no value for children as they were considered to be useless. My mother wrote back to my father and said, 'You look after the two children and I have to look after this youngest one.' She wouldn't leave her.

On Saturday morning – it was the 19th of December 1942 – they came to the synagogue and they ordered fifty strong, able-bodied men to come forward; they said they need them to do a specific job and when they finish this job they will release them. So the fifty strongest men managed to force their way to the front and then they were escorted to the woods. They were ordered to dig pits, five pits, long ones. When they finished digging they were ordered to undress. At that stage there was somebody there who had experienced this once before, and he realized what was about to happen. He screamed out aloud in Yiddish, 'Let's run!' Those who could think fast started running. The Nazis were taken aback and started shooting, but a few men got away.

That very evening we knew about this, because one or two of them managed to smuggle themselves back into the small ghetto, and they told us what has happened. The Nazis then made a party that evening, they all got drunk, and at the early morning, Sunday morning, the 20th of December, they took out a hundred people at a time from the synagogue and led them to the woods where they killed them, group after group; and by about eight o'clock in the morning they were all dead. I was asleep Sunday morning and I remember clearly how I woke up and I saw my father coming in; and he was crying. And I didn't ask him anything any more.

The following day, on Monday, my father bribed one of the Polish workers who was driving a lorry, and he went to the woods and he came back that evening with lots of photos and all kinds of memorabilia that he picked up. All the clothing – because they were told to undress – was taken to a selection place, a sorting place. So we knew almost instantly – it was no secret, if it had been a secret the Nazis wouldn't have taken the clothing to a place where Jews were working and sorting it out.

For the first time I realized . . . Well, I couldn't believe it, I couldn't accept that I'd lost my mother. Because, you know, when we were saved during that bombing raid in the first days of the war, my mother kept saying, if we could survive this disaster we will survive the war. She held this conviction with unwavering faith and infected us with the same belief. And now for the first time the spell broke. And there was my little sister . . . For a few days I just couldn't believe it that I have lost my mother. I just . . . I found it impossible to reconcile myself to it. I kept crying all the time – I mean, not in front of other people, because I felt ashamed to cry in front of other people – but I just couldn't contain myself from crying when I was alone.

Soon afterwards other disasters struck our family – we'd managed before to come out almost intact from the huge deluge, so to speak, but then after my mother and my sister were killed, two of my uncles were killed with fifty others shot in the back of the head in the Jewish cemetery. And two of my aunts were sent away to another concentration camp. We just slowly tried to settle down to the new life. We were anaesthetized all the time, because death was always looming in front of us. We came back from work and we saw people lying there . . . One day we came back, somebody was being searched and they found something on him which he was not supposed to have. They were kicking him; and when the poor fellow started to run they shot at him. This was winter, the snow was very high, and the blood as he was running was just pouring off him on this white snow. I see it all the time. And I see these two who tried to save their parents lying there every time we had to pass by them.

Nobody knew what was in store for us, from minute to minute, day to day. In this situation you simply don't know what you're doing; how is it possible, how can families be separated? They would say, 'Look, kill us all together.' But there was no choice. It was, 'You go here and you go there'; you don't know whether going here meant death or life, nobody knew. Not to go along with the order meant instant death, because we were completely helpless. We had to run – where were we to run? Even when we did go into hiding we weren't safe. For an ordinary person living an ordinary life, it is impossible really to understand. We were always frightened; yet I kept thinking to myself, it's not going to happen to me. The two thoughts can run separately. You see, every time I saw one of the murderers passing by, I kept thinking to myself, what is he going to do to me? Death was around us all the time.

But, I tell you, when bombs were falling, later, when we were in Germany, and we sometimes had to leave the factory and hide in the fields, I really was not afraid whatsoever about bombs. The Germans went for cover; it really didn't bother me. And I will say something that might sound very callous, but it isn't. About nuclear bombs. It doesn't at all bother me – well, it worries me like it worries every human being that we could be destroyed. But it doesn't worry me, in the sense that when I was earmarked to be killed, outside the people were living a normal life – if I could walk outside and be left alone I'd be like everybody else. Just outside, people were going to church, they were buying food, they were sleeping in a bed on sheets, but I was living like an animal. That was what was hurting. But the nuclear bomb, we are all in the same boat, I'm no different from you – it's a common problem that we have to face together and find a solution to it. But there, there was no one to speak up for me, nobody to give me shelter. God did not respond to our prayers, if I did pray.

For instance, I was later beaten up by a *Volksdeutsch* – they were ethnic Germans who had lived in Poland all their lives. When the Germans occupied Poland, the majority joined up with them. And there was one of those, about twenty years old, who I got to know at the glass factory where I first worked. When I met him he was very nice, very pleasant to me, and I always thought he was a friend. One day we'd been working already for twelve hours, and we were told to do another job and when this was finished we would be allowed to go into the camp. It was later, it was in 1944. So I got a permit to go back to the camp, and when I got there I showed it to the guard – and I'm sure he couldn't read it, because he was about to hit me. So I was running away; and just then two guards came up, and one of them was that so-called friend. I ran up towards him to say, 'Look, I've got this permit and he's not letting me in.' Instead of listening to me, he took off his rifle and started hitting me with the butt. He split my head, he split my forearm – I didn't run away from him because I couldn't believe he would do this to me. I was just standing there and looking at him and this permit was in my hand and blood was pouring down me. When he walked away I sat down there and I cried out of the sheer impotence – why did he do this to me? I was crying like a baby.

In the meantime we were still in the small ghetto. An existence in hell really. Then by July 1943 it was decided to liquidate the small ghetto. On the day of the selection my father, my sister, and my little cousin – her father had been killed and her mother sent to a camp, and my sister looked after her like a mother – were about to be sent to another place. Then my sister jumped off the lorry and ran up to the chief of the Gestapo and told him she had a brother inside and could she join him. He looked at her and he was rather taken aback and said, 'Yes, go in.' She was encouraged by this and she asked if my father and my little cousin could be allowed in as well; she pointed to the lorry where they were, and he ordered them to get off, and they came in with the others. So we were together.

Until November 27th 1944 we were put to work in a woodwork

factory. Then on that day we were ordered to go to the station and we were loaded into cattle-trucks and sent to Buchenwald – my father and I. My sister and my cousin were sent to Ravensbrück. We were for about two weeks in Buchenwald and then we were selected to be sent to another camp, Schlieben, where anti-tank weapons were manufactured. When our names were called – or rather numbers, we had in Buchenwald only numbers, mine was 94790 – my father was not called and he was left behind. So I was now separated even from my father. For the first time I was alone. He stayed in Buchenwald till about February, I learned afterwards, then he was sent on a transport to another camp. At the end of the war they marched them out of there, and when they reached the borders of Czechoslovakia there were rumours that the Americans were only a few miles away; at this point my father and a few other people decided to make a run for it. But they were rounded up and killed. That was just a few days before the end of the war.

I was in Schlieben till the 14th of April 1944 and then deported to Theresienstadt. I was there the last three weeks until I was liberated. We were liberated on the morning of the 9th of May. My little sister and cousin also survived; they were sent to Belsen from Ravensbrück, and both of them were liberated there.

When I was liberated I felt completely naked; I thought, what's going to happen, where am I going to go? I was fifteen. I went back to Poland to find out if anybody had been saved, who has come back. I went with a cousin of mine who was also liberated in Theresienstadt – he was a bit younger than me, thirteen years old. He was in a very poor state, very emaciated. We arrived in Poland, and we had to change trains at Czestochowa. This town is famous for its shrine where thousands of Catholics go every year on pilgrimages. While we were waiting at the station two Polish army officers came up and said, 'What are you doing here?' I was very surprised, because we had it written all over our faces where we came from, our hair was all shaved off and we were still not recovered. I told him, 'We were liberated in Theresienstadt and we are on our way to Piotrków.' We showed them our passes, and they said, 'Well, we'll have to take you to the police station.' And with all my experience I was still so naïve to believe ... Anyway, we went ahead and I was tired and I said, 'Where's the police station?' And they said, 'Shut your f****** mouth, you bloody Jew.' So I realized there and then that I had made a mistake and I thought, my God, what's going to happen to us now? For the first time, after all this I had experienced I began to think that now my luck has left me. They took us to a place that was completely deserted and then they took their revolvers out and they said, 'Get to the wall.' I wouldn't move. I said to them, 'What do you want? What have we done to you?' I kept on talking and talking. In the end one of them said, 'Oh, let's leave them, what the hell.' The officer turned round and said, 'You're very lucky, you're the first ones of your kind whom we didn't kill.' That was my welcome back to Poland.

I came to England in 1945; there was a committee, the CBS, that was set up before the war to help refugees, and they applied to the Home Office for permission to bring in a thousand children. In the end only 732 came to Britain. I was in the first group of 300. One and a half million children under sixteen had been killed.

In all honesty, I don't think religion played any part in the fact that I survived. I never thought in terms of religion at all. It was in the main a question of luck – not contracting typhoid, having capable parents who protected me, having a robust constitution. When I was a child, no matter who I wrestled with, I always used to beat them. And there's no question about it, confidence played a very important part in it – without it I would have been lost.

Afterwards ... On the one hand there was this terrible loss hanging over me, because on my mother's side there were seven uncles and aunts and numerous cousins, my father was one of ten – out of all the family only a few were not wiped out. On the other hand there was this feeling, this gratefulness that I was alive. It wasn't just a question of saying, 'Well, why did I survive? – I wasn't better than the others, I should have gone with them.' I don't think that was the case with most of the survivors, because if it were so we would have been all today in an asylum. The only way we could survive was to accept reality; the experience that no matter how much one describes it, no matter how much one talks about it, can't really be conveyed to anybody. How can one convey hunger to anybody? I haven't even said anything to you about hunger, the degrees of hunger – there are so many degrees of hunger. What people can do when they're hungry. When day after day there is no hope of getting an extra piece of bread. And the freezing cold, and having to march up and down to the whims of a crackpot. And not having anything to look forward to. And when we went back from work, seeing people just dropping and not taking any notice because we didn't have the strength to pick them up. How does one begin to think about it?

I have a very close friend with whom I was practically in every camp together. They came to his father and said, 'Look, either you bring your parents here or we will take your wife and your son and we'll send you away.' And this man had to make a decision. He survived, and he had to live with it. In the end he told his parents and they said, 'Look, we are old people, you are young people . . .' But he still had to live with it. Think how many people who are alive today had to go through this experience. In this respect I'm very lucky, I was never put into a position where I had to make a choice, where my life was balanced against somebody else's. Indirectly, yes, indirectly this happened. Because during the time of the deportation, during the last day, when the transport wasn't quite full, the Germans came into the glass factory and they were picking up at random anyone they could get hold of. And they came up to me and they kicked me and they said, 'Off you go.' But I turned round and I said, 'I'm a Pole.' Fortunately one of the Poles, who was an anti-Semite, and who really gave me a big hiding the first day I started work, that very man shouted out, 'Yes, he's a Pole.' And so somebody else was taken. I don't remember who it was, I don't think I remembered after a week who this person was – possibly I didn't want to remember it. But in a sense one could say . . . You know?

When I was liberated, I was thinking in terms of how to create a new life; I was even thinking like this when I was in the camps. I wasn't thinking in terms of revenge, I wasn't consumed with any hatred. I was very naïve too. You know what I was thinking? I was thinking that when I go back to my home town I will look for this *Volksdeutsch* who beat me, not to take him to court, but to challenge him to a fair fight! And give him the opportunity to defend himself against me – I mean, that's how naïve I was! I always believed in a fair fight. My mother was a very upright woman – with her, right and wrong were very clearly delineated. My whole family were like this really. But when you see what happens when strikes and demonstrations get out of hand, when you see what happens even when the football crowds go wild, doesn't it make you think that there is in all of us a kind of atavistic violence that if we let it go we can destroy ourselves? Control of it means having a country with checks and counter-checks and balances; we must have the will and the resolve to maintain a modicum – perhaps more than that – of civilization.

Yes, I do think of my family. I don't believe we'll meet in another life, but I do think a lot about them. I don't suppose that there is a day that goes by that in one way or another I don't think about them. My parents, my sister, my grandparents, my cousins, my aunts and uncles, my friends and neighbours. We were very close. I've never suppressed my thoughts about them, my sorrow. As long as I think about them, I know they are alive – they are alive in *me*. They still live – they are a part of me. I can tell you it gives me peace of mind to think about them. It's because I've thought so much that I can tell you the whole story like this, in all its details.